GENDER-LINKED VARIATION ACROSS LANGUAGES

---

*YOUSIF ELHINDI AND THERESA MCGARRY,
EDITORS*

GENDER-LINKED VARIATION ACROSS LANGUAGES

YOUSIF ELHINDI AND THERESA MCGARRY,
EDITORS

First published in 2013 in Champaign, Illinois, USA
by Common Ground Publishing LLC
as part of the On Diversity book series

Copyright © Yousif Elhindi and Theresa McGarry 2013

All rights reserved. Apart from fair dealing for the purposes of study, research, criticism or review as permitted under the applicable copyright legislation, no part of this book may be reproduced by any process without written permission from the publisher.

Library of Congress Cataloging-in-Publication Data

Gender-linked variation across languages / Yousif Elhindi and Theresa McGarry, editors.
    pages cm
Includes index.
ISBN 978-1-61229-222-9 (pbk : alk. paper) -- ISBN 978-1-61229-223-6 (pdf)
1. Language and languages--Sex differences. I. Elhindi, Yousif. II. McGarry, Theresa.

P120.S48G4744 2013
306.44--dc23

2013020261

Photo credit: Theresa Marie McGarry

Table of Contents

Acknowledgements viii

Contributors ix

Introduction 1
  Yousif Elhindi and Theresa McGarry

Chapter 1: The Role of Women in Māori Sound Change 5
  Margaret Maclagan, Ray Harlow, Jeanette King, Peter Keegan and Catherine I. Watson

Chapter 2: Negotiating Locality and Gender–Men, Women and Local Honorifics 22
  Anna Strycharz-Banaś

Chapter 3: Gender Variations in Hebrew 36
  Malka Muchnik

Chapter 4: Gender and the Sentence-final Particles in Japanese 50
  Naomi Ogi and Duck-Young Lee

Chapter 5: Gender Variation in Compliment Responses: A Case of the Malaysian Tamil Community 86
  Jariah Mohd Jan and Prabhalini Thevendiraraj

Chapter 6: Gender Variances in Chinese and Korean Requests: A Continuum Rather than Polarity 102
  Yong-Ju Rue and Grace Zhang

Chapter 7: Topic Introduction Elements in Single-gender and Mixed-gender Social Club Business Meetings in the US 128
  Theresa McGarry

Chapter 8: Metaphors in Distress: Gender Differences in Sudanese Arabic 156
  Yousif Elhindi

Chapter 9: Naming Places, Establishing Divides: Gender and Linguistic Territorialization among Sri Lankan Students 171
  Cala Zubair

Chapter 10: Linguistic Differentiation in the Ekegusii Language ... 181
  Martha Michieka and Hellen Ondari

Index 193

Acknowledgements

This book has been improved by the comments of Lori Donath and Tim McDowell. We also appreciate the help in editing from Carmen Stamey, Meghan Morrison, and Yousif Moohamed. Finally, we would like to thank our colleagues and chair in the Dept. of Literature and Language at East Tennessee State University for their continuous support of many kinds.

Contributors

Yousif Elhindi is an associate professor and the Director of the Linguistics Minor at the Department of Literature and Language at East Tennessee State University in Johnson City, Tennessee. Elhindi obtained a PhD from Oklahoma State University in 1995, his MA from the University of Sheffield in 1981 and his BA from the University of Khartoum in 1975. Before coming to ETSU in 1998, Elhindi taught at Oklahoma State University as well as King Faisal University in Saudi Arabia and Gezira University in the Sudan.

Ray Harlow is a retired Professor of Linguistics and an Honorary Fellow of the University of Waikato, Hamilton, New Zealand. His research interests include the Māori language, its history, structure, dialects, and literature; Polynesian languages more generally, especially their historical relationships; and issues in minority language maintenance. His recent publications include *A Māori Reference Grammar* (Pearson, 2001) and *Māori: A Linguistic Introduction* (Cambridge University Press, 2007).

Margaret Maclagan is an Adjunct Professor in Communication Disorders at the University of Canterbury in Christchurch, New Zealand where she taught phonetics and linguistics to speech pathology students. Her research interests include sound change over time in New Zealand English and Māori and language change in time over the course of Alzheimer's disease. She is a co-author of two books on New Zealand English (*New Zealand English: Its origins and evolution* (Cambridge University Press, 2004) and *New Zealand English* (Edinburgh University Press, 2008).

Jariah Mohd Jan is an Associate Professor in the Department of English at the Faculty of Languages and Linguistics, University of Malaya. Her research interests are interdisciplinary, centering on feminist linguistics and emphasizing the importance of language in understanding social processes. Her main research interests are gender and power issues in language, discourse and society, social networks and workplace discourse, and literature in ESL.

Jeanette King is an Associate Professor in Aotahi: School of Māori and Indigenous Studies at the University of Canterbury in Christchurch, New Zealand

and heads the bilingual theme of the New Zealand Institute of Language, Brain and Behaviour. Her research interests include aspects of change in the Maori language over time, non-verbal cues, and language ideology. She has published articles on aspects of Māori language, language revitalisation, Māori English and Māori immersion education.

Peter J. Keegan (Waikato-Maniapoto, Ngāti Porou) is a senior lecturer in Te Puna Wānanga, the Faculty of Education, University of Auckland, New Zealand. He coordinated the Māori language developments of Project asTTle (assessment tools for teaching and learning), a computer-based assessment tool for assessing literacy and numeracy in English and Māori. Peter's major research includes the structure and current use of Māori language, assessment/measurement and language testing especially in indigenous language contexts, vocabulary and the achievement of minority students.

Duck-Young Lee is a reader in Japanese at the Australian National University. His research interests include spoken discourse, the interface between grammar and pragmatics, and language teaching. His recent publications focus on special features of spoken conversation, such as the sentence-final particles *ne* and *yo* (Journal of Pragmatics, 2007) and personal pronouns in Japanese spoken discourse (Journal of Pragmatics, 2008), the interface between cognition and interaction (Journal of International Studies, 2011), the teaching of Japanese in the Australian context, such as 'Nihongo ga Ippai' [Japanese Ippai] (Hituzi Shobo, 2010), and Japanese education in the multicultural–multilingual society of Australia (Journal of Yokohama National University, 2010).

Theresa McGarry obtained a PhD in linguistics from the University of South Carolina in 2004, specializing in sociolinguistics and second language acquisition. She is now an associate professor and the coordinator of the TESOL Certificate Program at East Tennessee State University. Her dissertation studied the introduction of topics in single-gender and mixed-gender meetings of a social club.

Martha Moraa Michieka is an Associate Professor and director of the linguistics minor at East Tennessee State University. Her research interests include second language teaching, sociolinguistics and World Englishes. Email: michieka@etsu.edu

Malka Muchnik is senior lecturer at the Department of Hebrew and Semitic Languages at Bar-Ilan University in Israel, and her expertise is on Sociolinguistics, particularly language and gender. She is founder and editor of the journal "Israel Studies in Language and Society" and author of the book *Language, Culture and Society*, published in Hebrew, as well as many articles in this field. Her book *The Gender Challenge of Hebrew* has been accepted for publication by Brill.

Naomi Ogi is a lecturer in Japanese at the Australian National University. Her main research interests are in spoken discourse, pragmatics and the teaching of culture in language education. Her current research focuses on the interactional functions of Japanese sentence-final particles and their gender orientations, and attempts to demystify some aspects of how Japanese language can be associated with a particular gender of the speaker. Her recent publications include *Nihongo ga Ippai* [Japanese Ippai] (Hituzi Shobo, 2010) and 'The interactional functions of Japanese interactive markers *yo* and *sa*' (*Linguistics and the Human Sciences* 2012).

Hellen Kwamboka Ondari is a lecturer in Linguistics and former Chair of the Department of Languages and Literature, at the University of Eastern Africa, Baraton (UEAB). She holds a BA from UEAB and an MPhil from Moi University. Her research interests include second language teaching, sociolinguistics and pragmatics. Email: hellekwambo@yahoo.com

Yong-Ju Rue is a Visiting Fellow at Korean Research Institute in the University of New South Wales. She was awarded a Ph.D. in linguistics by Curtin University in 2007. She has been researching into the area of requests and has published a book on the topic. Her primary research area is Cross-Cultural Pragmatics. Email: y.rue@unsw.edu.au

Anna Strycharz-Banaś is currently a research fellow at the Meertens Institute in Amsterdam. Her main research interests focus on the use of specific linguistic features in the construction of identities, and especially the changes visible in those uses across time and across generations of speakers. She has investigated dialect levelling in Osaka Japanese, media representations of alternative Japanese femininities and communicative practices of expatriate Japanese women. She has also taught various linguistic and sociolinguistic courses in the UK and in New Zealand.

Prabhalini Thevendiraraj has 20 years experience in teaching the English Language. She holds a MA in ESL from University of Malaya and a BA Honours with Linguistics major, from University of Lancaster, UK. She spent 12 years teaching English Language including GCE O level English Language at secondary school level. She was actively involved in facilitation of NIE English Language workshops and conducted English Language teaching to foreigners. She is now a free lance tutor and provides editorial support for academic work.

Catherine I. Watson is a senior lecturer in the Department of Electrical and Computer Engineering at the University of Auckland, New Zealand. She has been working in acoustic phonetics for over 15 years, and has over 20 years experience in speech technology. Her research interests include sound change in New Zealand English and Māori, developing a computer-based visual feedback platform for learning Māori pronunciation, developing synthetic New Zealand English voices for healthcare robots, and mathematical modelling of ageing in speech production. She has over 80 peer reviewed publications.

Grace Zhang is an Associate Professor at Curtin University, Australia. She was awarded a Ph.D. in linguistics by the University of Edinburgh in 1996. She has published extensively on semantics, pragmatics and intercultural communication. Email: Grace.Zhang@exchange.curtin.edu.au

Cala Zubair's research is directed towards various sociolinguistic and structural components of Sinhala language varieties. Her ethnographic studies among Sinhalese youth examine register formation, gendered slang constructions, and language ideology. She also focuses on Sinhala syntax and semantics via research on (in)volitive verbs, causative/inchoative alternations, and non-canonically casemarked subjects. She received her Ph.D. from Georgetown University in 2011 and is an Assistant Professor of Sociolinguistics at SUNY Buffalo.

Introduction

Yousif Elhindi and Theresa McGarry, East Tennessee State University

Since the beginning of language and gender studies, the great majority of gender research has focused on English. However, the significant work that has been done in other languages, the best example probably being Japanese, has demonstrated and continues to demonstrate how much cross-linguistic work informs the understandings, research questions, and frameworks of the field. In fact, a key development in the field is the insistence on recognizing the particularity of genders, languages, and their interactions. In Coates and Pichler's words, "What used to be called 'language' is now seen instead as a heterogeneous collection of competing discourses. Gender is no longer viewed as monolithic or static but as multiple and fluid. Researchers have progressed to observing the discursive production of a wide range of femininities and masculinities, and have broadened the range of communities investigated, both geographically and also in terms of gay, lesbian, bisexual, and transgender studies" (569). We believe that the recognition of the importance of the fluidity of language and gender has been stimulated in part by the increasing attention to various languages and in turn points to the need for more work in more diverse languages. Thus, this volume presents a collection of studies that highlights the linguistic diversity of the language and gender research currently being pursued, to emphasize the value of such work for the formulation of theories and methods and to stimulate more research across languages.

Accordingly, we have selected the chapters with the goal of representing the current range of languages and topics investigated. We have resisted setting constraints on the contributors regarding investigative framework. We certainly believe that collections set in specific frameworks are valuable, and the discussion of which frameworks are more useful, and in what regards, is an essential one, but this work has a different purpose. We have provided a forum for new research that demonstrates the rapidly developing areas in the field and waited to see what would emerge. What we believe has emerged is a collection showing the variety not only of languages and areas investigated but also of methodologies. While some very important areas, such as language, gender, and sexuality, are not directly addressed by this volume, many other significant areas are addressed, and we believe the collection will be productive in stimulating further research for many years to come. The aim of this volume is to present language-gender research from diverse languages spanning a wide range of questions and methodologies.

The history of language and gender studies has been summarized astutely by other researchers; a recent example is Coates and Pichler 2011. Therefore, this introduction does not attempt a historical overview. Rather, the goal is to contextualize the various studies in the following chapters with regard to previously investigated questions and especially with regard to some of the currently emerging and developing issues in the field.

The first study engages the longstanding question of the relationship of gender to language change. Maclagan et al. investigate sound change in Maori, analyzing data from three groups of subjects born between 1871 and 1992. Despite Maori's minority status, they find that the sound changes follow a typical pattern, and the women can be seen as assuming their usual roles in language change, i.e. leading in changes below the level of consciousness and somewhat more conservative in changes that have risen above that level. The situation, they conclude, is like that described by Holmes (1997) with regard to New Zealand English; women's language sets the standard of usage.

The second paper also deals with generational change but relates to a key current issue identified by Coates and Pichler, that of the significance of ideologies in structuring both language and society. Anna Strycharz-Banaś investigates the correlation between gender and the use of the local referent honorific suffix *haru* among three generations in Osaka Japanese and argues that research attempting to find a correlation between gender and honorifics in Japanese fails to capture the complexity of the phenomenon. The suffix appears to have become associated with a particular local identity that is no longer attractive for younger women, while simultaneously acting as a resource for indexing this kind of local identity among younger men. Thus, Strycharz-Banaś concludes, changing ideologies must be taken into consideration when the use of honorifics is explained.

Malka Muchnik investigates a third diachronic change, with regard to Hebrew gender-marking on various word classes, instantiated by the word representation in dictionaries, in professional nouns, and in the use of proper names. The use of many feminine forms, she finds, having been reintroduced when the language was revitalized, has once again decreased over the last few decades, and even conscious changes to increase the use of feminine forms have not succeeded. The unmarked masculine forms, Muchnik argues, are more salient and preferred than their feminine counterparts, even when speakers reference women and their actions. She adds that gender differences in Hebrew are also evident in the preference for masculine lexical items. This, she believes, reflects the prestige Hebrew-speaking communities ascribe to masculine forms. Thus, ideologies about gender and about language also explain this imbalance. Moreover, the results could inform in multiple interesting ways the construction of gender and the sources of the socio-cultural models that frame that construction.

Jan and Thevendiraraj shift the focus to the pragmatic level with their analysis of responses to compliments in Malaysian Tamil. The responses of 20 Malaysian Tamil professionals in their 30s to the Discourse Completion Test, considered in light of their responses in semi-structured interviews, suggests an interactive effect of gender and age on the strategy chosen to comply with politeness maxims. Men and women in their early 30s and mid-30s were more inclined to accept compliments. Among the participants in their late 30s, the men also followed that pattern, but the women deflected or rejected more compliments than they accepted. The authors interpret these findings as suggesting differing degrees of importance the speakers accord to the Agreement Maxim and Modesty Maxim as described in Leech's Politeness Principle, relating, they argue, to both traditional and changing aspects of Malaysian Tamil culture.

Ogi and Lee continue the examination of the pragmatic level with their investigation of the significance of the sentence-final particle *wa* in spoken Japanese. Based on an analysis of a spoken language corpus and a Japanese *manga* collection, they find that *wa* constructs speaker's female gender by indexing the cultural notion of *onna-rashisa* 'womanliness' established and consciously propagated in the Meiji era. The arbitrary and intentional association of the particle with that ideological notion demonstrates, they argue, how society members can conceptualize and adapt gender-specific values. Moreover, the particle also indicates the speaker's firm attitude towards the interlocutor, and this dual functionality makes it a versatile pragmatic linguistic form.

Rue and Zhang take the discussion of pragmatic-level gender construction into Mandarin and Korean with a study of how request speech acts construct gender in the framework of the Cross-Cultural Speech Act Realization Project. Previous cross-cultural analysis indicated that in choosing request strategies, Chinese speakers attend more to the degree of familiarity between interlocutors, while Korean speakers appear more attuned to status than familiarity. When speaker gender is also accounted for, it turns out that, overall, men are more direct than women and Koreans are more direct than Chinese. However, gender variance is present in most but not all aspects of request making, suggesting a continuum of gendered variance that supports the fluidity of gender categories.

The following chapter does deal with English and was included because it focuses on an area rarely dealt with in terms of gender, that of topic introduction, specifically its linguistic elements. McGarry analyses a Community of Practice based on membership in an outdoor sports club and investigates the speech of women in single-gender and mixed-gender meetings. The results, like those of Rue and Zhang, are complex, with regard to both speaker gender and group composition. Overall, the women try harder to link their topics to previous discussion and involve the other participants in topic development, show less certainty that their topics will be accepted or understood, and use directives in response to varying contexts. Thus, the analysis brings together previous findings relating to specific linguistic features such as directives, aspects of men's and women's topic introductions such as degree of abruptness, and gender style accommodation, and it emphasizes the local situatedness of the functions of gender-indexing speech behaviors.

While the chapters discussed so far deal with gender-preferential issues, Elhindi examines gender-exclusive differences in the lexicon and discourse properties of Sudanese Colloquial Arabic, a variety spoken in Northern and Central Sudan. Terms used only by women include certain terms of endearment, exclamations and interjections, while a smaller set of terms used only by men perform oaths. Most of these gender-exclusive expressions, he argues, are metaphorical in nature and reflect traditional gendered social roles such as cooking, lamenting deceased loved ones, and divorce initiation. Their importance in constructing gender is evident in the overt chastisement of boys who have not yet acquired the social properties of the words and mistakenly use a feminine expression.

Zubair takes up a lexical issue in Sinhala and brings us back to the importance of ideologies with regard to the contesting of local boundaries and identities in Sri Lanka. Names given to university campus places by a specific group reference and construct in-group significance and ethno-linguistic exclusion. The male students' general acceptance and the female students' general resistance of these terms and their implications indicate corresponding positions in regard to local ideologies and degrees of ethnic tolerance, indicating that the place names function as points of orientation.

In the final chapter, Michieka and Ondari turn to the ideology of researchers. Investigating nouns referencing women and pronouns in Ekegusii, an indigenous Southwestern Kenyan language, they argue that the western based feminist framework distorts the Kisii reality. While not disputing male dominance in the community, they explain the gendered linguistic practices as indicating not female subordination or male domination but the differing roles of women and men in the society. A locally accountable framework, they insist, is indispensable.

We believe this volume takes forward the crucial shift, going back to Bucholtz and Hall (1995), among others, from conceptualizing the gender-language relationship as a monolithic mapping to approaching it as a crosscutting, situated, and practice-based process in which identities and relationships are continuously constructed and reconstructed. In the formidable task of explaining this process in all its complexity, analyses from many languages will be essential, and we hope that we have contributed in this regard.

References

Coates, Jennifer, & Pia Pichler. 2011. New directions in language and gender research. In Jennifer Coates & Pia Pichler (eds.), *Language and gender: A reader,* 569-572. Malden, MA: Wiley-Blackwell.

Holmes, Janet. 1997. Setting new standards: Sound change and gender in New Zealand English. *English World Wide.* 18:107-42.

Hall, Kira, and Mary Bucholtz. 1995. Introduction. In Kira Hall & Mary Bucholtz (eds.), *Gender articulated: Language and the socially constructed self,* 1-22. New York: Routledge.

Chapter 1: The Role of Women in Māori Sound Change

Margaret Maclagan[1], Ray Harlow[2], Jeanette King[3], Peter Keegan[4] and Catherine I. Watson[5]

Abstract: The sound system of Māori, the language of the indigenous people of New Zealand, has changed dramatically over the 200 years that it has been in contact with English. This chapter uses data from three groups of people with birthdates between 1871 and 1992 to trace the development of the pronunciation of vowels and diphthongs in modern Māori. Changes in the vowel system have been influenced by concurrent changes in the pronunciation of New Zealand English. As has been found for other languages, Māori women play the traditional role of leading in non-stigmatized sound changes, but being more conservative when changes are noticed and stigmatized. We can see no effect of the break in the intergenerational transmission of Māori on the traditional roles in sound change as played by Māori women over time.

Introduction

Many researchers have found that women are in the lead in both phonological and syntactic language change (see, for example, Cheshire 2002; Coates 1998, 2004; Eckert 1989; Labov 1990, 2004; Wolfram and Schilling-Estes 1998). Similarly, women have been found to be leading sound changes in New Zealand English (Maclagan, Gordon and Lewis 1999; Woods 1997). The role of women is complex: when sound change is below the level of consciousness, women are usually in the lead, but if a sound change rises above the general level of consciousness in the community so that it becomes stigmatized, women usually pull back. Women are often noted as using more standard forms than men (e.g.,

[1] University of Canterbury
[2] University of Waikato
[3] University of Canterbury
[4] University of Auckland
[5] University of Auckland

Cheshire 1982; Trudgill 1974) and this has been explained as women using the language as 'symbolic capital' (Bourdieu 1991) because of their lesser status in the linguistic market place (Trudgill 1983; Yaeger-Dror 1998) or because of their roles as caregivers to young children (Labov 1990; Trudgill 1983). However Holmes (1997) considered that, rather than using standard language forms out of a sense of inadequacy, women's language actually sets the standard of usage which is then followed by others. Women have been observed both leading change in New Zealand English (NZE) and pulling back when change becomes stigmatized (Maclagan, Gordon and Lewis 1999). However little is known about the role of women in sound change in Māori, the language of the indigenous people of Aotearoa/New Zealand.

Māori belongs to the Eastern Polynesian family of languages, a language family that is regarded as having had a particularly stable vowel system over time (Krupa 1982:2,15).[6] However, since Māori has been in contact with English in New Zealand (NZ), its vowel system has changed dramatically. Some of these changes appear to have been in direct response to the external influence of NZE and others seem to be a mixture of language internal factors as well as external ones (see Harlow et al. 2009 for a description of internal changes and Maclagan et al. 2009 for a description of a change that is both external and internal).

In this chapter, we will describe the changes that have taken place in the Māori vowel system over the last 100 or so years, focusing on the role of women. This analysis is possible because we have data from 10 men and two women born in the late nineteenth century and recorded between 1946 and 1948. Although Europeans had settled NZ by the time these speakers were born, they nevertheless provide an indication of an early state of Māori pronunciation. These recordings will be compared with recordings from both Māori men and women born approximately 50 and 100 years later in order to give an indication of the changes the Māori language has undergone since European settlement of NZ.

Historical Background

According to the archaeological evidence, Māori have been in NZ for about 750 years (Anderson 2009). The first Europeans to spend enough time in NZ to have any influence on the language of the indigenous people were whalers and sealers who had varying degrees of contact with the indigenous people from the very late 1700s on. Māori have been in increasing contact with Europeans over the last 200 years. Over this time, the number of speakers of Māori has declined dramatically,

---

[6] Descriptions of Polynesian languages with much in the way of fine phonetic detail are difficult to find; most restrict themselves to the statements that there are five vowels and distinctive vowel length. However, those few which do contain some comment on phonetic detail (e.g. Kuki 1970 for Tuamotuan, Elbert and Pukui 1979 for Hawaiian, Shibata 1988 for Mangaian in the Southern Cook Islands) provide nothing which would indicate that the pronunciation of the vowels by the MU speakers is anything other than the system in place since at least the breakup of Central Eastern Polynesian languages, the subgroup to which all the languages just named as well as Māori belong (Biggs 1978: 697; Krupa 1982: 2-3). See Blust (2009) for an overview.

so that, by the late twentieth century the language was seriously compromised (Benton 1991). There has been a determined effort at revitalization since the 1980s (Benton and Benton 2001), so that there are now a number of young first language speakers of Māori. All Māori in NZ now speak English, most with native fluency, though there are a few areas, such as in the Ruātoki valley in the North Island of NZ, where older people still use Māori in everyday conversations. Māori is still the language of ritualized welcome (pōwhiri) and other ceremonies on marae (Māori communal areas with a meeting house). In recent times, pōwhiri have also become common in schools, the public service sector and in greeting of overseas dignitaries and celebrities.

Māori Phonology

Māori has ten consonants /p, t, k, m, n, ŋ, f, w, r, h/ and five short vowels /i, e, a, o, u/ which are paired with five corresponding phonemically contrastive long vowels /i:, e:, a:, o:, u:/. Sequences of mid or low vowels followed by a higher vowel usually combine to form diphthongs, at least within morphemes. There are also some long diphthongs, all of the shape long mid or low vowel plus a short higher vowel, e.g. /a:i/, /o:u/. Sequences of appropriate vowels may form long vowels or diphthongs across morpheme or word boundaries.

In this paper we will focus on the five most common diphthongs /ai, ae, au, ou, ao/, and on the five long-short pairs of monophthongs. The long vowels are usually interpreted as two adjacent short vowels. The contrast /a/ ~ /a:/ enjoys a much higher frequency and functional load compared with the other pairs to the point that Bauer suggests that Māori may actually have six vowels rather than five (Bauer 1993: 537). Māori syllable structure is very straightforward; the onset is zero or a single consonant, and the rhyme is a short or long vowel or a diphthong or long diphthong: σ = (C)V(V(V)).

Data

The data analyzed for this chapter come from material gathered by the MAONZE (Māori and New Zealand English) project over the last ten years (see King et al. 2011 for an overview of the project). The MAONZE database contains recordings of a total of 62 speakers with approximately the same number of men and women (see Table 1). The speakers are divided into three main groups: historical speakers born in the nineteenth century, modern day elders and modern day young speakers. Table 1 gives details of the birth dates, as well as the ages of the speaker groups at the time they were recorded. The historical male elders and two of the historical female elders were recorded by the Mobile Disc recording unit of the NZ broadcasting service (for details see Gordon et al. 2004). These recordings were obtained from Radio New Zealand Sound Archive/Ngā Taonga Kōrero. Recordings of the other six female historical elders and two of the modern day female elders were sourced from the Radio NZ Sound Archives, the TVNZ Archive and a recording made by Radio Ngāti Porou. Another two of the modern day female elder recordings come from the Radio Kahungunu archive.[7] Although six of the historical female elders were born between 1895 and 1916, they were recorded in the 1990s. They had therefore had considerably more interaction with Pākehā[8] with, presumably, effects on their own Māori pronunciation. In some of our analyses it has proved illuminating to separate these speakers into their own group, called the Intermediate Female elders). The majority of the modern day elders and young speakers were recorded between 2001 and 2009 by members of the MAONZE team. Speakers recorded by the MAONZE team were recorded for approximately an hour in Māori and an hour in English. Both English and Māori recordings are available for most of the historical speakers. These recordings vary in length from approximately ten minutes to well over an hour. The analysis is based on a total of 427,700 words of Māori.

Table 1: Overview of the MAONZE corpus

Speaker group	No. of speakers	Coding	Year of birth	Age at recording	No. of words
historical male elders	11	HME	1871-1885	62-77	37,700
historical female elders	8	HFE	1881-1916	55-67	21,200
present day male elders	10	ME	1925-1938	64-79	72,900
present day female elders	12	FE	1918-1944	63-87	165,200
present day young males	10	YM	1969-1984	21-35	64,800
present day young females	11	YF	1975-1992	17-32	65,900

Analysis

The recordings were transcribed using Transcriber (http://trans.sourceforge.net/en/presentation.php) and analysed in PRAAT (version 4.125 or later Boersma and Weenink 2009). Where possible, 30 stressed tokens of each of the short and long vowels were analysed acoustically for each speaker and plotted on vowel charts. In addition, analysis was made of the five most common diphthongs. It was not

---

[7] The copyright for the Mobile Unit recordings is held by Sound Archives Ngā Taonga Kōrero (www.soundarchives.co.nz). Copyright for the television recordings is held by Television New Zealand Ltd. Radio Ngāti Porou hold the copyright for part of the recordings used for one of the modern day female elder speakers and Te Reo o Ngāti Kahungunu Inc. hold the copyright for recordings for two of the modern day female elder speakers. Grateful acknowledgements go to Joe Te Rito who supplied the Te Reo o Ngāti Kahungunu recordings.

[8] Pākehā is the usual term within New Zealand for non-Māori of European origin.

always possible to obtain 30 suitable tokens for all vowels as some vowels like /u:/ and diphthongs like /ou/ and /ao/ are relatively less frequent in Māori text than the others.

Results

Monophthongs

We first discuss the results for the monophthongs. The results for the historical elders, both the men and the two oldest women, show the balanced vowel plots that could be expected for a Polynesian language.[9] The mid vowels, /e:, e/ and /o:, o/ are well below the high vowels and the high back vowels /u, u:/ are at the back of the quadrilateral. Because women's vocal tracts are shorter than men's, their formant frequencies are higher and while it is possible to do some vowel normalisation and lessen the differences between men's and women's values, this often introduces other artifactual effects. In this paper we use the same scales for all the men's plots and all the women's plots. By making the vowel plots approximately the same size, it is possible to compare the men's and women's patterns visually. Our comments will be based on a comparison of the patterns, rather than specific formant frequencies or statistical analyses. Already in Figure 1, it can be seen that there are differences between the HME and the HFE: the women's mid vowels /e:, e, o:, o/ are relatively closer to the high vowels /i:, i, u:, u/ than are the men's. We know that this pattern also appears in the production of similar vowels in the English speech of contemporary Pākehā (Gordon et al. 2004). The /æ/ and /ɒ/ vowels were raising in NZE in the late nineteenth century, so here it appears that the Māori women are following their Pākehā compatriots and leading this change in Māori pronunciation. The women also have /a:/ and /a/ slightly closer together, so that the qualitative difference between them may be slightly less for the women than for the men. However the women's /u:/ and /u/ are slightly farther back than the men's, which is different from the NZE of the time, where /u/ was already quite central.

---

[9] For people not used to reading acoustic plots, they are plotted in this way so that the acoustic results match the place of articulation in the mouth. The position of the vowel on the quadrilateral approximates the highest position of the tongue, with the lips to the left of the plot and the back of the tongue to the right.

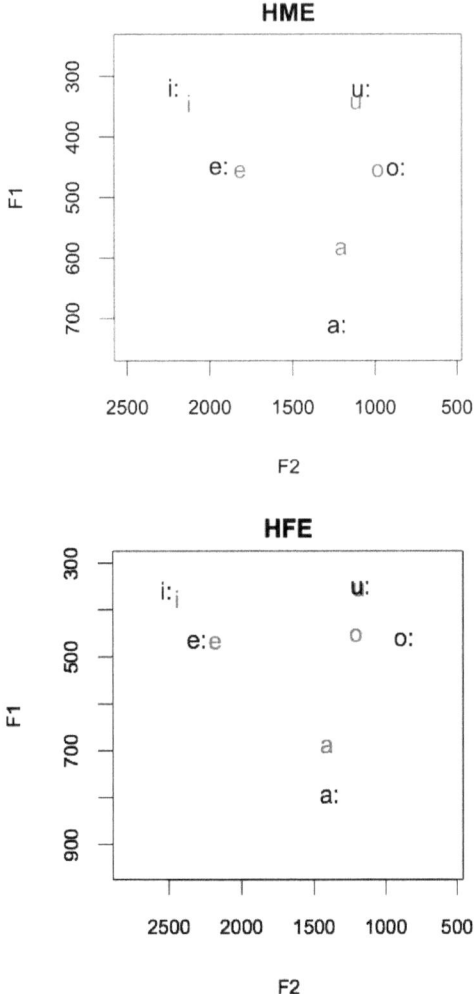

Figure 1: Formant plots of the mean values for the vowels of the historical male elders and the historical female elders. The formant frequencies are plotted in Hz.

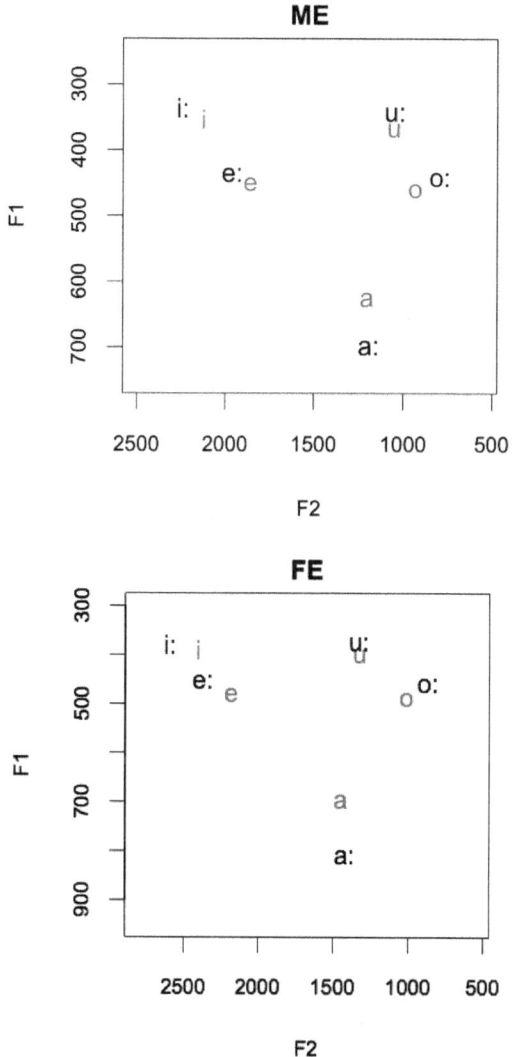

Figure 2: Formant plots of the mean values for the vowels of the present day male and female elders. The formant frequencies are plotted in Hz.

When the vowel plots of the present day male and female elders are compared (Figure 2) the mid vowels are closer to the high vowels for both men and women and the men have caught up with the women in terms of bringing /a/ closer to /a:/. However /u:/ and /u/ have still not moved forward to match NZE. Although the mid vowels have risen considerably for the women, the five pairs of vowels are still distributed fairly evenly around the vowel space for the men. This changes when we come to the young speakers (Figure 3).

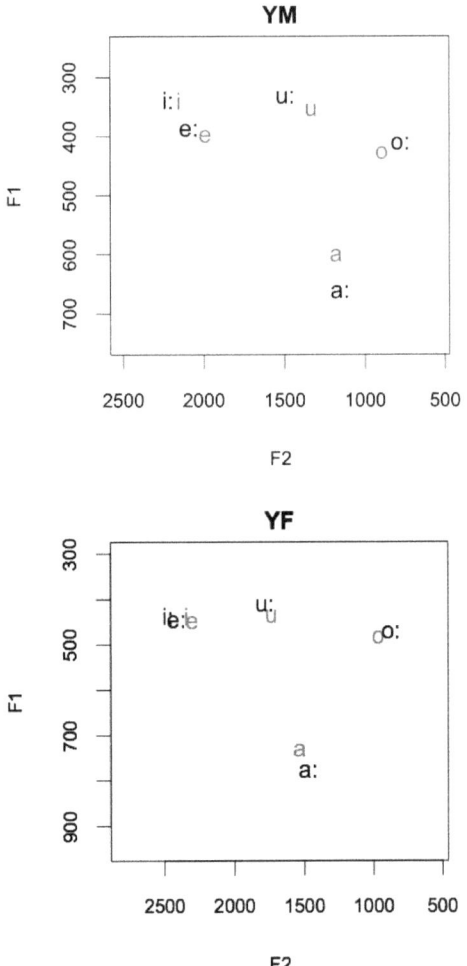

Figure 3: Formant plots of the mean values for the vowels of the present day young male and female speakers. The formant frequencies are plotted in Hz.

In Figure 3 we see that /u:/ and /u/ are now central for both groups of young speakers. They have moved considerably more towards the front than for any of the older groups, and are in a similar position to those of current young NZE speakers (Hay, Maclagan and Gordon 2008). The young women are in the lead. /a:/ and /a/ are now much closer together for both the men and the women and it would be very difficult to hear any qualitative difference between them. In addition, the women's /a:/ and /a/ are more central than the men's, though not yet as central as modern NZE /a/ and /ʌ/. The mid vowels have raised for the men so that they are now closer to the high vowels than for the FE in Figure 2. The most striking change, however, is the extent to which the mid vowels have risen for the young women. /i:, i, e:/ and /e/ all occupy the same acoustic space, and the vowels can no longer be said to be evenly distributed round the vowel space. The extent of the overlap in the high and 'mid' vowels is demonstrated in Figure 4 where the distributions of the vowel tokens are shown in the ellipses. The ellipses contain 95% of the data, so that the extreme outliers are omitted. The ellipses show the extent of the overlap for the long and short tokens for each vowel pair, and emphasize that /i:, i, e:, e/ really all do occupy the same acoustic space. A similar graph is given for the two oldest of the historical female elders who were recorded in the 1940s to show that although the ellipses for /i:, i/ and /e:, e/ overlap, the overlap is considerably less than for the young females.

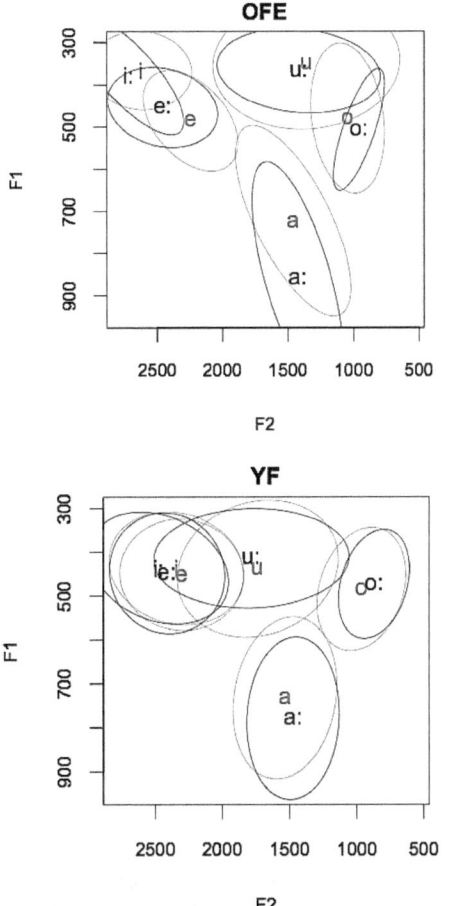

Figure 4: Plots of the mean values for the vowels of the two oldest historical female elders and the young female speakers together with ellipses that contain 95% of the tokens for each vowel. Formant frequencies are plotted in Hz.

In these results so far, women are playing their traditional role and leading in changes that do not seem to have been noticed by the community. We can see them also playing their role in maintaining standards if we separate out the two groups of female elders, those who were recorded in the 1940s, the oldest female elders (OFE), and those who were recorded in the 1990s, the intermediate female elders (IFE). In Figure 5 the vowel plot of the OFE is contrasted with the plot of the IFE. It can be seen that the OFE actually had relatively central /u:/ and /u/

sounds. The IFE, however, have retracted the high back vowels, /uː/ and /u/, so they are again as far back as for the HME in Figure 1. We interpret this as indicating that initially women led a change towards centralizing the high back vowels, but that Māori speakers had become aware of this process and that the IFE were reacting against it.[10]

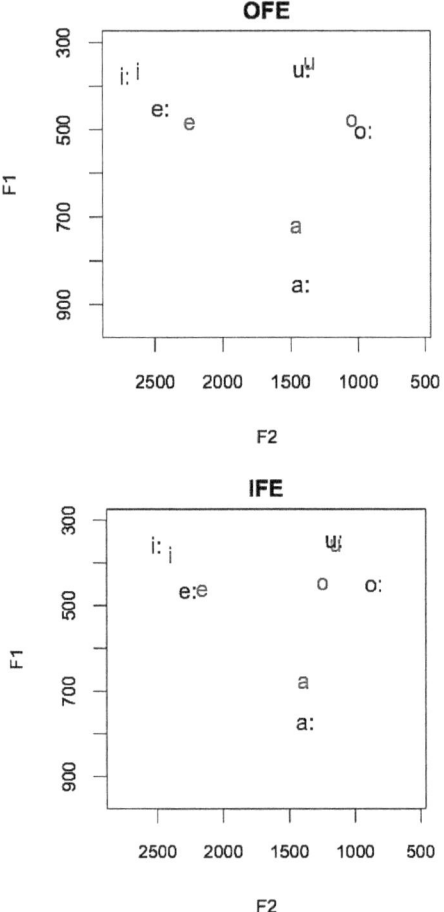

Figure 5: Plots of the mean values for the vowels of the historical female elders and the intermediate female elders. Formant frequencies are plotted in Hz.

Diphthongs

When we consider the diphthongs, the historical speakers, both men and women, have distinct starting points for all five diphthongs (see Figure 6). They have similar ending points for /au/ and /ou/ and different ending points for the other

---

[10] Winifred Bauer notes that one of the speakers she worked with for her 1993 book *Māori* ridiculed the very front pronunciation of words like *tū*, 'stand' and *runga* 'top' (location) (personal communication, 9 May, 2012).

diphthongs. In the diagrams for the diphthongs, the diphthongs are represented by arrows, with the identifying symbol placed at the end point. The diphthong arrows are plotted against the ellipses for the short vowels so that it is possible to see where the starting and ending points are with respect to the speakers' short monophthongs. For both the men and the women the diphthongs start and finish within the ellipses of the short vowels which are their first and second elements. The only exception is /ae/ for the women, where the second element only reaches the edge of the /e/ ellipse, perhaps to heighten the contrast with /ai/. For both men and women, the diphthongs that move towards the high vowels, /ai/ and /au/, start in very similar positions, and considerably higher than /ae/ and /ao/, which move towards the mid vowels.

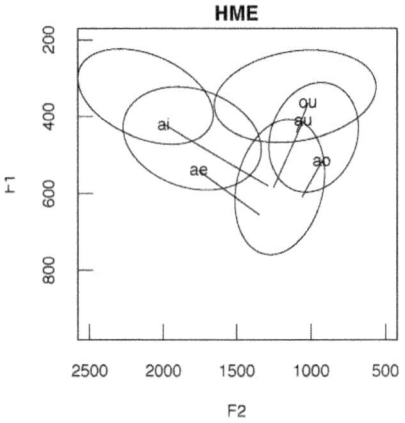

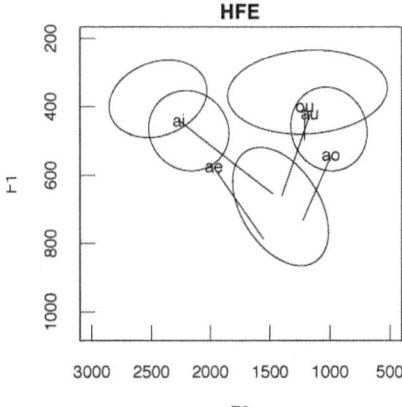

Figure 6: Diphthong plots for the historical male and female speakers. The arrow represents the direction of movement with the diphthong symbol placed at the end point. The ellipses represent 95% of the tokens for the short vowels. Formant frequencies are plotted in Hz.

When we move to the present day elders (Figure 7), the first observation is that the second elements of both /ai/ and /ae/ hardly reach the ellipses for their associated short vowels for the men. /ai/ still reaches the centre of the /i/ ellipse for the women. The historical elders had similar ending points for /au/ and /ou/, the two diphthongs moving towards /u/. For the present day elders, the starting points for these diphthongs have also become much more similar so that it is difficult to hear a difference between the diphthong pairs. Although /u/ did not seem to have fronted for the present female elders (Figure 2), the second elements of /au/ and /ou/ in Figure 7 are fronter for the women than for the men so that the angles of the diphthong trajectories are different. In similar fashion to the historical speakers, /ai/ and /au/ start in very similar positions, and their starting points are still higher than /ae/ and /ao/.

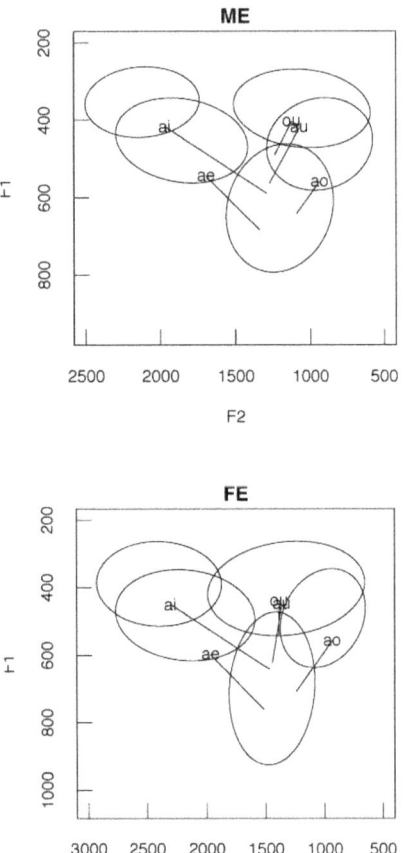

Figure 7: Diphthong plots for the present day male and female elders. The arrow represents the direction of movement with the diphthong symbol placed at the end point. The ellipses represent 95% of the tokens for the short vowels. Formant frequencies are plotted in Hz.

Figure 8 shows the diphthongs for the young speakers. The most obvious change is in the two front diphthongs, /ai/ and /ae/. For the young men, the starting points are very close; for the young women, the starting and ending points for both diphthongs are now virtually identical – as are the ellipses for their ending points /i/ and /e/. Here, as elsewhere, the young women are leading in the change. The diphthong pair /ou/ and /au/ are even more similar for the young men than for the present day elders, but the young women have different starting points.

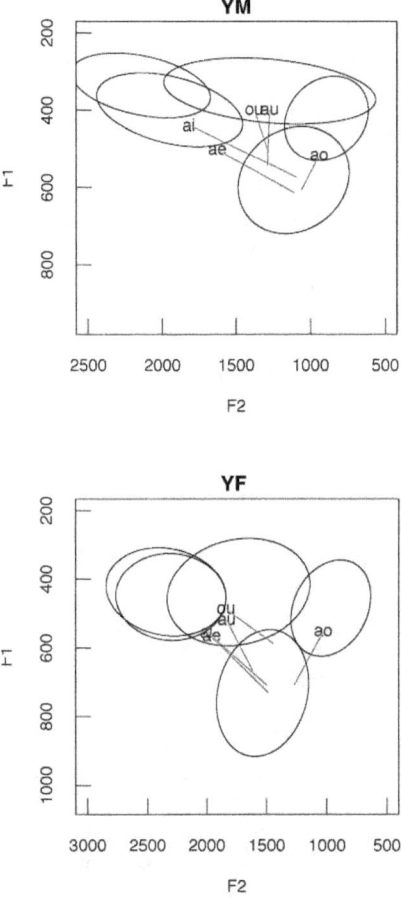

Figure 8: Diphthong plots for the young male and female speakers. The arrow represents the direction of movement with the diphthong symbol placed at the end point. The ellipses represent 95% of the tokens for the short vowels. Formant frequencies are plotted in Hz.

We do not yet have sufficient data, but it is possible that women are starting to withdraw from a change that could lead to the merger of these two diphthongs. As /u:/ and /u/ fronted for the young speakers (see Figure 3) so the ending points of /au/ and /ou/ have fronted, and the modern diphthongs sound very different from those of the historical elders. In our analysis, we have noted that the most fronted versions of /ou/ occur in the pronouns (*mātou, tātou, koutou, rātou*). As has been found in other cases, common words are often in the lead in sound change (Bybee 2002; Phillips 2001).

Discussion and Conclusion

In the material presented here, women can be seen as fulfilling their usual roles in language change for the Māori language. They are leading in changes that are below the level of consciousness, and somewhat more conservative in changes that have risen above the level of consciousness and have become stigmatized. In the development of NZE, it was noted that sound changes initially lagged in some regions and proceeded faster in others, but that, in time, the sound changes occurred everywhere (Gordon et al. 2004). And similarly, men usually catch up with changes led by women. This appears to be true for the sound changes we have been studying in Māori. Initially, the historical female elders were ahead in the fronting of /u:/ and /u/. The intermediate female elders pulled back and produced very back conservative versions of these vowels but the young females are again in the lead. Similarly we have found that, rather than shortening the long vowels as the men were doing, the present day female elders actually produced longer long vowels. But the young women produce long vowels that are somewhat shorter than the men (King et al. 2010). Overall, there appears to be less difference between the vowel systems of the young men and women than between men and women of earlier generations. Although women have been in the lead, men are rapidly catching up with the standards that women seem to be setting.

Because there was a generation when Māori was not transmitted from parents to children (Benton 1991), we wondered whether the traditional gender role patterns would be observable for the younger generations of Māori speakers. We cannot find any evidence of this break in the speech of modern young Māori. The young speakers we have recorded can be divided into two groups: those who learnt Māori as a first language (L1), albeit alongside English, and those who learnt it as a second language (L2) after they started school. There is a slight difference between the experiences of the young men and the women. None of the parents of the L1 young men spoke to them in Māori – they learnt their language from frequent early interaction with grandparents and then at kōhanga reo (Māori language nests) and kura kaupapa Māori (Māori medium schools). At least one of the young women was raised by L2 parents who spoke to her in Māori. L2 Māori speaking parents raising L1 children is not unusual in NZ at present, although for the vast majority of students learning in the medium of Māori, the school remains the only place where they are exposed to a significant amount of Māori.

Although differences can clearly be found in syntax for young L1 and L2 speakers (Bauer 2011) and even between the young men and women (Bauer personal communication, April, 2012) we have not found marked differences in their phonology. The vowel spaces of the young L2 men are larger than those of the young L1 men, perhaps reflecting a greater care in their speech (Watson et al. 2008). The speech of first and second language speakers of Māori is clearly an area that would reward further study. Apart from the work of Bauer (2011) we are not aware of other work examining differences between men's and women's syntax. This would be another fruitful area for study.

Along with many other minority languages in the world whose situation is similar, Māori has been subjected to colossal pressure from a major language leading both to its continuing very precarious position demographically and sociolinguistically, and to contact phenomena in phonetics, in syntax and in vocabulary. Nonetheless we believe that this study shows that normal processes of change, and in particular, the role of women speakers in its progress continue to operate despite disruption of transmission. It would be hard to argue that female speakers of Māori speak as they do out of any subconscious feeling of insecurity or inferiority, and Holmes' point mentioned in the introduction is surely the case. While it remains true that oratory, one of the most highly valued oral arts where Māori is still very much the preferred language, is mostly the preserve of men, women have equally high-status oral arts and are very much at the forefront of the efforts to maintain the language in all ways, as parents, teachers, and policy makers. Māori women's contribution to the future of Māori and its shape in that future cannot be overestimated and certainly requires ongoing research.

References

Anderson Atholl. 2009. Origins, settlement and society of pre-European South Polynesia. In Giselle Byrnes (ed.) *The New Oxford History of New Zealand*. South Melbourne, Vic.: Oxford University Press Australia and New Zealand, pp. 21-46.
Bauer, Winifred, with William Parker and Te Kareongawai Evans 1993. *Māori*. London: Routledge.
Bauer, Winifred. 2011. The changing use of the manner particles of Māori. Linguistics Society of New Zealand 19th Biennial Conference, 17-18 Nov 2011.
Benton, Richard. 1991. *The Māori language: dying or reviving?* Hawaii: East-West Center.
Benton, Richard and Nena Benton. 2001. RLS in Aotearoa/New Zealand 1989-1999. In Joshua Fishman (ed.) *Can threatened languages be saved?* Clevedon: Multilingual Matters, pp. 423-50
Biggs, Bruce. 1978. The history of Polynesian phonology. In Stephen Wurm and Lois Carrington (eds) *Second International Conference on Austronesian Linguistics: Proceedings*. Pacific Linguistics C-61. Canberra: Australian National University, pp 691-716.
Blust, Robert. 2009. *The Austronesian Languages*. Canberra: Australian National University.
Boersma, Paul & David Weenink. 2009. Praat: doing phoneticsby computer (Version 5.1.05) [Computer program]. Retrieved May 1, 2009, from http://www.praat.org/
Bourdieu, Pierre. 1991. *Language and symbolic power*. Cambridge: Harvard University Press,
Bybee, Joan. 2002. Word frequency and context of use in the lexical diffusion of phonetically conditioned sound change. *Language Variation and Change*. 14: 261-90.
Cheshire, Jennifer. 1982. *Variation in an English dialect*. Cambridge: Cambridge University Press.
Cheshire, Jennifer. 2002. Sex and Gender in Variationist Research. In J. K.

Chambers, P. Trudgill and N. Schilling-Estes (eds). *The Handbook of Language Variation and Change*. Oxford: Blackwell, pp. 423-43.
Coates, Jennifer, 1998 *Language and Gender: a Reader*. London: Blackwell
Coates, Jennifer. 2004. *Women, men and language: a sociolinguistic account of gender differences in language*. 3rd ed. London: Pearson Longman.
Eckert, Penelope. 1989. The whole woman: sex and gender differences in variation. *Language Variation and Change* 1:245-67.
EckertPenelope. 2000. *Linguistic variation as social practice*. Malden, MA: Blackwell.
Elbert, Samuel H. and Pukui, Mary K. 1979. *Hawaiian Grammar*. Honolulu: the University of Hawaii Press.
Gordon, Elizabeth, Campbell, Lyle, Hay, Jennifer, Maclagan, Margaret, Sudbury, Andrea and Trudgill, Peter. 2004. *New Zealand English: its origins and evolution*. Cambridge: Cambridge University Press.
Harlow, Ray, Keegan, Peter, King, Jeanette, Maclagan, Margaret and Watson, Catherine. 2009. The changing sound of the Māori language. In James N. Stanford and Dennis R Preston. (eds). *Variation in Indigenous Minority Languages*. Amsterdam/Philadelphia: Benjamins. pp. 129-52.
Hay, Jennifer, Maclagan, Margaret and Gordon, Elizabeth. 2008. *New Zealand English*. Edinburgh: Edinburgh University Press.
Holmes, Janet. 1997. Setting new standards: sound change and gender in New Zealand English. *English World Wide*. 18:107-42.
King, Jeanette, Watson, Catherine, Maclagan, Margaret, Harlow, Ray, Keegan, Peter. 2010. Maori women's role in sound change. In J. Holmes & M. Marra (eds) *Femininity, Feminism and Gendered Discourse*. Newcastle upon Tyne: Cambridge Scholars Publishing. pp. 191-211.
King, Jeanette, Maclagan, Margaret, Harlow, Ray, Keegan, Peter and Watson, Catherine I. 2011. The MAONZE project: changing uses of an indigenous language database. *Corpus Linguistics and Linguistic Theory*.7 (1):37-57.
Krupa, Viktor. 1982. *The Polynesian languages: A guide*. Languages of Asia and Africa. Vol. 4. London: Routledge and Kegan Paul.
Kuki, Hiroshi. 1970. *Tuamotuan phonology*. Pacific Linguistics B-17. Canberra: Australian National University.
Labov, William 1990. The intersection of sex and social class in the course of linguistic change. *Language Variation and Change*. 2:205-51.
Maclagan, Margaret, Gordon, Elizabeth and Lewis, Gillian. 1999. Women and sound change: conservative and innovative behaviour by the same speakers. *Language Variation and Change*. 11 (1):19-41.
Maclagan, Margaret, Watson, Catherine I., Harlow, Ray, King, Jeanette and Keegan, Peter. 2009. /u/ fronting and /t/ aspiration in Māori and New Zealand English. *Language Variation and Change*. 21(2):175-92.
Phillips, Betty. 2001. Lexical diffusion, lexical frequency and lexical analysis. In Joan Bybee and Paul Hopper, *Frequency and the emergence of linguistic structure*. Amsterdam: Benjamins. pp 123-36.
Shibata, Norio. 1988. Language of Mangaia: A Linguistic Sketch. In Kazumichi Katayama and Akira Tagaya (eds) *People of the Cook Islands – Past and Present*. Rarotonga: The Cook Islands Library and Museum Society. pp. 303-50.

Trudgill, Peter. 1974. *The social differentiation of English in Norwich*. Cambridge: Cambridge University Press.

Trudgill, Peter. 1983. *On Dialect*. New York: Blackwell

Woods, Nicola. 1997. The formation and development of New Zealand English: Interaction of gender-related variation and linguistic change. *Journal of Sociolinguistics*. 1:95-125.

Wolfram, Walt and Schilling-Estes, Natalie. 1998. *American English: Dialects and Variation*. Oxford: Blackwell.

Watson, Catherine I., Maclagan, Margaret, King, Jeanette, and Harlow, Ray. 2008. The English Pronunciation of Successive Groups of Maori Speakers. *Proceedings of the 9th Annual Conference of the International Speech Communication Association (Interspeech 2008) incorporating the 12th Australasian International Conference on Speech Science and Technology (SST 2008)*. ISSN 1990-9772. pp. 338-41.

Yaeger-Dror, Malcah. 1998. Factors influencing the contrast between men's and women's speech. *Women and Language*. 21 (1): 40-6.

Chapter 2: Negotiating Locality and Gender– Men, Women and Local Honorifics

Anna Strycharz-Banaś, University of Edinburgh

Abstract: Osaka Japanese has been shown to be linked by its speakers (and speakers of other varieties of Japanese) with masculinity on the one hand, but also different kinds of femininity on the other. By looking at one specific linguistic feature – local referent honorific suffix haru – and the change in its use across generations, we can observe different use of the form by men and women. To understand this variation it is necessary to look not only at the general patterns of use, but also at the ideologies surrounding the local variety, and the feature under study (cf. Okamoto 1998).

In line with previous findings (Maeda 1980; SturtzSreetharan 2004) haru occurs much more (though, unlike in most previous studies, not exclusively) in female speech. A significant drop in the use of this form among women is observed when we compare the older and middle age cohorts, who use it frequently, to the younger age cohort, whose use of this honorific is close to zero. On closer analysis of metalinguistic comments and use of the form in interactions, it appears, however, that the form is perceived (and used) differently by younger men and younger women. While younger women tend to avoid using the form, younger men use it more often.

The local honorific suffix haru seems to have become associated with a particular local identity (traditional Osaka woman). It appears that this kind of identity is no longer attractive for younger women, and this is mirrored in a decrease in the use of haru in the younger age cohort. On the other hand, with the image of Osaka men as comedians increasingly present in national media (especially TV), haru seems to have become a resource for indexing this kind of local identity among younger men. The form can thus index different meanings for different people in the same speech community (Johnstone & Kiesling 2008; Eckert 2009). Meanings available for and utilized by (mostly) women seem to be different than those indexed by the same form when used by (mostly younger) men.

Introduction

Honorifics in Japanese have been widely studied in relation both to politeness phenomena in general and to their link with gender. While numerous previous approaches have clearly outlined gendered norms in the use of honorification, over the past few decades more and more research using empirical evidence has questioned this approach, arguing that a straightfoward link between any linguistic feature and a predetermined social category demands a more detailed explanation. While on an ideological level honorification may be a component of women's language, when honorifics are used in real interactions by real speakers, the research has consistently shown their multifaceted nature.

In this chapter we explore the relationship between the use of local honorifics found in Osaka Japanese and gender. We argue that though there may be a correlation between use of the form and gender of the speaker, in order to understand this correlation we need to uncover some locally constructed ideologies available to the speakers, and their link with both gender and the use of honorification.

Osaka Japanese Honorifics

Osaka Japanese (OJ is one of the dialects of Japanese which has its own unique system of marking honorification, different from that of Standard Japanese. With regards to verbal honorific marking, there are two kinds we can distinguish: addressee honorification, and referent honorification. Addressee honorification is said to work along the speaker: addressee axis, allowing the speaker to express respect for the addressee, but also marking the more general polite demeanor or formality of the situation (Ide 1990). Dialectal addressee honorification as such is not present in OJ[1]. Referent honorification, on the other hand, is used to show respect towards the referent of the utterance, who may, but does not have to, be the addressee.

In the discussion in this chapter we focus on one of the local honorific verbal suffixes – *haru*. It has been suggested in previous research that local referent honorifics are most widely used honorific resources, both for referring to a third person, and for addressing the other party in conversation (Miyaji 1987, 1996; Seiichi 1992). Moreover, some researchers have suggested that in informal conversations among OJ speakers, if any referent honorific was used, it was *haru* (SturtzSreetharan, 2008).

Haru is thus a referent honorific suffix which can be used either to refer to a third person (1 and 2), or to to address (3 and 4), and it can be used with (1 and 3) or without (2 and 4) SJ addressee honorification, as in the examples below. All of

---

1 Some sources (e.g. Sato 2003) suggest that there exists a local form for the addressee honorific/polite copula form, i.e. OJ dasu for SJ desu. Okamoto (1998) argues this form has become obsolete, and this is supported by the fact that there are no occurrences of dasu in my corpus.

the examples are taken from the corpus of spontaneous Osaka speech described in the section on data and methods[2].

(1) Ano   hito   mo   mochiron   shinji-te-harun   desu
    That   person   too   of.course   believe-PROGR-OJ.RH   AH
    yo
    SJ.SFP
    Of course he also believes in it

(2) Moo   sugu   shime-hat-ta   wa
    Already   soon   close-OJ.RH-PAST   OJ.SFP
    They closed soon after

(3) Nani   yuu-te-harun   desu-ka   honto ni
    What   say-PROGR-OJ.RH   AH-QP   really
    Really what are you saying?

(4) Shinu   made   benkyooshi-haru   ne
    Die   until   learn-OJ.RH   SJ.SFP
    You will study until you die, won't you?

What makes OJ honorifics particularly interesting for the study of language and gender is that OJ as a variety has come to be perceived as indexing a number of features, from traditionally being linked with gentle and elegant femininity (as depicted e.g. in Junichiro's novel *Sasameyuki*) to now being often associated with either rough masculinity (e.g. associated with a stereotypical villain characters in film) or the speech of comedians. How do these meanings associated with OJ translate into the ideologies surrounding the use of local honorification? And how do Osakan men and women make sense of the changing ideologies and perceptions in their use of local honorifics?

Honorifics and Gender

Japanese honorific marking has long been a hallmark for studying politeness, specifically in relation to its gendered nature. The use of honorifics is one of the most commonly talked about differences between the speech of men and women in Japan (e.g. Jorden & Noda 1987, Ide 1990, Niyekawa 1990, Shibatani 1990, [Shibamoto] Smith 1992). Polite language has been shown to be linked with the speech of women, who were claimed not to have access to rude or impolite linguistic resources (Ide 1990). It has been suggested that indeed the uniqueness of women's language derives from their use of honorification (Sugimoto 1997).

---

[2] Glossing conventions: AH – addressee honorific; RH – referent honorific; SJ – Standard Japanese; OJ– Osaka Japanese; SFP – sentence final particle; QP – question particle; PAST – past tense marking; PROGR – progressive; DAT – dative; ACC – accusative; SUB – subject; MASC – masculine; COP – copula; QUOT – quotative; : - prolonged sound; = mark latching s; capital letters mark a significantly louder ; (.) short pause

The view that the use of honorification is distributed along the lines of gender distinction has been challenged by some (e.g. Okamoto 1997, Yamaji 2008) when analysing spontaneous interactions. With regards to the local honorific suffix *haru* SturtzSreetharan (2006) and Maeda (1961) claim that men are not heard using this form. Other sources suggest, however, that *haru* is not sex-exclusive (Horii 1995). We will look at not only the distribution of this local honorific in the speech of men and women, but also at their perceptions of its use, as well as interactions, to be able to address the question of gender in a more nuanced way.

This Study

This chapter sets out to examine the role of gender and locality in relation to linguistic practices in use, specifically to the use of one of the local honorific suffixes – *haru*. It has been suggested that to have a fuller understanding of any given linguistic feature, we need to combine several aspects of its existence. John Gumperz argued long ago for the 'closer understanding of how linguistic signs interact with social knowledge in the discourse' (1982, 29), and in the same vein Michael Silverstein called for the study of the total linguistic fact, which is 'an unstable mutual interaction of meaningful sign forms contextualized to situations of interested human use mediated by the fact of cultural ideology' (1985, 220). This view of the study of language urges us to provide a more multi-faceted investigation of the use of linguistic signs. In the discussion which follows we will therefore look into the distribution of the form across age and gender groups, the use of this form in interaction, and linguistic and cultural ideologies expressed in metapragmatic comments by the speakers themselves. While the link between the overt comments and the use of any linguistic (and indeed not only linguistic) sign is not straightforward, metapragmatic discourses can serve as one of the interpretive frames that are involved in shaping daily interactions (Hanks 1993). Therefore, the way certain linguistic resources are perceived and stereotyped is important in understanding the use of language as a social process, at the same time also allowing us to acknowledge that linguistic ideologies are also subject to change (Okamoto 1997). In the analysis of the distributional data we will present an apparent time picture across three age cohorts, but in the discussion of ideologies we will focus on the youngest group of speakers.

Data and Methods

Methods and Grammatical Context

For the quantitative analysis, tokens of *haru* were counted out of all contexts in which the use of a referent honorific would have been warranted. While there are other possible honorific features available at hand, *haru* accounts for 85% of all referent honorifics used in the corpus, and thus overshadows any other form. Other OJ honorifics are used in a very restricted context, and SJ honorification is found only in the speech of two older men.

The finding that *haru* is the main referent honorific used by OJ speakers is in line with previous research (SturtzSreetharan 2008), which has shown that in informal conversations if any honorific is used at all, it is always *haru*. We will then consider *haru* as the prevalent form of referent honorification used by OJ speakers in informal conversations.

To be able to discuss the distribution of this form across generations and genders, all of the contexts in which the use of *haru* would have been warranted were taken into account. The verbs included in the analysis are finite verbs with a clear human referent (whether it is the addressee or a third person, present or absent), except for reference to children and babies. There were overall 17 child/baby references, none of them containing any kind of honorific marking.

Verbs excluded were ones offering general statements without a clear referent (translated with a generic subject 'you', e.g. 'you work all day and in the end it seems like there is no money in your bank account') as well as self-references (where referent honorific marking is not possible). Passives were excluded altogether (Iwasaki 2002), as was the verb *oru* 'be'. In SJ the verb *oru* is a humble equivalent of the verb *iru* 'be'. In OJ, however, it is said that *oru* is a local equivalent of *iru*, and has no humbling quality. Since the meaning of this verb seems ambiguous, it was excluded from the analysis. In the corpus there are 71 uses of *oru* and none of them have any honorific marking.

Overall, 381 tokens of *haru* out of 2731 possible contexts were taken into account and analyzed.

Sample

Data used in this discussion come from a corpus collected during fieldwork in Osaka in 2008. The corpus consists of over 38 hours of recorded spontaneous interactions, each involving 2-4 speakers of Osaka Japanese. The sample consists of 44 speakers, 21 men and 23 women, divided into three age cohorts (Table 1).

Table 1. The sample of speakers, divided into age and gender.

	Younger	Middle	Older
Women	8	9	7
Men	6	7	8

Following Dubois and Horvath (1999), age was treated as a sociological, as well as chronological, variable (see also Eckert 1997). The participants were assigned into cohorts based on their chronological age, but the lines separating the older, middle and younger groups were drawn according to the shared socio-cultural experiences of each group, with special emphasis placed on the sociolinguistic situation of OJ relevant for the given cohort (see below).

The sociolinguistic situation of OJ has been changing in recent years, and its status and perceptions (and possibly therefore also use) have been undergoing some changes. This may have had a different impact on the perceptions of the local variety by speakers from different age groups, as we shortly explain below.

The *older group* is composed of people who are 60 and above. People in this group experienced immediate post-war Japan and were involved in rebuilding the country. Members of this group were in education between 1930s and 1960s, and the educational agenda of the day is what sets them significantly apart from the other two age cohorts.

Not unlike in other parts of the world, in the pre-war period there seems to have been no recognition of dialects in schooling, and the use of standard language was promoted throughout the country using different platforms. Standard language was seen as a source of national identity (a policy which continued long afterwards), and as one of the significant factors in creating the image of a homogenous society and uniting the nation. Immediately after WWII, while the national drive towards homogeneity (both linguistic and cultural) was not as intense as it had been previously, the pressure of language standardization continued until the mid 1960s (Carroll 2001, 183). During this period, the teaching of correct language was to be achieved not only through schools, but also through the radio (Carroll 2001). This underlines the role Japanese media have had in language education and in shaping attitudes towards the language spoken in the country. The huge influence of national media in shaping attitudes regarding linguistic varieties continues to this day.

Speakers from the *middle* age cohort were faced with a different approach as far as teaching and language education was concerned. Their school years fell between the late 1960s and early 1990s, when new guidelines were put in place, and school curricula began to change their view of and attitude towards dialect varieties. Gradually code-switching began to be the prescribed norm, with school children taught to use the local and standard varieties where appropriate (Carroll 2001, 186).

The *younger* age group is composed of people whose school years fall between the 1990s and the present (some are still in education at universities). The official teaching curricula have not changed in the recent years, and the official guidelines are the same as they were in the times of their parents' education. What has changed, however, is the recognition of OJ, its presence in the media and attitudes towards it both within and outside Osaka. One of the most visible aspects of it is the increasing presence of OJ in the national media, especially in TV dramas and comedy programs. OJ is, however, also used in commercials and shows for children.

One of the first initiatives to introduce OJ in the public sphere outside the local area was *Osaka-ben de shaberu DAY* ('A Day of Talking in Osaka Dialect') in 1993 - all day on NHK One Radio only OJ was spoken. The importance of this can be appreciated if we recall that media (and especially radio) had previously been used to promote the correct use of 'good' language, and many of the older generation informants were still surprised by the presence of OJ in national media. For the younger age group, however, this is the sociolinguistic reality – their variety is recognized, liked, and even imitated (Onoe et al. 2000). With an increasing number of Osaka-born comedians appearing on TV, the city has begun to be associated with entertainment more than anything else. Anecdotal evidence suggests that people from other parts of Japan consider Osakans to be 'funny guys', and students in other parts of Japan have been reported to use OJ when trying to sound funny (Pawel Dybala – personal communication). OJ has become a valuable commodity not only in the local circles.

Results and Discussion

Quantitative Analysis

The table below presents the use of *haru* by the three generations of speakers in the form of an apparent time picture. The number of possible contexts where *haru* could have occurred is followed by the number of tokens of *haru* in these contexts, and the percentage is calculated in brackets. In line with what some previous findings suggested, it is then clear that (i) the use of the form is different in different generations, and (ii) men use this honorific significantly less than women. However, an interesting shift can be observed in the youngest generation of speakers.

Table 2. The distribution of *haru* in different age and gender groups (number of all possible contexts / number of tokens of *haru* (percentage))

	Older	Middle	Younger
Women	152/393 (39%)	161/636 (25%)	14/449 (3.2%)
Men	28/434 (6.5%)	9/251 (3.6%)	17/208 (8.2%)

In the youngest generation, men and women behave in a rather unexpected way with regards to the use of *haru*. While younger women follow the trend visible in the other two age cohorts, that is their use of *haru* keeps steadily declining, younger men seem to be reversing this trend, by using the form more than younger women, and also more than men from older and middle age cohorts. While the number of tokens is indeed quite small in the younger age cohort overall, the difference between younger men's and younger women's use of the form is statistically significant ($p=0.0102$).

From the distributional patterns alone, we can see that there is a combined effect of age and gender on the use of local honorification. In the discussion below we will focus on the interesting pattern we are observing in the younger generation – the almost complete disappearance of the form from the repertoire of younger women, and the way younger men seem to be picking up its use.

The shared histories of three generations with regards to the status of OJ suggest that the younger generation is actively participating in a kind of cultural renaissance. While OJ has always been a vital variety of Japanese, and its relationship with Standard Japanese might involve a different amount of influence from that exerted on other varieties of Japanese, the increasing vitality of OJ on a national scale has been especially visible in the recent years. It is therefore possible that the pattern we are observing is akin to what has been termed 'recycling' by Dubois & Horvath (1999) in their research on Cajun community – the increasing value of OJ has affected the use of certain local features in such a way that they are now beginning to be used by groups of speakers in whose speech the feature had not been present previously, or not to that degree.

An interesting question that emerges from observing this pattern is whether younger men and women use this form in the same way. Do they take it to fulfill the same discourse function? Is the form linked with the same sets of social attributes by these two cohorts? We will explore the possible answers to these questions by examining the metapragmatic comments of the speakers which occurred during the interviews, and the way in which *haru* is used in interactions.

Metapragmatics

Paying attention to the metapragmatic discourse surrounding the use of certain linguistic features allows us to look into the ideologies of their use[3]. While the relationship between ideologies and the actual use of language is not straightforward, it is nonetheless important to incorporate the metapragmatic comments, especially when the feature we are interested in has such a high social load. We will thus look briefly at the metapragmatics surrounding the use of *haru* to be able to add another dimension to the analysis of the shift we have seen in the previous section.

While the older and middle age cohorts of speakers in the corpus – both men and women – generally tend to agree that the form can be seen as indexing femininity and politeness, younger speakers seem to have developed a new set of meanings that is attached to this form. The ideology of the use of *haru* seems therefore to have shifted in a new direction, evolving from being perceived as an index of politeness, and refined elegant femininity, to being associated with more specific kinds of locally available identities.

Younger women in the sample have overall been rather dismissive of the use of *haru*. In Standard Japanese the use of referent honorification, especially without addressee honorification, has been shown to evoke images of mature and refined femininity. While reflexes of this kind of index can be seen in the older and middle generations of OJ speakers, who claim the form sounds feminine, younger women overall have come to associate it with a traditionally stereotyped image of an Osaka woman, who has come to be known throughout Japan as *Osaka-no obachan*. This kind of local persona is not in line with the iconicized Japanese womanly woman (e.g. Shibamoto 1985) and is usually characterized as being loudmouthed, stingy and badly dressed (Maegaki 2005, SturtzSreetharan 2008). *Osaka-no obachan* is an image recognizable throughout Japan that constitutes a particularly salient local cultural stereotype. The younger women have thus come to associate the use of this local referent honorific with a local icon that they do not wish to be associated with. With this we are provided with an example of 'the use of a sign with an image of personhood' (Agha 2002, 31) – while *haru* is still undoubtedly seen as indexing femininity, it is a very different kind of femininity, one that younger women do not want to associate with.

An entirely different set of meanings seems to be associated with *haru* when we look at the comments provided by younger men. For them, the form has come to be linked with someone who is 'a true Osakan' and also 'a comedian'. This kind of cultural stereotype – that Osaka people are funny, or that all comedians come from Osaka – can be seen promoted in the media. *Haru,* thus, at least on an ideological level, for the younger men seems to have become a marker of local identity, one that is often linked with being funny. We can then begin to

---

[3] For the purpose of this discussion ideology here is understood, following Silverstein, as 'sets of beliefs about language articulated by users as a rationalization or justification of perceived structure and use' (1979, 123).

understand the increase in use of this form among younger men, who clearly see it as a valuable asset that will link them with the desirable local identity. These different 'images of personhood' available to different groups of speakers are therefore affecting the perception of locally available forms. The images available to any given person are definitely gender-specific, but the link between the form and the fixed social category (gender) is mediated by local ideologies.

To what extent these new emerging meanings directly affect the use of *haru* is impossible to tell. However, we cannot neglect the fact that younger women, who have come to associate the form with an unwanted local identity, are dropping its use, while younger men, who have come to see it as being an index of desirable localness, seem to be picking up its use in terms of frequency.

To further explore ways in which the form is used among younger men and women, and enrich our understanding of the different practices, we will now briefly turn to examining the interactional functions of *haru*.

Interactional Analysis

Let us turn to the interactional functions of *haru* visible in the conversations of younger speakers. We will briefly analyse prototypical uses found in this age cohort, and show differences in their use between men and women.

Younger men overwhelmingly use *haru* to address the listener, in a seemingly prescriptive manner, to convey respect. In the following excerpt three men are talking about their career prospects and ambitions. At one point one of them admits to wanting to proceed and do a PhD, while the other says he wants to be a comedian.

1. Jun: chirigaku   ni   kyoomi   ga   aru   no de-
           geography   DAT   interest   ACC   have   because
           (It's) because I am interested in geography-

2. Taka: sugo:i   na::
           great   OJ.SFP
           That's great

3. Taka: ore   wa   manzai (.)   ano (.)
           I.MASC   SUB   manzai   well
           As for me, well, manzai…
   {looking at Jun}

4.   sonna   shinu   made   benkyooshi-haru   ne
           like.that   die   until   study-OJ.RH   SJ.SFP
           So you will study until you die
   {all four laugh}
                                            (OsakaI, ASTJ, Taka and Jun, 01'20'24)

Throughout the conversation the unmarked way of addressing each other is with plain verb forms, that is without either addressee or referent honorification. This is one of the few exceptions, which suggests the use of honorific in this example is socially and interactionally meaningful in the given context. Taka, while the remark in line 4 is made in a joking tone, honestly admires Jun's perseverance in continuing education, as we learn from later in the conversation. The honorific used in line 4 can then be seen as an expression of respect, but the laughter and joking tone suggest that *haru* here fulfills more than one function. It is also interesting that it is used in an utterance directly following Taka's manzai reference. It is therefore not unlikely that *haru* in this utterance both conveys respect and adds a comical effect to the utterance. It might then be used to add to the comical persona Taka is crafting for himself. In the follow-up interview later on Taka was one of the people who suggested that this local honorific is also used by comedians.

The function of *haru* appears to be very different when used by younger women. There are two prototypical functions the form fulfills in the speech of younger women: to index solidarity and to create a comical effect. For space considerations we will provide an example of the first function and briefly discuss the other.

In the following interaction, the conversation revolves around different areas of Osaka, and the topic boils down to who lives where. The participants are two young women, Kaori and Junko, the researcher and a young man, Kenji. All of the participants have known each other for an extended period of time.

1. Kaori: minami   ga   suki   nan   desuka=
          south   ACC   like   AH-QP
          Do you like the south (of Osaka)?

2. Anna: =zu::tto   minami   (.)   minami   ga   suki
          All the time south   south   ACC   like

          desu   yo=
          COP.AH   SJ.SFP
          It's always been the south (.) I like (living in) the south

3. Junko: Nagai   kooen   yatta(-ra)   chikai   desu =
          Nagai   park   OJ.COP-POT   close   COP.AH

          ne
          SJ.SFP
          If it's Nagai park it's close, isn't it?

4. Anna: dakara   koko   kara   tooi=
          therefore   here   from   far
          That's why it's far from here

5. Junko: TOOI   desu   yo   ne::
          far   COP.AH.   SJ.SFP   SJ.SFP
          It's far isn't it?!

6. Kenji: Matsubara   tte   nani   sen

		Matsubara QUOT what line
		What line is Matsubara (on)?

7.	Junko:	Kintetsu minami sen desu
		Kintetsu south line COP.AH
		It's Kintetsu southern line

{…}

8.	Junko:	Nani sen desu-ka
		what line COP.AH-QP
		What line are you on?

9.	Anna:	Kintetsu=
		Kintetsu

10.	Junko:	Kintetsu sen not-te-harun desu-ka
		Kintetsu line get.on-PROGR-OJ.RH AH-QP
		You use Kintetsu line?

11.	Anna:	un
		yeah

12.	Junko:	ua: SUGO::I
		wow great!

(OsakaI, KKJ, Junko, Kaori, Kenji & Anna, 00'41'17)

The unmarked way of addressing me in this interaction is, for all three of the speakers, the use of addressee honorification and, for the most part, SJ sentence-final particles. In line 10, however, we can see that Junko uses *haru* to address me, and this is the only time she uses *haru* towards me in the whole recording. In line 8 Junko asks me what train line I take and when my response turns out to be Kintetsu – the same line she also takes – she responds with a polar question as if asking for confirmation. We can see from this, as well as her further reaction in line 12 ('wow, great!'), that she finds it quite exciting. Later on in the conversation it becomes clear also that the other two speakers, Kaori and Kenji, had trouble placing that neighbourhood on the map, and weren't too sure where the train line was. It is then clear that the fact I was also on the same train line placed me within Junko's in-group. The function of *haru* in this interaction can then be seen as a way of marking solidarity, or placing the addressee within the speaker's in-group.

Another common way of using *haru* among younger women is to make a joke, or to create a comical effect. Very often it was accompanied by a change in pitch to higher, and the utterance containing it was always welcomed by laughter by the other participants. Interestingly, this comical intent seems to be common to all ages and genders.

Conclusions

We have looked at the use of a local referent honorific among three generations of Osaka Japanese speakers. While there is a clear distribution of this form along the distinction of gender, there is an unexpected turn of events in the younger generation of speakers, where men are beginning to use this form much more. The explanations for this pattern are rooted in local perceptions and local changing ideologies – it is thus not a direct effect of gender we are seeing, but one mediated through locally crafted ideologies.

The perceptions of the same form can differ in the same speech community (cf. Johnstone and Kiesling 2008), and these differences impact the use of the given linguistic feature. While in the example discussed above there are clear gender differences in the use of the local form, stating merely that these differences in the use of the form are linked with gender of the speakers would be an oversimplification.

The questions, of course, that remain to be asked are – what would be the pattern if we looked into the practices of young women who do associate themselves with the image of an *Osaka-no obachan?* What about women who associate themselves with the comedians or aspire to be one? These questions still need to be explored

References

Agha, A. 2002. "Honorific registers." In *Culture, interaction and language*, edited by K. Kataoka and S. Ide, 21-63. Tokyo: Hitsujishobo.

Carroll, T. 2001. *Language planning and language change in Japan.* Richmond, Surrey: Curzon Press.

Dubois, S. and B. Horvath 1999. "When the music changes you change too: Gender and language change in Cajun English." *Language Variation and Change 11*: 287-313.

Dunn, C. D. 2010. "Information structure and discourse stance in a monologic 'public speaking' register of Japanese." *Journal of Pragmatics* 42: 1890-1911.

Eckert, P. 1997. "Age as a sociolinguistic variable." In *The handbook of sociolinguistics,* edited by Florian Coulmas, 151-167. Oxford: Blackwell Publishing.

Eckert, P. 2008. "Variation and the indexical field." *Journal of Sociolinguistics 12 (4)*: 453-476.

Gumperz, J.J. 1982. *Discourse strategies.* Cambridge: Cambridge University Press.

Hanks, W. 1993. "Metalanguage and pragmatics of deixis." In *Reflexive language*, edited by J. Lucy, 127-157. Cambridge: Cambridge University Press.

Hill, B., S. Ide, S. Ikuta, A. Kawasaki and T. Ogino. 1986. "Universals of linguistic politeness. Quantitative evidence from Japanese and American English." *Journal of Pragmatics 10*. 347-471.

Horii, R. 1995. *Osaka kotoba jiten.* Tokyo: Tokyoodoo.

Ide, S. 1982. "Japanese sociolinguistics. Politeness and women's language."

    Lingua 57: 357-385.
Ide, S. 1990. "How and why do women speak more politely in Japanese?" In *Aspects of Japanese women's language,* edited by S. Ide and N.H. McGloin, 63-79. Tokyo: Kuroshio.
Iwasaki, S. 2002. *Japanese*. Amsterdam & Philadelphia: John Benjamins Publishing Company.
Johnstone, B. and S. F. Kiesling. 2008. "Indexicality and experience: Exploring the meanings of /aw/ -monophtongization in Pittsburgh." *Journal of Sociolinguistics 12 (1):* 5-33.
Jorden, E. H. and M. Noda 1987. *Japanese: The spoken language.* New Haven: Yale University Press.
Maeda, I. 1961. *Osaka-ben nyuumon.* Tokyo: Asahi shinbunsha.
Maegaki, K. 2005. *Doya! Osaka no obachangaku.* Osaka: Shooshisha.
Miyaji, H. 1987. "Kinkihoogen ni okeru taiguuhyoogenunyoojoo no tokushitsu." *Kokugogaku 151*: 38-56.
Miyaji, H. 1996. "Hoogen keigo no dookoo." In *Hoogen no genzai,* edited by Takahashi Kobayashi, Koichi Shinozaki and Takuichiro Onishi. Tokyo: Meiji Shoin.
Niyekawa, A. 1990. *Minimum essential politeness: A guide to Japanese honorific language.* Tokyo, London: Kodansha International.
Okamoto, S. 1997. "Social context, linguistic ideology and indexical expressions in Japanese." *Journal of Pragmatics* 28: 795-817.
Okamoto, S. 2004. "Ideology in Linguistic Practice and Analysis: Gender and Politeness in Japanese Revisited." In *Japanese language, gender and ideology. Cultural models and real people,* edited by S. Okamoto and Janet S. Shibamoto Smith, 38-56. Oxford & New York: Oxford University Press.
Onoe K., S. Kasai and K. Wakaichi. 2000. "Osaka no kotoba, Osaka no bunka. Interview." *Gengo 29(1)*: 14-39.
Seiichi, N. 1992. "Kansai dialect as a regional standard. The diffusion of Osaka-type treatment expressions." *Handai Nihongo Keknyuu 4:* 17-33.
Shibamoto, J. 1985. *Japanese women's language.* New York: Academic Press.
Shibatani, M. 1990. *The languages of Japan.* Cambridge: Cambridge University Press.
Silverstein, M. 1979. "Language structure and linguistic ideology." In *The elements: A parasession on linguistic units and levels,* edited by P. R. Clyne, W. F. Hanks and C. L. Hofbauer, 193-247. Chicago: Chicago Linguistic Society.
Silverstein, M. 1985. "Language and the culture of gender: At the intersection of structure, usage and ideology." In *Semiotic mediation: Sociocultural and psychological perspectives,* edited by E. Mertz and R. J. Parmentier, 219-259. Orlando, FL: Academic Press.
SturtzSreetharan, C. 2006. "Gentlemanly gender? Japanese men's use of clause-final politeness in casual conversations." *Journal of Sociolinguistics 10*: 70-92.
SturtzSreetharan, C. 2008. "Osaka aunties: Negotiating honorific language, gender and regionality." *Proceedings of the Sixteenth Annual Symposium about Language and Society - Austin. Texas Linguistic*

Forum. Austin: University of Texas. 163-173.
Yamaji, H. 2008. "Manipulation of honorifics in first-encounter conversations in Japanese." Unpublished PhD diss., Tucson: The University of Arizona.

Chapter 3: Gender Variations in Hebrew

Malka Muchnik, Bar-Ilan University

Abstract: Hebrew is gender marked for almost all content words and inflected function words. Masculine forms are unmarked, while feminine words are derived from them, with a suffix added to the masculine, which is the base form and also serves for generic use. Masculine forms are also used generically, and are therefore more salient than the feminine. In some cases they could have been replaced by feminine features, which would have made them more visible. However, this option is not widely applied, and masculine features are often preferred. Moreover, feminine grammatical forms tend to disappear, therefore increasing the generic use of the masculine. In this chapter, I argue that this trend reflects the greater prestige ascribed to masculine forms.

Grammatical Gender in Hebrew

Grammatical gender characteristics are mostly evident in nouns, although Hebrew presents gender differentiation in almost all parts of speech. Masculine nouns are unmarked, while feminine forms are regularly marked by the suffixes *–a* or *–(V)t*. The fact that animate nouns are divided into masculine or feminine based on a semantic-biological principle is not surprising when compared to other languages (Corbett, 1991; Dahl, 2000). However, although the Hebrew system is dichotomic, it is not balanced, and while unmarking usually indicates masculine nouns, many unmarked nouns are feminine. Consider, for example, the feminine nouns *'em* ('mother'), *pilegeš* ('concubine'), *tsipor* ('bird'), *tsfardea'* ('frog') and *'ez* ('goat'), which present no feminine suffix. Similarly, many inanimate nouns, such as *kaf* ('spoon'), *'erets* ('country'), *'ir* ('city, town'), *beten* ('stomach') and *na'al* ('shoe') are feminine, despite the lack of suffix, while some non-suffixed nouns can be used either as masculine or as feminine, such as *kos* ('glass, cup'), *derex* ('way'), *sakin* ('knife'), *ruaḥ* ('wind') and *šemeš* ('sun'). The opposite phenomenon does not exist, i.e. there are no nouns with a feminine suffix used as masculine.

Not only animate and inanimate nouns, but also , personal, possessive and demonstrative pronouns, verbs and inflected prepositions, as well as cardinal and ordinal numerals are gender marked in Hebrew, and syntactic rules require gender agreement for all of these parts of speech. Masculine forms are considered the base forms, and feminine forms are marked and derived from them. Therefore, Hebrew words can be described as [+ MASC] or [− MASC], and this can be seen as a reflection of a negative attitude towards the feminine features, as claimed by Spender (1985).

The following example illustrates the markedness of feminine words in Hebrew.

(1) *hamankalit*   *haneḥmada*   *hazot*   *kibla*
    the-CEO [FEM]   the-nice [FEM] the-this [FEM] received [FEM]

   hamankalit   *'et*   *štei*   *ha'ovdot*
   the-CEO [FEM]   [ACC]   two [FEM]   the-workers [FEM]

   haḥadašot,   *dibra*   *'itan*
   the-new [FEM],   talked [FEM]   with-them [FEM]

   vehisbira   *lahen*   *'et*
   and-explained [FEM]   to-them [FEM]   [ACC]

   'avodatan
   work-of-them [FEM]

   'This nice female CEO received the two new workers, talked to them and explained their work to them.'

In the above sentence, we can see that almost all words are marked for the feminine, with the only exceptions being the article (*ha–*), the accusative preposition (*'et*), and the particle denoting 'and' (*ve–*). Beside the suffixes *–a* or *–(V)t* added to the basic masculine form, mostly in nouns and adjectives, feminine second person plural in past tense verbs and pronominal, possessive and prepositional inflections present the suffix *–n* instead of the masculine *–m*. From example (1), we could have concluded that feminine forms are widely visible in Hebrew, but as I will show below, feminine features are actually on the wane, and in many cases masculine or generic features replace them. This may be seen as a normal and universal process of simplification, but in a language where almost every word is marked by gender, the decreasing presence of feminine forms is quite salient.

The gradual decline of feminine grammatical forms is not new, and some evidence can be found as early as in the later books of the Bible, and to a greater degree in Mishnaic Hebrew of about 2000 years ago. The best known examples of this are the disappearance of the feminine second- and third-person plural in future tense and imperative mood, which presents the prefix *t-* and the suffix *–na*, as well as the feminine personal pronoun for the same persons, and the corresponding suffix *–n* for all inflected possessive and prepositional forms. In the first case, the feminine form is replaced by the masculine, using the prefix *y-* and the suffix *–u*. In the second case, the feminine suffix is replaced by the masculine *–m*.

Interestingly, after its development was arrested for close to 1700 years, revitalized spoken Hebrew returned to the old biblical feminine forms mentioned above. However, over the past two decades they have once again begun disappearing, remaining only in high-level registers of the spoken and written language. This process is exemplified in (2), where changes from feminine to masculine forms are shown.

(2)   *banot,*   *'ate**m** telx**u***   *limkomoteixe**m***
        girls,   you will-go [MASC]   to-your-places [MASC]

        veteḥaku   *'ad šeḥavroteixe**m***
        and-you-will-wait [MASC]   until that-your [MASC]-friends [FEM]

        *yavo'**u***   *'aleixe**m***   *veyaḥlif**u***
        will-come [MASC]   to-you [MASC]   and-will-replace [MASC]

        *'etxe**m***
        you [MASC]

        'Girls, you will go to your places and wait until your female friends come to you and replace you.'

The sentence in (2) presents many masculine features, although it is addressed to females. If it were formulated in the feminine, this is how it would have been phrased:

        (3) banot, 'ate**n** telax**na** limkomoteixe**n** veteḥake**na** 'ad šeḥavroteixe**n** tavo'**na** 'eleixe**n** vetaḥlef**na** 'etxe**n**

The sentence in (3) is grammatically correct and up until only a few years ago these kinds of formulations were used, typically by female teachers or commanders addressing their female students or soldiers. When I presented this sentence to native speakers and asked them if they would use it, they responded that they would not use it, because it sounds to them old-fashioned and arrogant. In contrast, they reported that the sentence in (2), where grammatical masculine forms are used, seems absolutely natural. Moreover, attempts to change the masculine "neuter" forms and use feminine forms instead among a group of women speakers did not succeed, even among a group of feminists, who claimed that this would make them sound like "snobs" (Jacobs, 2004).

In an ethnographic study among gays and lesbians in Israel, Levon (2010) found that women in this group tended to use more gender-specific morphology and avoided the generic use. He observed that in some cases they consciously corrected themselves from generic masculine forms to feminine-specific forms. This was explained as part of the commitment of lesbian women to feminism and to the use of non-sexist language. However, when looking at the example in his study, presented in (4), we can see that the female speaker mostly uses masculine forms when referring to lesbian women in the group (Levon 105).

(4) *hanašim   šehem   kvar   pe'ilot*
    the-women   that-they [MASC]   already   activists [FEM]

   hem   smolaniyot   feministiyot   še'ixpat
   they [MASC]   left-wing [FEM]   feminist [FEM]   that-care

   lahem   meha'aravim   velo
   to-them [MASC]   from-the-Arabs   and-not

   me'atsmam   ke'ilu   'im   'anaḥnu noflim   'az
   about-themselves [MASC]   as-if   if   we fall [MASC]   then

   'anaḥnu   tsrixim   lihiyot be'ad   kol   hamiskenim
   we need [MASC]   to-be   in-favor   all   the-miserable

   'The women who are already activists are the left-wing feminists who only care about the Arabs and not about themselves. Like if since we fall, we need to be in favor of all the have-nots.'

From this example, we see that even when consciously trying to avoid masculine forms used as generic, the feminists used them naturally, because they are widely accepted in the language.

Gender Representation in Dictionaries

Hebrew dictionaries generally state the grammatical gender of nouns. However, in cases of regular animate nouns, gender is not indicated, because the convention is that the entries are presented in the unmarked masculine form. The feminine suffix is regularly added in brackets, while in cases where there is a different meaning for each gender, they are listed separately. In all cases, the masculine form is placed first, with the feminine after it. Adjectives and participles have four forms – masculine singular, feminine singular, masculine plural and feminine plural[1]. In these cases too, dictionaries only present the masculine singular form, while the inflectional suffixes are written in brackets. Verbs have inflectional forms for all persons, and the convention is that they are presented in the third-person masculine singular.[2]

From the aforementioned conventional documentation in dictionaries, it is clear that masculine forms are far more visible than feminine ones. Moreover, it is interesting to look not only at the quantitative aspect of gender representation,

---

[1] For a more detailed description of Modern Hebrew morphology, see Schwarzwald, 2001, 2011.

[2] They were traditionally presented in the past tense, but some new dictionaries prefer the present, which is actually a participle and has four forms. In this case too, entries are presented in the masculine.

but also the qualitative aspect. For this purpose, we will consider here two pairs of words – *'iš* ('man') versus *'iša* ('woman'), and *gever* ('gentleman') versus *geveret* ('lady'), as presented in different dictionaries.

In the first comprehensive dictionary on Modern Hebrew by Ben Yehuda[3] (1960), we find the following meanings for the word *'iš*:[4] man, male, male animal, husband, brave, hero, owner of, habituated to, one another, somebody, one to every, each, nobody, men, sir and individual. The parallel word, *'iša,* only presents these meanings: woman, wife, anyone and female animal. Moreover, all submeanings for the masculine are widely illustrated with examples from the different Hebrew epochs, while very few examples are provided for submeanings for the feminine. However, after the meanings of the word *'iša* ('woman'), a long list of proverbs with the word is presented, all of them regarding characteristics attributed to her – beauty, goodness, evil, gluttony, jealousy, frivolity, pitifulness, talkativeness, witchery and chastity. The meanings presented for the word *gever* ('gentleman') are man, hero, everyone, flowery use of man, cock (figurative) and penis. For the parallel feminine form, *geveret* ('lady'), the dictionary presents totally different meanings: mistress, ruling country (figurative), Madame.

The following meanings are presented in the dictionary by Even-Shoshan (1975) for the word *'iš*: person, man, husband, male animal, hero, brave man, somebody, nobody, inhabitant and honorific form of address. The meanings listed for the word *'iša* are human female, spouse of a man, female animal and somebody. The meanings that appear beside the word *gever* are man, person, male, brave man and hero, while the meanings for the parallel form *geveret* are polite form of address, servant's master, ruler and lady. In this case too, we clearly see that although the number of meanings presented is similar, they are completely different.

These are the meanings for *'iš* in the dictionary by Choueka (1997): man, person, adult person, husband, spouse, nobody, inhabitant. After the main entry, 77 subentries are listed, explaining idioms that contain this word. For the parallel form *'iša*, the following meanings are listed: female adult person, spouse, somebody who exhibits femininity. Only nine idioms containing this word are presented subsequently. The meanings presented for the word *gever* are man, adult male, somebody who has manly qualities (such as courage, audacity, power, decisiveness), and everybody respects him. For the form *geveret*, we find the following meanings: polite form of address, respectable or elegant woman, servant's master.

Interestingly, all three dictionaries state that one of the meanings of *'iš* is 'husband,' as opposed to *'iša* ('wife'), but the regular term used for husband is *ba'al*, which literally means 'owner, lord.' Only a few feminists use *'iši* ('my man') as opposed to *'išti* ('my wife,' lit. 'my woman'); the drive to introduce this term did not widely succeed. When looking at the Dictionary of Hebrew Idioms and Phrases (Rosenthal, 2009), we find 75 idioms with the word *'iš*, none of them

---

[3] Eliezer Ben Yehuda was the driving force behind the revitalization of spoken Hebrew at the end of the nineteenth century. The dictionary was first published in 1940.
[4] The English meanings listed here, sometimes odd, are the original translations given in the dictionary, which despite being monolingual presents lexical translations into German, French and English.

related to 'husband,' the only approximate exception being *'iš mišpaḥa* ('a family man'). The number of idioms containing the words *'iša* and *ešet*, its constructed form, is only eleven, four of them related to 'wife.' The word *ba'al* appears in 31 idioms and, in this case too, they are not related to the meaning 'husband,' except for *ba'al mišpaḥa* ('a family owner').

As we have shown, Hebrew dictionaries clearly distinguish between masculine and feminine words, not only in terms of the number of entries, but also in the quantity and quality of definitions presented for each. This is true in dictionaries representing both formal and informal language. Livnat (2006) examined the MS Word thesaurus for Hebrew, and found that when parallel masculine and feminine forms are presented, different meanings are provided for each gender. For example, the feminine word *metapelet* ('nursemaid') refers to childcare, and the synonyms presented are *o per* ('au pair') and *'omenet* ('nanny'), whereas the masculine form *metapel* is presented as a synonym for *terapist* ('therapist') and *psixoterapist* ('psychotherapist').

Muchnik (2007) conducted a study designed to reveal the connotative meaning of words and expressions according to gender and their use in the popular language, as reflected in the *Dictionary of Israeli Slang* (Rosenthal, 2005). The analysis included (a) forms marked for only one gender, i.e. when the corresponding form was not included in the dictionary, and (b) parallel forms for both sexes, when the meaning presented for each case is different. Unlike the greater number of meanings and idioms regarding the masculine form found in the aforementioned dictionaries, in this case the vast majority of expressions were found for the feminine form, due to negative connotations based on social stereotypes of women. Derisive expressions presented were mostly related to women's physical appearance, age and sexual behavior, as well as negative characteristics, such as stupidity, nagging, and maliciousness. In contrast, characteristics attributed to men were courage and strength.

Following are examples of gender differentiation found in slang expressions.[5] Men are presented as *gever la'inyan* ('a talented and impressive male'), *gever gever* ('having typical male attributes, usually used ironically'), and *yatsa gever* ('passed a tough test'). Unlike this, women are presented as *ptsatsa blondinit* ('a blonde bombshell'), *blondinit metumtemet* ('a dumb blonde'), *ptsatsat min* ('a sex bomb'), *betula ba'ozen* ('a woman feigning modesty, ostensible virgin'), *zkeine bobe* ('an old nag'), *yaxne* ('a gossip and nag, generally a woman'), *yente* ('an aging nag'), *tsatske* ('a promiscuous young woman'), *maxšefa* ('witch'), *klafte* ('a wicked woman, a woman who is evil'), *bičit* ('a bitch'), *kusit* ('an attractive young woman, usually with pronounced sexual appearance and behavior'), and *čapačula* ('dismissive term for a woman'.[6]

---

[5] All definitions in parentheses are literal translations of the definitions in the dictionary (Rosenthal, 2005).
[6] Some of the words are borrowed, such as *bobe, yaxne, yente, klafte* and *tsatske* from Yiddish, *bičit* from English, *kusit* from Arabic, and *čapačula* from Turkish through Ladino.

The Use of Professional Names

One of the well-known asymmetric fields regarding grammatical gender in many languages is the denomination of professions. According to Pauwels (1998, 2003), gender equality may be achieved by either neutralization or specification of gender. In some European languages, special forms designating female professions or occupations have been eliminated, such as poet**ess** in English, *professeure* in French, *avvocatessa* ('lawyer') in Italian, *supervisora* in Spanish, and *Lehrerin* ('teacher') in German, and the basic male forms are mostly used for either sex indistinctly. The inverse process is gender specification, i.e. adding feminine suffixes to existing masculine forms, for example *Pilotin* in German, and *docteure* in French. Gender neutralization could be achieved by creating new forms, such as the English *chairperson, spokesperson, cleaning person*, etc. (cf. Guil, 2006; van Compernolle, 2009).

Pauwels (1998: 191) contends that gender changes may be accepted more easily if they do not affect the structure of the language, whereas if they run counter to natural language, they may be rejected. In the case of Hebrew, using different forms for each gender, and adding missing feminine forms for some professions, could be perceived as a natural process, because this is in conformity with the regular grammatical structure. However, this process does not always occur. Some professions are only related to women, and parallel masculine forms are not used, although they could be easily obtained by back formation, e.g., *katvanit* ('typist'), *šinanit* ('dental hygienist'), *saya'at* ('dental assistant'), *kosmetika'it* ('cosmetician'), *manikuristit* ('manicurist'). Some religious roles are only filled by men, and consequently no feminine forms are used, although in these cases too there is no grammatical impediment, e.g., *kavran* ('undertaker'), *šohet* ('ritual slaughterer'), *'avre*x ('married Yeshiva student'), and *mekubal* ('a man who studies the Kabbalah') (see Livnat, 2006). However, in recent years, when women started filling some previously only masculine roles in liberal communities, new feminine terms were coined such as *hazanit* ('female cantor'), *mohelet* ('female circumciser'), *gaba'it* ('female synagogue treasurer'), *soferet stam* ('female scribe'). The feminine derivation is sometimes performed automatically even in cases where there is no need for it. For instance, a male laureate of an important prize is called *hatan ha-pras* (lit. 'groom of the prize'), and a female laureate is called *kalat ha-pras* (lit. 'bride of the prize'), but sometimes we find the derived (non-existing) form from the masculine, *hatanit*.[7]

Despite the quasi-automatic derivation for gender, in cases where men work in a "feminine" profession, or when women work in a "masculine" profession, the terms to be used are not self-evident. In some instances, terms are used differently for each gender, such as *rav* ('rabbi') versus *rabanit* ('rabbi's wife'), and therefore female rabbis are referred by the masculine form *rav*[8] or by the derived form *raba*. Another interesting case is *ganenet* ('female kindergarten teacher'), as opposed to *ganan* ('gardener'). There is no accepted differentiating term to refer

---

[7] Similarly, the feminine word brit**a** was derived from the masculine *brit* ('circumcision'), and is used to refer to the celebration of a new-born female.
[8] See below about the female intentional use of masculine forms of address.

to a man who serves as a kindergarten teacher,[9] and although the term *ganen* was proposed, many speakers use the expression *ganenet mimin zaxar* ('kindergarten teacher [FEM] of masculine gender'). This is a derisive term, only comparable with the expression *zona mimin zaxar* ('whore [FEM] of masculine gender').

Some professions have completely different names depending on gender. Traditionally, the term *ḥayat* ('tailor') was only used for men, while the equivalent term for women is *toferet* ('seamstress'). Although both terms can be derived, the potential words *ḥayetet* or *tofer* are not used at all. Interestingly, in recent years a more prestigious term was coined, *me'atsev 'ofna* ('fashion designer'), which is generally used in the masculine form, although there is a parallel feminine term, *me'atsevet 'ofna*. The feminine term *toferet* remained in use for unprestigious sewing. Similarly, the term *me'atsev se'ar* ('hair stylist') was coined to replace the term *sapar* ('barber'), and although it exists in its derived feminine form *me'atsevet se'ar*, the old feminine term *saparit* is still being used to refer to an unprestigious female hairdresser, even with a derisive connotation.

A recent change in Israeli society is the one made by some women in political, economic and academic prestigious positions. Being aware of the power of language, these women prefer to be addressed with the masculine form, for example *mazkir ha-'aguda* ('association's male-secretary') instead of *mazkirat ha-'aguda*, or '*ozer ha-sar* ('male-assistant to the minister') instead of '*ozeret ha-sar*. It could be claimed that this originated in the pragmatic use of these terms. Thus, while the masculine form *mazkir* ('secretary') mostly refers to a person fulfilling an important voluntary or elective administrative function, the feminine form *mazkira* is associated with a clerical position in an office. Similarly, '*ozer* ('assistant') can be widely used, including for prestigious functions, whereas '*ozeret* is mainly associated with 'maid.'[10] However, women's preference for masculine terms is also found when there is no semantic difference between forms, such as *gizbar* ('male treasurer'), *nasi* ('male president'), *mankal* ('male CEO'), *yošev roš* ('chairman'), *direktor* ('director'), instead of the feminine forms *gizbarit*, *nesi'a*, *mankalit*, *yoševet roš* or *direktorit*, respectively. It thus appears that masculine forms are perceived as being more prestigious and powerful, and therefore some women prefer to use them, creating an alternative identity and manipulating normative language.

The aforementioned examples could be seen as designed to create new neutral forms, which do not regularly exist in Hebrew, because as we have seen, the language is highly marked for gender. Nonetheless, some terms exist only in the masculine form, and especially salient are official terms such as *'osek murše* ('licensed dealer'), *nišom* ('taxpayer'), *'iš kešer* ('contact man'), *tošav vatik* ('senior citizen'), whereas the respective grammatical forms *'oseket muršet*, *nišoma*, *'ešet kešer* and *toševet vatika* are possible, but not used at all. Another term used in the masculine for both sexes is *mišne* ('vice'), as in *hamišne lamankal'* ('assistant CEO'). Recently, a woman in the position of vice president of the court addressed the Hebrew Academy of Language and asked if she may be

---

[9] The official term is *ganan yeladim* ('children's kindergarten teacher [MASC]').

[10] *See Livnat (2006) on this kind of semantic difference according to gender.*

called in the feminine form *mišna*,[11] and the response was positive, adding another possibility – *mišnet*. This was officially published by the Hebrew Academy in November 2012 together with the surprising approval of the words *roša* ('feminine head, chief') and *rošat* (the same in construct state). The terms *mišna*, as in *hamišna lanasi* ('feminine vice president') and *roša*, as in *rošat miflaga* ('party head') and *rošat mahlaka* ('department head'), were rapidly adopted and are now regularly used in the media, but we still need time to see if they will be widely used by all speakers and by women in these positions.

A clear discriminative case is the use of military ranks, as well as parallel ranks in the police force and prison service. Low-rank names are used both in masculine and feminine forms, such as *tura'i / tura'it* ('private'), *tiron / tironit* ('recruit'), *samal / samelet* ('sergeant'), *šoter / šoteret* ('police officer'), *soher / soheret* ('warden'). In contrast, high-rank names are only used in the masculine when referring to both genders. For example, *segen* ('lieutenant'), *seren* ('captain') in the army, *pakad* ('chief inspector'), *nitsav mišne* ('commander') in the police, and *meyšar* ('first lieutenant'), *gundar* ('major general') in the prison service. In 2011, the first female major generals were appointed in the Israel Defense Forces and in the Israel Prison Service, but both of them are referred to with the masculine words *'aluf* and *gundar*, respectively. In the case of the army, the decision was made by the Chief of Staff, despite the fact that the Academy of the Hebrew Language recommended the use of *'alufa*, and despite the fact that this feminine word already exists, but is mostly used meaning 'female champion.' The potential feminine word *gundarit* is never used either. The parallel feminine rank in the Israel police has existed since 1989, and in this case, too, the woman is called *nitsav* ('major general [MASC]'); although the feminine word *nitsevet* exists, it is used to refer to an extra in the film industry.

A similar phenomenon can be seen in academic ranks, where masculine forms are used referring to women, such as *martse baxir* ('senior lecturer') or *madrix doktor* ('Ph.D. instructor'), instead of *martsa bexira* or *madrixa doktorit*. Foreign words are also used in academic spheres without derivation for the feminine. For example, the titles Doctor and Professor are used for males and females alike, although there are potential parallel feminine forms, *doktorit* and *profesorit*, but they are seldom used and are limited to nouns, like in *geveret levi hi doktorit / profesorit* ('Ms. Levy is a Doctor / a Professor'), but are never used as a title before a name, such as *doktorit / profesorit levi* ('Dr. / Prof. Levy'). Even when adding a Hebrew noun or adjective to a foreign word, only masculine forms are used for both genders, e.g. *profesor haver* ('associate professor') or *profesor male* ('full professor'), while the feminine forms *havera* or *mele'a* are never used. Other foreign academic terms such as *dekan* ('dean') or *rektor* ('rector'), could be used in the feminine forms *dekanit* and *rektorit*, but very often appear in the masculine (neutral?) form when referring to females. In contrast, some foreign terms referring to females are always used in the feminine, such as *fizika'it* ('female physicist'), *matematika'it* ('female mathematician')*, statistika'it*

---

[11] This word may be confused with Mishnah, a collection of oral tradition writings dating from 200 CE.

('female statistician'), *psixologit* ('female psychologist'), which proves that foreign words are not an impediment.[12]

The feminization of some professions in recent decades brought about linguistic changes. These changes did not introduce feminine words instead of the previous masculine terms, but used neutral expressions containing inanimate nouns. For instance, instead of *bet sefer la'aḥayot* ('female-nurses' school'), the neutral term used is *bet sefer lesi'ud* ('nursing school'), and similarly, the old name *bet midraš / seminar lemorim vegananot* ('institute for male-teachers and female-kindergarten-teachers') was replaced by *mixlala leḥinux* ('college of education').

Despite the aforementioned changes, professional associations still use only masculine names, ignoring the fact that in many of them women are the majority, such as in the case of teachers, who have two associations, both of which use the generic masculine form – *histadrut hamorim* and *'irgun hamorim* ('association of teachers [MASC]').[13] Women in Israel are also becoming the majority of writers and journalists. That said, in these cases too, the associations use generic nouns – *'agudat hasofrim* and *'agudat ha'itona'im* ('association of writers [MASC] / journalists [MASC]'), although they could have added feminine nouns – *'agudat hasofrim* [MASC] *vehasofrot* [FEM] and *'agudat / 'irgun ha'itona'im veha'itona'iyot*, 'association of [MASC] and [FEM] writers,' and 'association of [MASC] and [FEM] journalists,' respectively. The official meeting place for writers is also referred to in the masculine, *bet hasofer* ('house of the [MASC] writer'), and the same is true for a parallel place for journalists, which is called *bet ha'itona'im* ('house of the [MASC] journalists').

The Use of Proper Names

Another field in which gender variations can be perceived is the use of proper names. Like other nouns, most masculine names in classical Hebrew are unmarked, e.g., Dan, Gad, David, Shim'on, Me'ir, Yo'av, Ehud and Nadav. Most traditional names presenting the suffixes *–a* or *–(V)t* are feminine, e.g., Din**a**, Chan**a**, Penin**a**, No**a**, Asna**t**, Efra**t**, Yehudi**t**, but we find some feminine names presenting no suffix such as Na'omi, Ya'el, Tamar, Michal, Merav, Esther and Miriam. In Biblical Hebrew there is not always a dichotomic grammatical differentiation between names of men or women. For example, we find some names of men with a typical feminine suffix such as Aday**a**, Ahav**a**, Be'er**a**, Shel**a**, Simch**a**, Yon**a**, Gina**t**, Nacha**t**, Ana**t**, Peda**t**, while several names containing feminine suffixes are used for both males and females, such as Avi**a**, Tzviy**a**, Ataliy**a**, Eif**a**, Shelomi**t**. In Modern Hebrew, names with feminine suffixes tend to be used only for women, where unmarked names may be used for both sexes. Some names expected to be masculine, such as **Avi**gail, **Avi**tal, **Avi**shag, **Achi**no'am, were used in the past and are still used for females. These

---

[12] On women's preference for being addressed in the masculine, see Muchnik, in press. On the trend of switching genders, which only reported about women using masculine forms and not the other way around, see Tobin, 2001 and Sa'ar, 2007.

[13] Similarly, the special room for teachers at school is still called *hadar morim* ('[MASC] teachers' room').

names are particularly interesting, because although they are unmarked concerning suffixes, they contain a clear male reference as prefix (*'avi* = 'father of,' *'achi* = 'brother of').

In traditional Hebrew writings, we find many more masculine than feminine proper names. The reason for this is that only a small number of women are mentioned, and in many cases women are referred to solely as somebody's daughter, wife or sister, not as central figures in their own right. Because of the absence of feminine names, a significant number of new names were introduced in Modern Hebrew, and as we will see below, in the first stage there was a clear differentiation between names given to men or women, mostly according to grammatical gender. This differentiation has weakened over the course of time, and many of the names that were initially only used as masculine are used nowadays for both sexes.

Proper names in Modern Hebrew have undergone different waves of changes regarding gender, probably motivated by the desire to achieve gender equality. These waves seem to be parallel to the waves of feminist movements. The first trend was deriving feminine names from existing masculine names, such as Shmu'el**a**, Micha'el**a**, Jo'el**a**, Isra'el**a**, Netan'el**a**, Refa'el**a** (from Shmu'el, Micha'el, Jo'el, Isra'el, Netan'el, and Refa'el, respectively). All of these names carry the suffix *–'el*, and are considered theophoric names, as the word *'El* means 'God,' and when deriving them into the feminine form, the suffix *–'ela* could be understood as 'Goddess,' which was clearly not the intention. Another interesting feminine name is Re'uven**a**, derived from Re'uven, which originally means 'look, [it's] a boy,'[14] and therefore adding the feminine suffix *–a* seems very odd.

This derivational method was applied through the '70s, when a new trend arose, and the suffixes *–t* and *–it* were used to introduce new feminine names, such as Rina**t**, Yif'a**t**, Eina**t**, Yotva**t**, Sagi**t**, Kalani**t**. Some of the names were aimed to replace existing names ending in *–a*, such as Sar**it**, Tov**it**, Devor**it**, Mir**it**, Pnin**it** (from Sar**a**, Tov**a**, Devor**a**, Mir**a** and Pnin**a**, respectively, which were perceived as old-fashioned). At the same time, some names started being used as masculine-feminine pairs, such as Tzach-Tzach**it**, Gal-Gal**it**, Paz-Paz**it**, Gur-Gur**it**. These processes led to a more equal attitude to both genders and contributed to a greater saliency of feminine names.

We also witnessed a complex and contrasting process, consisting of first adding the feminine suffix *–a* to masculine names, then changing it into *–it*, e.g., Dan > Dan**a** > Dan**it**; Ilan > Ilan**a** > Ilan**it**. A newer opposite process consists of deducting feminine suffixes, such as Or**a** > Or**it** > Or; Aviv**a** > Aviv**it** > Aviv; Dror**a** > Dror**it** > Dror; Ziv**a** > Ziv**it** > Ziv; Yon**a** > Yon**it** > Yon. The deducted forms Or, Aviv, Dror, Ziv, Yon and the like serve both as masculine and feminine names, and in most cases replace the marked feminine forms. Thus, a new remarkable trend in the last decade is the use of unisex names without any suffix. Some of these names originate in the shortening of existing feminine names by back formation, such as Ofir, Shir, Li'or, Shoshan, Yarden (from Ofir**a**, Shir**a**, Li'or**a**, Shoshan**a** and Yarden**a** respectively), and are used now for both sexes.

Not only the morphology of names is interesting in Hebrew, but also the semantic aspect, because most proper names are existing words, and therefore

---

[14] A more recent version is Re'ubat, meaning 'look, [it's] a girl'.

have a specific meaning. This can help us see the topics associated with male or female names and serve as evidence of the social expectations from each gender. Thus, for example, many female names are names of flowers, some of them originally Hebrew, such as Vered ('rose'), Shoshana ('lily'), Rakefet ('cyclamen'), Sigal/Sigalit ('violet'), Kalanit ('anemone'), Chavatzelet ('pancratium') and Nurit ('buttercup'), while others are foreign names adopted in Hebrew, e.g., Dalia, Iris, Lilach and Yasmin. Some of them have a masculine gender, but they are never used for male names. Only in recent years have some flower names been used for both sexes, e.g., Shoshan ('lily'), Savion ('groundsel'), Sachlav ('orchid'), Sayfan ('gladiola') and Narkis ('daffodil'), all of them grammatically masculine.

Gems are another source of popular female names, whether by using Hebrew nouns, such as Penina ('pearl'), Margalit ('pearl'), Shoham ('onyx'), Bareket ('agate'), Yahaloma / Yahalomit[15] ('diamond') or by borrowing or adapting foreign nouns, e.g., Sapir / Sapirit[16] ('sapphire'), Inbar ('amber') and Topaz ('topaz'). Similar names for women are Zehava and Zehavit, originated from *zahav* ('gold'), as well as the older name Golda, borrowed from Yiddish. The principle we have mentioned regarding names of flowers also holds for gems – when they are grammatically masculine, they have recently come into use for both sexes.

Names of big and strong animals were traditionally given only to men, such as Arie / Shachal / Layish ('lion'), Dov ('bear'), Ze'ev ('wolf').[17] These names do not regularly have a parallel feminine form. Unlike them, animal names used for women, either exclusively or as derivation from masculine names, are inspired by non-aggressive or small animals, e.g. Ayala / Ayelet ('doe'), Tzviya / Tziviya ('gazelle'), Ofra ('fawn'), Talia ('lamb'), Rachel / Rechela ('ewe'), Ya'el / Ye'ela ('goat'), Devora ('bee'), Tzipora ('bird'), Tzofit ('sunbird') and Kanarit ('canary').

Even more suggestive is the use of feminine adjectives denoting personal qualities in traditional names for women such as Yafa / Yafit ('pretty'), Tova / Tovit ('good'), Na'ava ('beautiful'), Aliza ('joyful'), Adina ('delicate'), Ahuva ('beloved'), Chinanit ('graceful'), Temima ('innocent') and Metuka ('sweet'). Although all of these names are feminine adjectives, the parallel potential masculine forms are never used as male names, and therefore the social expectations regarding men and women are clear. We find these names among adult females, but they are no longer commonly given.

As opposed to them, we find masculine future verb forms used for names of men, and from them we can infer the expectations of them: **Y**arim ('he will raise'), **Y**akim ('he will establish'), **Y**iftax ('he will open'), **Y**ig'al ('he will redeem'), **Y**ariv ('he will fight'), **Y**avin ('he will understand'), **Y**adin ('he will judge'), **Y**ir'am ('he will make noise'), **Y**isgav ('he will be sublime'), **Y**isge ('he will prosper'), **Y**izhar ('he will shine'). None of these names have a parallel form

---

[15] The feminine suffixes –a and –it were added to the original word Yahalom.

[16] Here too, the suffix –it was added to the masculine form Sapir.

[17] In Biblical Hebrew, we also find Chamor ('donkey'), Nachash ('snake'), and Shu'al ('fox'), but they are no longer used as proper names.

used as a female name, although it is morphologically possible by changing the initial *Y-* into *T-*.[18]

The clear trend over the past two decades is towards unisex names. As a consequence of this preference, most forms in current use are grammatically masculine, while only a small number of names remain in the feminine, and those are used only for women. Among the hundreds of popular unisex names we find, for example, Ofir, Guy, Dor, Tamir, Oren, Yuval, Ron, Omer, Shai and Tomer, which were previously used only for the masculine. From the semantic point of view, many of the unisex names are taken from nature, e.g., Agam ('lake'), Ofek ('horizon'), Almog ('coral'), Gefen ('vine'), Eshel ('tamarisk'), Gal ('wave'), Yam ('sea'), Sahar ('moon'). It is impossible to know the gender of these unmarked names; when teachers receive a list of their students, it states "boy" or "girl" beside the name.

The new trend in the use of names in Hebrew and Arabic was addressed in research conducted by Rosenhouse (2002). She states that the changes perceived in name giving in Modern Hebrew are related to the loss of gender differentiation in plural forms of the verb, in syntactic agreement and in intimate discourse. Indeed, it appears that the unification of names for both sexes is only one of the many socio-cultural phenomena occurring in recent decades such as gender equalization in fashion, hairstyles or jewelry. However, the vast use of unmarked names cannot be seen only as a process of gender equality in the language, but rather as the preference of masculine at the expense of feminine forms.

Conclusions

In this chapter I have shown that although Hebrew presents a dichotomic masculine-feminine division in lexical and grammatical features, when looking at the actual use of the language, it is clear that this division is not symmetrical. In terms of grammar, we have seen that unmarked nouns, regularly associated with the masculine, may also serve for the feminine, but not the opposite. Feminine forms of verbs, pronouns and related pronominal inflexions tend to disappear, and the parallel masculine forms replace them. The lexical field was exemplified by the word representation in dictionaries, in professional nouns, and in the use of proper names. In all cases we can see that masculine forms are preferred, and when a semantic differentiation is presented, masculine forms are perceived as more prestigious, while feminine forms are often seen as derisive.

References

Ben Yehuda, Eliezer (1960). A Complete Dictionary of Ancient and Modern Hebrew. New York & London: Thomas Yoseloff.
Choueka, Yaacov (1997). Rav-Milim. Center for Educational Technology, Yedioth Aharonot, Sifrei Hemed & Steimatzky.
Corbett, Greville (1991). Gender. Cambridge: Cambridge University Press.
Dahl, Östen (2000). "Elementary gender distinctions". In: B. Unterbeck & M. Rissanen (eds.). Gender in Grammar and Cognition. Berlin & New York:

---

[18] The only exception is **Ta'ir**, derived from **Y**a'ir ('he will illuminate').

Mouton de Gruyter, 577-593.
Even-Shoshan, Abraham (1975). Hamilon Heḥadaš [The New Dictionary]. Jerusalem: Kiryat Sefer.
Guil, Pura (2006). "Word's Spanish Thesaurus: Some limits of automaticity". In: E. Thüne, S. Leonardi & C. Bazzanella (eds.). Gender, Language and New Literacy: A Multilingual Analysis. London & New York: Continuum, 153-168.
Jacobs, Andrea (2004). Language Reform as Language Ideology: An Examination of Israeli Feminist Language Practice (Ph.D. dissertation). Austin: The University of Texas.
Levon, Erez (2010). Language and the Politics of Sexuality: Lesbians and Gays in Israel. New York: Palgrave Macmillan.
Livnat, Zohar (2006). "Gender online in Hebrew: New technology, old language". In: E. Thüne, S. Leonardi & C. Bazzanella (eds.). Gender, Language and New Literacy: A Multilingual Analysis. London & New York: Continuum, 169-181.
Muchnik, Malka (2007). "Gender differences as social messages in Hebrew slang expressions". Cahiers d'Analogie et Diachronie 4: 327-347.
Muchnik, Malka (2012). "Male CEO or female CEO? Is it possible to avoid sexism in Hebrew?" In: M. Muchnik & T. Sadan (eds.). Research on Modern Hebrew and Jewish Languages. Jerusalem: Carmel [Hebrew], 487-505.
Pauwels, Anne (1998). Women Changing Language. London & New York: Longman.
Pauwels, Anne (2003). "Women and men as language users and regulators". In: J. Holmes & M. Meyerhoff (eds.). The Handbook of Language and Gender. Oxford: Blackwell, 550-570.
Rosenthal, Ruvik (2005). Dictionary of Israeli Slang. Jerusalem: Keter [Hebrew].
Rosenthal, Ruvik (2009). Dictionary of Hebrew Idioms and Phrases. Jerusalem: Keter [Hebrew].
Rosenhouse, Judith (2002). "Personal names in Hebrew and Arabic: Modern trends compared to the past". Journal of Semitic Studies 47 (1): 97-114.
Sa'ar, Amalia (2007). "Masculine talk: On the subconscious use of masculine linguistic forms among Hebrew- and Arabic-speaking women in Israel". Signs: Journal of Women in Culture and Society 32 (2): 405-429.
Schwarzwald, Ora (2001). Modern Hebrew. Muenchen: Lincom Europa.
Schwarzwald, Ora (2011). "Modern Hebrew". In: S. Weninger (ed.). The Semitic Languages: An International Handbook. Berlin: de Gruyter, 523-536.
Spender, Dale (1985). Man Made Language. London: Routledge & Kegan Paul, 2nd edition.
Tobin, Yishai (2001). "Gender switch in Modern Hebrew". In: M. Hellinger & H. Bussmann (eds.). Gender across Languages: The Linguistic Representation of Women and Men. Amsterdam & Philadelphia: John Benjamins, vol. I, 177-198.
van Compernolle, Rémi (2009). "What do women want? Linguistic equality and the feminization of job titles in contemporary France". Gender and Language 3 (1): 33-52.

Chapter 4: Gender and the Sentence-final Particles in Japanese

Naomi Ogi and Duck-Young Lee, Australian National University

Abstract: This study discusses the use of the Japanese sentence-final particle *wa*, which is widely known as a female-speech marker in the language. In Japanese, sentence-final particles are one of the most frequently used linguistic items in spoken conversation, and as pointed out by many studies (McGloin, 1990; Ide and Sakurai, 1997; Hayashi, 2000; Katagiri, 2007), it is difficult and unnatural to have a conversation without using these particles. Reflecting their significance, numerous studies have been dedicated to the issue of these particles from an early stage in the study of modern Japanese. However, the attention has mainly been paid to ne and yo, which are the most frequently used among the sentence-final particles, and many aspects of the other particles, including our target particle *wa*, are still to be unveiled.

This study aims at investigating the function of *wa* and its connection with the specific gender, i.e. female, and sheds light on some aspects of how our language can be associated with a particular gender of the speakers. Invoking the interactive nature of *wa*, the study first clarifies the linguistic property of the particle. Based on the linguistic distributions of the particle including its co-occurrence restrictions with modal expressions as well as with certain sentence types, the study will show that the function of the particle is to convey the speaker's monopolistic attitude, through which the speaker attempts to deliver an utterance towards the hearer in a firm manner.

The study further discusses its relationship with the female-specific values of gentleness, non-assertiveness and gracefulness. It will be shown that what underlies these feminised values is the notion of onna-rashisa 'womanliness', the ideal goal of which is the ryoosai-kenbo 'a good wife and wise mother'. It will also be shown that the notion was established during the Meiji era (1868-1912) in response to the need at the time, and that it was further promoted and widely spread by the Meiji writers who adopted genbunitchi 'the unification of spoken and written language styles' in their novels.

As a whole the study suggests that the development of wa as the female-speech marker for the notion of onna-rashisa 'womanliness' was not directly motivated by the linguistic property of the particle, but rather it was deliberately established in order to differentiate female speech from male speech. In this line of argument, the study further suggests that *wa* is a unique linguistic tool which possesses ambivalent functions; that is, on the one hand it conveys the speaker's firm attitude towards the hearer, and on the other hand it indicates the feminised values of womanliness, which were arbitrarily associated with the particle.

Keywords: Japanese sentence-final particles, gender and language, female-speech marker wa, spoken conversation, onna-rashisa 'womanliness'

Introduction[1]

This study discusses the use of the sentence-final particle *wa* in Japanese, which is widely known for marking the gender of the speaker as being a female (Uyeno, 1971; Tanaka, 1977; Ide, 1982; Reynolds, 1985; Cheng, 1987; Mizutani and Mizutani, 1987; McGloin, 1990; Miyazaki et al., 2002). For example, in the following utterances, no sentence-final particle is attached to the utterance in (1), while *wa* is attached in (2).[2]

(1) *Kinoo   Tanaka-sensei o   daigaku de   mimashita.*
    yesterday Mr. Tanaka   OBJ   university at saw
    'I saw Mr. Tanaka at the university yesterday.'

(2) *Kinoo   Tanaka-sensei o   daigaku de   mimashita wa.*
    yesterday Mr. Tanaka   OBJ   university at saw   WA
    'I saw Mr. Tanaka at the university yesterday-WA.'

Both (1) and (2) denote the same propositional information, 'I saw Mr. Tanaka at the university yesterday', and yet native speakers of Japanese will immediately notice that (2) with *wa* differs from (1) in that its speaker is a female while (1) does not in particular indicate the information about the gender of the speaker. In addition to this gender specification, they will also feel that (2) with *wa* is uttered in a two-way conversation, and indicates the speaker's certain 'message' or 'attitude' towards the hearer in delivering the propositional information. (Details will be provided through the later discussions.) (1) is 'neutral' in this regard, and may be used to simply describe the propositional information. It may be used in a monologue, and when used in two-way conversation, it could be informative to the hearer but this is only by virtue of the conversational setting that 'while I am talking you are the hearer and are supposed to pay attention to my talk'. As such, the investigation of *wa* is interesting because it does not only involve the socio-

---

[1] We would like to thank Geng Song, Steven Lee and Peter Hendriks for their invaluable comments and assistance with this study. However, we are solely responsible for all errors and misinterpretations.
[2] The abbreviations used in the glosses are the following: BE:Various forms of the be verb; CD:Conditional; LK: Linker; NEG: Negative marker; NOM: Nominaliser; OBJ: Objective marker; PROG:Progressive form; QT: Quotation; QUE: Question marker; SUB: Subjective marker; TOP: Topic marker

cultural dimension of our language use as to how it is associated to a particular gender, but it also involves the interactional dimension of spoken conversation, which is related to the general function of the particle in spoken discourse. It is also interesting to know the background of how this particle came to indicate a particular gender.

In Japanese, sentence-final particles are one of the most frequently used linguistic items in spoken conversation, and as pointed out by many studies, it is difficult and unnatural to have a conversation without using these particles (McGloin, 1990; Ide and Sakurai, 1997; Hayashi, 2000; Katagiri, 2007). Reflecting their significance, numerous studies have been dedicated to the issue of these particles. However, the attention has mainly been paid to *ne* and *yo*, which are the most frequently used among the sentence-final particles, and many aspects of the other particles are still to be unveiled. The use of our target particle, *wa*, including its connection with the gender, has also not been fully explored, despite its well-known role as the gender marker. There are some studies on the particle (e.g. Uyeno, 1971; Cheng, 1987; McGloin, 1990; Miyazaki et al., 2002); however they are limited to stating the related facts and cannot provide a convincing account for the function and gender issue of the particle based on an empirical analysis. (A summary of previous studies will be provided in later discussion.)

In Western societies the 'dominance' approach (e.g. Trudgill, 1972; Lakoff, 1975; Zimmerman and West, 1975), the 'difference' approach' (e.g. Maltz and Borker, 1982; Tannen, 1990, 1993, 1996) and the 'social construction' approach (e.g. McElhinny, 1995; Eckert and McConnell-Ginet, 2003; Holmes and Stubbe, 2003) are widely acknowledged as major approaches to the relationship between gender and language. In Japanese society the gender-distinction in language use has mainly been discussed in close connection with the notion of *-rashii* '-like, -ly' as in *otoko-rashii* 'manly' and *onna-rashii* 'womanly' (Jugaku, 1979; Falconer, 1984; Ide and McGloin, 1990; Reynolds, 1990). (Detailed discussion will be provided in the section "Development of the Notion of *Onna-rashisa* 'womanliness'.) Adopting the notion of *onna-rashisa* 'womanliness', the present study aims at investigating the function of *wa* and its connection with the specific gender. Ultimately it attempts to shed light on some aspects of how our language can be associated with a particular gender of the speaker.

Note that our target particle *wa* is reported to sometimes be used in monologues as well (Miyazaki et al., 2002; Nakazaki, 2004). While further investigation is needed to clarify this issue, we exclude such a usage of the particle from the scope of the current study since the purpose of this study is to reveal the mechanism of how the interactional function of the particle is related to its use by a specific gender. Further, there is another *wa* which may be used by male speakers as well (Tanaka, 1977; McGloin, 1990; Hattori, 1992; Miyazaki et al., 2002; Aizawa, 2003). This *wa* is generally distinguished from the females' use of *wa* in terms of intonation. That is, *wa* by female speakers typically carries a rising intonation, while *wa* by male speakers carries a falling intonation.[3] This *wa* with a falling intonation is sometimes treated as a dialect feature in particular

---

[3] According to some research (e.g. Hattori, 1992; Oota, 1992; Aizawa, 2003), *wa* with a falling intonation may be used by female speakers as well.

regions such as Kansai and Hokkaido (Hattori, 1992; Washi, 1997; Aizawa, 2003). As the current study focuses on the Tokyo-standard variety of modern Japanese,[4] we deal with *wa* with a rising intonation, which is in principle used by female speakers only, in order to avoid an unnecessary dispute with respect to the issue of dialects.

The data for this study consists of two types of sources[5] which are drawn from two-way conversations, in considering the fact that *wa* is basically found in an interactional conversation setting only. The former consists of one-hundred-and-sixteen conversations of approximately twenty-four hours in total. It includes conversations in a wide variety of settings such as telephone, first meeting, and chat between friends. The latter is of Japanese comics which have widely been read by Japanese people. As Kabashima (1990) reports, language used in comics overlaps with that used in spontaneous conversation to a large extent, and thus in terms of language use, these comics are deemed to be an ideal data source for the current analysis apart from that of spontaneous conversation.

This study is organised as follows. In the next section, we first summarise the general features of sentence-final particles, which is important for understanding the nature of *wa*. We then introduce the involvement-based approach (Lee, 2007) adopted into our analysis of the functions of the target particle, and show that the general function of the particle is to indicate the speaker's attitude of inviting the hearer's involvement in a monopolistic manner. The section "Development of the Notion of *Onna-rashisa* 'womanliness'" will then explore the unique features of *wa*. We will demonstrate that the unique property of the particle is to indicate the speaker's 'firm attitude' in delivering the utterance within a monopolistic manner. "*Wa* and Gender Specification" will be devoted to discussions of its connection with the gender. In particular, the section will provide explications of the key notions of female-specific values in Japanese, i.e. *onna-rashisa* 'womanliness', and the background about how *wa* was recognised and used nationwide by female speakers. The final section of this chapter presents concluding remarks.

---

[4] According to Koyama (2004), standard varieties, such as the Modern-Tokyo Standard Japanese, are consciously articulated, ideologically prescribed normative standards which are in principle accessible to anyone ('public' in a strong sense) and speakers' behavioural and ideological (dis)loyalty to which indexes their group identities and power-statuses. Throughout the current study the term 'Japanese' indicates the Tokyo-standard variety of modern Japanese.

[5] Data sources: Adachi, Mitsuru. 1992. Tatchi. Vol. 1-11. Tokyo: Shoogakkan; Kamio, Yoko. 1993. Hana yori Dango. Vol. 1-20. Tokyo: Shuueisha; Usami Mayumi. 2007. BTS ni yoru Tagengo-hanashikotoba Koopasu - Nihongo Kaiwa 1 (Nihongo-bogo-washa Dooshi no Kaiwa) 2007 [The Corpus of Spoken Language in Multi Languages by 'Basic Transcription System': Japanese Conversation 1 (Conversations between native speakers of Japanese)]. Tokyo University of Foreign Studies.

Monopolistic Nature of *Wa*

General Features of Sentence-Final Particles

There are some general features which are shared by sentence-final particles (hereafter, SFPs) including *wa*. First, SFPs are frequently used in spoken language (typically face-to-face conversation), whereas they are rarely found in written language (typically expository prose) (Uyeno, 1971; Sakuma, 1983; Oishi, 1985; Maynard, 1989; McGloin, 1990; Hasunuma, 1998; Hayashi, 2000; Yonezawa, 2005; Katagiri, 2007; Izuhara, 2008). This fact suggests that the functions of SFPs are closely related to certain properties peculiar to spoken discourse.

The second point is that the use of SFPs does not affect the truth-condition of the propositional information of an utterance, and yet it plays an important role for the hearer's interpretation of the utterance (Uyeno, 1971; Sakuma, 1983; Chino, 1991; Kose, 1996, 1997; Hasunuma, 1998). This point is exemplified in (3) below, which is extracted from Kose (1997). (The English meaning and connotation of each utterance is also given by Kose (1997).)

(3) a. *Taroo wa   uta   ga   umai   yo.*
 Taro   TOP song SUB is.good.at YO
 'Taro sings well, (I tell you).'

b. *Taroo wa   uta   ga   umai   zo.*
 Taro   TOP song SUB is.good.at ZO
 'Taro sings well, (damn it!).'

c. *Taroo wa   uta   ga   umai   wa.*
 Taro   TOP song SUB is.good.at WA
 '(Oh), Taro sings well...'

d. *Taroo wa   uta   ga   umai   sa.*
 Taro   TOP song SUB is.good.at SA O
 'Taro sings well, (naturally).'

e. *Taroo wa   uta   ga   umai   ne.*
 Taro   TOP song SUB is.good.at NE
 'Taro sings well, (doesn't he?)' (Kose, 1997: 119)

All the sentences have the same truth-conditional value with respect to the propositional information, i.e. the speaker's positive judgement about Taro's ability of singing, *Taroo wa uta ga umai* 'Taro sings well'. Further, as specifically indicated in the brackets, each particle conveys a different nuance such as 'I tell you' with *yo*, 'damn it' with *zo*, 'Oh' with *wa*, 'naturally' with *sa* or 'doesn't he?' with *ne*, and these different nuances associated with the different particles delineate the hearer's different interpretations of the given utterance.[6] What is observed in these examples is that SFPs function beyond the mere conveyance of information, and are closely related to the non-referential meaning of language.

The third point is that the use of SFPs has certain effects on the interpersonal relationship between the speaker and the hearer. For example, some point out that the use of SFPs softens or strengthens the tone of the utterance (e.g. Uyeno, 1971; Suzuki, 1976; Masuoka, 1991; Izuhara, 1996; Lee, 2007), and some note that SFPs are used more frequently in casual settings than in formal settings (e.g. Uyeno, 1971; Oishi, 1985; Maynard, 1989; Oota, 1992; Lee, 2007). Further, it is widely known that some SFPs are mainly used by either male speakers or female speakers (Uyeno, 1971; Tanaka, 1977; Ide, 1982; Reynolds, 1985; Cheng, 1987; Mizutani and Mizutani, 1987; McGloin, 1990; Miyazaki et al., 2002). These effects of SFPs imply that the socio-cultural connection should be included in a full analysis of the functions of SFPs.

In light of the above general features of SFPs, the current study assumes that the functions of SFPs are more closely related to the interactional aspect of language than to the informational aspect of language, and takes an interactional approach[7] to the function of our target particle, *wa*. In the next section, 'Incorporative vs. Monopolistic Attitude and *Wa*', we outline the involvement-based approach (Lee, 2007), which will be adopted into our analysis of the function of *wa*.

Incorporative vs. Monopolistic Attitude, and Wa

Involvement is a fundamental element for the initiation and maintenance of verbal interaction. It is seen as a prerequisite to the success of any conversational encounter, and created and maintained by the consistent use of a variety of linguistic forms and strategies (Arndt and Janney, 1987; Besnier, 1994; Daneš, 1994; Lee, 2007). A prominent expression of involvement often has an important role in the interaction of speech events, which is typically realised through linguistic exchanges that show a high level of tenseness and intimacy, or in Daneš' (1994) terms, 'more-than-normal' signalling cues of participants' emotions and attitudes.

Lee (2007) adopts the notion of involvement in connection with the role of a speaker's attitude in conversation, and characterises SFPs *ne* and *yo* as the incorporative and monopolistic particle, respectively. Observe (4) below.

(4) a. *Eiga,   omoshirokatta.*
        movie   was.interesting
        'The movie was interesting.'

---

[6] Note that these interpretations of the given particles are not comprehensive ones. We present them here for the purpose of demonstrating the point under discussion. See later discussions for the connotations delivered by the use of our target particle *wa* as well as of *ne* and *yo*.
[7] What we mean by 'interactional approach' is not situated in sequentially based approaches such as turn-taking systems. Rather, it focuses on the effect of the speaker's use of the particles on the hearer, and how the particles operate within social contexts.

b. *Eiga,   omoshirokatta   ne.*
    movie   was.interesting   NE
    'The movie was interesting.'

c. *Eiga,   omoshirokatta   yo.*
    movie   was.interesting   YO
    'The movie was interesting.' (Lee, 2007: 367)

Lee (2007) notes that, while these utterances convey the same propositional information, i.e. the speaker's positive evaluation of the movie, each utterance differs from the others in delivering the attitude of the speaker towards the hearer. (4a), without either *ne* or *yo*, indicates the speaker's attitude of unilaterally delivering his/her positive evaluation of the movie, without 'markedly' inviting the hearer's involvement. Being a 'simple' statement without involvement, it may also be used in monologue or written language. In contrast, (4b), with *ne*, invites the hearer's involvement in the way that the speaker encourages the hearer to align with his/her positive evaluation. This can roughly be glossed as 'I think that the movie was interesting. Don't you think so?' Further, (4c), with *yo*, invites the hearer's involvement in the way that the speaker enhances his/her position as a deliverer of his/her positive evaluation. This can roughly be paraphrased as 'Listen. I tell you that the movie was interesting'. (5) below is a summary of the functions of *ne* and *yo* extracted from Lee (2007: 369).

(5) Functions of *ne* and *yo* (Ø = no sentence-final particle is appended)

	Marked involvement	*Speaker's attitude*
Ø	no	Unilateral delivery toward the partner
ne	yes (Incorporative)	Aligning the contents and feeling of the utterance with the partner
yo	yes (Monopolistic)	Enhancing of the position as the deliverer toward the partner

In what follows, we expand the above approach to the analysis of our target particle *wa*, and show that this particle shares the monopolistic nature with *yo*. First, consider (6) below which illustrates the use of *ne* identified as an incorporative particle by Lee (2007).

(6) O: *Masaka   konna   shinya ni   okyakusan   ga*
        by.no.means   this   late.at.night   customer   SUB

        korareru   no   kana   to   omottara   ippai
        come   NOM   I.wonder.if   QT   think-CD   lots

        kite-itadaite   hontoo   ureshikatta   desu   ne.
        come   really   was.glad   BE   NE
        'I didn't think by any means that customers would come (to see my film) at such a late time, but in fact lots of people came and I

was really glad.'

> K: *Nee.*
> NE
> 'NE (I fully understand how you felt).' (Lee, 2007: 368)

In this example, speakers O and K are talking about a film in which O featured as a main character. The film was shown very late at night, and because of this O did not expect that many people would come to see it. O expresses his happiness in finding that in fact many people had turned up, and uses *ne*. By adding *ne* here, O wishes to align with K with regard to his happiness. In responding to this, K uses *Nee* (the variant of *ne*), and shows her full alignment with O. Note that here K's role is as a receiver of O's utterance, so the use of the monopolistic particles *yo* and *wa,* instead of *Nee*, is not acceptable, since these particles, as we assume, signal the speaker's attitude of enhancing his/her position as a producer of the utterance rather than as a receiver of the other participant's utterance. As such, *ne* as an incorporative particle may be used when the speaker expects to be a receiver of, and indicates his/her alignment towards, the other participant's utterance, while *yo* and *wa* cannot be used in the same manner as *ne* due to their monopolistic nature.

The following examples (7) and (8) further illustrate that *yo* and *wa* share the monopolistic nature.

(7) A: *Konna   insei   ite   ii   n*
       such.as.this postgraduate.student exist   good   NOM

   daroo   ka.
   suppose   QUE
   'I wonder if it's ok to live sort of postgraduate life.'

   B: *Iyaa, juujitsushiteru   desho?*
       well   is.fulfilled   suppose
       'Well. You're having a fulfilled life, right?'

   A: *Juujitsushitenai   yo.*
       is.full-PROG-NEG   YO
       'It's not fulfilled.'   (CFF2)

In (7) A and B are talking about A's life, who is a postgraduate student. Just before this dialogue, A has expressed her concern that she has spent most of her time doing many other things rather than studying. In the first utterance in (7) she further expresses her worries if this is acceptable as she is a postgraduate student who is supposed to study very hard. Then B remarks that A's life (or what she is doing) is fulfilled. In the last line, A denies this by saying *juujitsushitenai* 'It's not fulfilled', and uses *yo* here. It is obvious that even without *yo* A is already taking a role of the message deliverer by virtue of the conversational setting. Nonetheless, A employs *yo* and markedly invites B's involvement through which she is committed to enhance her position as a speaker. By doing so, she attempts to draw B's exclusive attention to her view that is against B's, and makes sure that B more carefully listens to her. As a result, her view and feeling of denial are reinforced.

As assumed in the current study, this monopolistic nature of *yo* is shared by *wa*, and thus they are often interchangeable with respect to the speaker's monopolistic attitude. In fact, *yo* in (7) above can also be replaced with *wa* as shown in (8) below, while A's monopolistic attitude is sustained.

(8) A: *Juujitsushitenai   wa.*
         is.full-PROG-NEG   WA
         'It's not fulfilled.'

Although an utterance with a different particle indicates a different nuance, as native speakers of Japanese may easily notice, *wa* and *yo* commonly indicate the speaker's attitude, 'Listen. I have something to tell you', by which they markedly draw the hearer's attention to the utterance and make sure that the hearer more carefully listens to what the speaker says. Given that these particles share the monopolistic nature, this provides the primary reason for the fact that these particles are basically found only in two-way conversation, which presumes the existence of a hearer, and requires the dynamics of interaction between the conversation parties.

In this section we have discussed the general function of *wa*, i.e. signalling the speaker's monopolistic attitude. In the next section, we examine the unique features of *wa*.

The Function of *Wa*

We first summarise some distributional facts, focusing on its co-occurrence restrictions with commands/requests/proposals and some modal expressions. We will then outline previous studies of the particle, and examine the function of the particle on the basis of its co-occurrence restrictions and other relevant facts.

Relevant Facts

As pointed out in some studies, *wa* cannot be used with commands (Cheng, 1987; Miyazaki et al., 2002), requests (Uyeno, 1971; Miyazaki et al., 2002) or proposals (Miyazaki et al., 2002; Asano, 2003).

(9)   a.   *   *Ima   ike   wa.*
                now   go   WA
                'Go now.'

      b.   *   *Ima   ikinasai   wa.*
                now   go   WA
                'Go now.'

(10) a. * *Ima   itte   wa.*
         now   please.go   WA
         'Please go now.'

   b. * *Ima   itte kudasai   wa.*
         now   please.go   WA
         'Please go now.'

(11) a. * *Ima   ikoo   wa.*
         now   let's.go   WA
         'Let's go now.'

   b. * *Ima   ikimashoo   wa.*
         now   let's.go   WA
         'Let's go now.'

Example (9) illustrates that *wa* cannot co-occur with a command, *ike*[8] 'Go (abrupt)' or *ikinasai* 'Go (more formal than *ike*)'. Similarly, (10) shows that the use of the particle is impossible with a request, *itte* 'Please go (casual)' or *itte kudasai* 'Please go (formal)'. Furthermore, (11) shows that the particle cannot be used with a proposal, *ikoo* 'Let's go (casual)' or *ikimashoo* 'Let's go (formal)'.

Another interesting fact with regard to the use of *wa* is observed in its co-occurrence restriction with modal expressions. As illustrated in (12) and (13) below, the particle cannot be used with the modal expression *deshoo*[9] 'suppose', while it can with the other modal expressions, *rashii* 'it seems', *yoo(da)* 'apparently', *soo(da)* '(hearsay)', *(ni)chigainai* 'must (be)'[10] and *kamoshirenai* 'may (be)', as also pointed out by many researches (Uyeno, 1971; Miyazaki et al., 2002; Asano, 2003; Kashiwagi, 2006).

(12) * *Akiko   mo   konya   no   paatii   kuru   deshoo   wa.*
       Akiko   also   tonight   LK   party   come   suppose   WA
       'I think Akiko will also come to the party tonight.'

---

[8] Ike 'Go' sounds vulgar and is not normally used by female speakers. The female particle*wa* is added here for the purpose of illustration.

[9] Modal expressions in (12) and (13) are all casual forms except *deshoo*. As pointed out by Asano (2003) and Kashiwagi (2006), daroo (the casual version of *deshoo*) sounds quite masculine and its use is generally limited to male speakers. Instead of *daroo*, female speakers normally use *deshoo* for the same function even in casual conversation, and it is the reason for the use of *deshoo* in this female   with *wa*.

[10] To the best of our knowledge, there have been no studies which discuss the co-occurrence possibility between *wa* and *(ni)chigainai*. It seems that the combination between *wa* and *(ni)chigainai* is rare as we also could not find the case where *wa* is used with *(ni)chigainai* in our data. We have asked 20 native speakers of Japanese if this co-occurrence is possible: for example, *Akiko mo iku ni chigainai wa* 'Akiko will surely go, too-WA'. All of them answered that it was possible.

(13) a. *Akiko   mo   konya   no   paatii   ni   kuru   rashii   wa.*
       Akiko   also   tonight   LK   party   to   come   seem   WA
       'It seems that Akiko will also come to the party tonight.'

   b. *Akiko   mo   konya   no   paatii   ni   kuru   yooda*
       Akiko   also   tonight   LK   party   to   come   apparently

      wa.
      WA
      'It looks like Akiko will also come to the party tonight.'

   c. *Akiko   mo   konya   no   paatii   ni   kuru   sooda   wa.*
       Akiko   also   tonight   LK   party   to   come   hear   WA
       'I hear that Akiko will also come to the party tonight.'

   d. *Akiko   mo   konya   no   paatii   ni   kuru   ni chigainai*
       Akiko   also   tonight   LK   party   to   come   must

      wa.
      WA
      'Akiko will surely come to the party tonight, too.'

   e. *Akiko   mo   konya   no   paatii   ni   kuru   kamoshirenai*
       Akiko   also   tonight   LK   party   to   come   may

      wa.
      WA
      'Akiko may also come to the party tonight.'

Previous Studies

Cheng (1987) compares *wa* with another SFP *yo* and notes that *yo* can be used with sentences like commands which attempt to control the hearer's future action (e.g. *Ima ike yo* 'Go now-YO', *Ima itte yo* 'Please go now-YO' and *Ima ikoo yo* 'Let's go now-YO'), while *wa* cannot (Examples were given in (9), (10) and (11) earlier). According to Cheng (1987), this is because the nature of *yo* is to let the hearer know the speaker's thoughts or judgement for the hearer's benefit (*jibun no ninshiki handan shita koto o aite ni shirasete yaru*), while the nature of *wa* is to convince the hearer of the speaker's thoughts or judgement for the speaker's benefit (*jibun no ninshiki handan shita koto o aite ni nattokushite morau*). Cheng (1987) concludes that *wa* is used when a female speaker is committed to convey her thoughts or judgement towards the hearer 'for the sake of herself'.

    As will be discussed in the section "*Wa*: Delivering the Utterance in a Firm Manner", Cheng's (1987) account provides some useful information for an analysis of *wa*; that is, the particle does not particularly indicate the speaker's special consideration on the hearer's side. Nonetheless, Cheng's (1987) definition of *wa* has a shortcoming that it cannot differentiate an utterance with *wa* from that without *wa*. Compare (14a) and (14b) below ((14a) is drawn from our data set and (14b) is its duplication with *wa* omitted).

(14) a. *Katchan   ga   inakunatte   dare yori mo*
         Katchan   SUB   has.gone   more.than.anyone.else

   kanashinda   no   Tatchan   yo.   Sore   wa
   was.sad   NOM   Tatchan   YO   that   TOP

   machigainai   wa.
   certain   WA
   'After Katchan died, the person who was sad more than anyone
   else was Tatchan. That's definitely true.'   (T3)

 b. *Katchan   ga   inakunatte   dare yori mo*
     Katchan   SUB   has.gone   more.than.anyone.else

   kanashinda   no   Tatchan   yo.   Sore   wa
   was.sad   NOM   Tatchan   YO   that   TOP

   machigainai   wa.
   certain   WA
   'After Katchan died, the person who was sad more than anyone
   else was Tatchan. That's definitely true.'   (T3)

In (14a), the speaker says that the person who was the saddest with Katchan's death was Tatchan, and she uses *wa* when she further states that what she has just said is definitely true. According to Cheng (1987), (14a) with *wa* would be interpreted as such that the speaker is committed to indicate her judgement, *Sore wa machigainai* 'That's definitely true', towards the hearer for the sake of herself (the speaker). In other words, the utterance does not indicate 'the speaker's consideration of the hearer's side'. A noteworthy point is that the descriptive statement (14b) without *wa, Sore wa machigainai* 'That's definitely true', also indicates the speaker's commitment to convey her judgement towards the hearer without particularly considering the hearer's side. This reveals that (14a) with *wa* and (14b) without it are indistinguishable within Cheng's (1987) account.

There are also many studies that have accounted for the use of *wa* in terms of its illocutionary force. For example, some claim that the particle indicates the speaker's insistence (Uyeno, 1971; Nihongo Kyooiku Gakkai, 1987; Tanaka, 1989) or the speaker's 'strong emotional feeling' (McGloin, 1990). Interestingly, some other studies see that the particle has the effect of 'softening' the tone of the utterance (Oda, 1964; Suzuki, 1976; Kuwayama, 1981; Ide, 1982; Chino, 1991; Masuoka and Takubo, 1994; Usami, 2006). Note that these concepts, 'insistence, strong emotional feeling' and 'softening the tone of the utterance' can be seen as opposite views of each other. It is thus interesting to see how such opposite interpretations are possible for an identical particle, *wa*. However, no previous studies have provided a convincing account for these contrasting views to the particle. In the section "Expression Effects of *Wa*" we will discuss these views in connection with the function of the particle proposed in the next section.

Wa: Delivering the Utterance in a Firm Manner

Definition

In the section "Relevant Facts", we have seen that *wa* cannot be used with *deshoo* 'suppose', while it can with the other modal expressions. In considering this restriction as well as other relevant facts to be discussed later in this section, we shall first propose the function of *wa* as follows:

(15) The function of *wa*
    Wa signals the speaker's monopolistic attitude of delivering the content and feeling conveyed in the utterance in a firm manner.

This definition first of all clearly states that the particle is monopolistic in nature. Thus, the particle shares the general function of enhancing the speaker's position as a message deliverer, with *yo*.[11] It further specifies the unique feature of *wa* that the speaker delivers the utterance to the hearer in a firm manner.

Here, 'in a firm manner' means that the particle delivers the utterance with the speaker's confidence in what she says. In other words, by using *wa*, the speaker further specifically adds her feeling that she is very firm about what is conveyed in the utterance. With this in mind, observe (16) below.

(16) a. *Hanako   wa   gakusei   da.*
          Hanako   TOP   student   BE
          'Hanako is a student.'

      b. *Hanako   wa   gakusei   da   wa.*
          Hanako   TOP   student   BE   WA
          'Hanako is a student.'

The declarative statement without *wa* in (16a) indicates that the speaker is certain about Hanako being a student. By adding *wa* to this statement as in (16b), the speaker attempts to deliver her certainty further in a firm manner, implying 'I am certain about Hanako being a student and I am firmly stating my certainty to you'. The speaker's attitude of firm delivery is associated with her feeling that she has confidence in her judgement that Hanako is a student.

Co-occurrence Restriction with Modal Expressions

Having defined the function of *wa* as above, we now consider the function in connection with the co-occurrence restriction of the particle with modal expressions. Recall that *wa* cannot be used with *deshoo* 'suppose', while it can

---

[11] In fact wa shares this monopolistic function with other SFPs *zo, ze, sa* as well as *yo*, while *ne* and *na* share the incorporative function. See Ogi (2011) for details.

with the other modal expressions *rashii* 'it seems', *yoo(da)* 'apparently', *soo(da)* '(hearsay)', *(ni)chigainai* 'must (be)' and *kamoshirenai* 'may (be)'. In order to account for this restriction of the particle, below we first clarify the linguistic behaviour of *deshoo* (*daroo*), in comparison to the other modal expressions.

A number of Japanese linguists agreed that *rashii*, *yoo(da)* and *soo(da)* differ from *(ni)chigainai*, *kamoshirenai* and *daroo*,[12] in terms of the speaker's attitude towards the truth-value or factual status of the proposition (cf. Miyazaki, 1993; Moriyama et al., 2000; Miyazaki et al., 2002; Johnson, 2003; Narrog, 2009). Broadly speaking, the former expressions, *rashii*, *yoo(da)* and *soo(da)*, are seen as specifying the evidence/ground based on which the speaker judges the truth-value of the proposition ('evidentiality' in Miyazaki et al.'s (2002) term, or 'evidentials' in Johnson's (2003) and Narrog's (2009) term), and the latter, *(ni)chigainai*, *kamoshirenai* and *daroo*, expresses the way or degree of the speaker's conviction in judging the truth-value of the proposition ('suppositionals' in Johnson's (2003) term). To put it differently, when *rashii*, *yoo(da)* and *soo(da)* are used, they indicate what evidence the speaker has in judging the truth-value of the proposition — whether he/she has gained the propositional information through visual or other sensory impressions such as hearing or feeling. On the other hand, when *(ni)chigainai*, *kamoshirenai* and *daroo* are used, they do not denote evidence for the truth-value of the proposition[13], but rather indicate in what way or how much the speaker is certain about the proposition being true (Moriyama, 1989; Miyazaki, 1993; Asano, 2003).

Having noted that *daroo* is a suppositional, and differs from evidentials, our next question is then how it differs from the other suppositionals, *(ni)chigainai* and *kamoshirenai*. First, focusing on *(ni)chigainai* 'must (be)' and *kamoshirenai* 'may (be)', it is well known that they differ from each other in terms of the degree of the speaker's certainty of the proposition being true; more precisely, *(ni)chigainai* represents the high degree of the speaker's certainty while *kamoshirenai* expresses the low degree (Teramura, 1984; Masuoka, 1991; Nitta, 1991; Miyazaki, 1993; Masuoka and Takubo, 1994; Moriyama et al., 2000; Narrog, 2009). This difference is reflected in their different linguistic behaviour, as illustrated in the following examples extracted from Miyazaki (1993).

---

[12] For the purpose of presentation, hereafter we use *daroo* as a representative form of *daroo* and *deshoo*.

[13] This is not to say that the speaker does not have any grounds for his/her judgement (certainty) when he/she uses *(ni)chigainai*, *kamoshirenai* or *daroo*. For example, Asano (2009) claims that *(ni)chigainai* indicates the speaker's strong certainty which is based on his/her current knowledge or relevant information. What we mean by "they do not denote evidence" is that the focus of the suppositionals is not on specifically indicating the source of the speaker's judgement.

(17) a. *{Kitto/ ??Tabun/ *Moshikasuruto}* kare wa
surely maybe perhaps he TOP

konai ni chigainai.
come-NEG must
'{Surely/?? Maybe/* Perhaps} he will surely not come.'

b. *{*Kitto/ ??Tabun/ Moshikasuruto}* kare wa.
*surely maybe perhaps he TOP

konai kamoshirenai.
come-NEG may
'{* Surely/?? Maybe/Perhaps} he may not come.'
(Miyazaki, 1993: 41)

(17a) and (17b) show the co-occurrence restrictions of *(ni)chigainai* and *kamoshirenai* when paired with adverbs that indicate different degrees of certainty, respectively. As pointed out in many studies, the possibility/impossibility of co-occurrence of each modal expression with these adverbs is due to their semantic properties (cf. Masuoka, 1991; Nitta, 1991; Miyazaki, 1993; Masuoka and Takubo, 1994; Miyazaki ct al., 2002). Since *(ni)chigainai* represents a high degree of certainty, as shown in (17a) it can be used with *kitto* 'surely,' which also indicates a high degree of certainty, while it cannot with *moshikasuruto* 'perhaps', which indicates a low degree of certainty. In contrast, *kamoshirenai* in (17b) represents a low degree of certainty, and it can be used with *moshikasuruto*, whereas it cannot with *kitto*. Bearing the above facts in mind, let us observe the following.

(18) *{Kitto/ Tabun/ Moshikasuruto}* kare wa konai
surely maybe perhaps he TOP come-NEG

daroo.
suppose
'{Surely/Maybe/*Perhaps} I don't think he will come.'
(Miyazaki, 1993: 41)

Example (18) shows that *daroo* may co-occur with any adverbs that indicate various degrees of certainty from high to low. This suggests that, unlike *(ni)chigainai* and *kamoshirenai*, a genuine property of *daroo* is not to specifically indicate a high or low degree of certainty of the truth-value of the proposition.

Another noteworthy fact with regard to the difference between *daroo* and *(ni)chigainai/kamoshirenai* is that *daroo* can co-occur with the question marker *ka*, while *(ni)chigainai* and *kamoshirenai* cannot (Miyazaki, 1993; Johnson, 2003 for *(ni)chigainai*; Miyazaki, 1993; Asano, 2003 for *kamoshirenai*). Examples in (19) below are drawn from Miyazaki (1993).

(19) a. *Ashita   wa   hareru   daroo   ka.*
       tomorrow TOP   sunny   suppose QUE
       'I wonder if it will be sunny tomorrow.'

   b. * *Ashita   wa   hareru   ni chigainai   ka.*
        tomorrow TOP   sunny   must   QUE
        'It must be sunny tomorrow.'

   c. * *Ashita   wa   hareru   ni kamoshirenai   ka.*
        tomorrow TOP   sunny   may   QUE
        'It may be sunny tomorrow.'   (Miyazaki 1993: 42)

In close connection with these facts, Asano (2003) points out that the nature of the question marker *ka*, which indicates one's uncertainty, is the reason for its possible/impossible co-occurrence with the given modal expressions. According to Asano (2003), *kamoshirenai* involves one's uncertainty; thus its combination with *ka*, another expression of one's uncertainty, is semantically redundant, and as a result, their co-occurrence is not allowed. Needless to say, this point made by Asano (2003) is also applicable to *(ni)chigainai*, which is the same as *kamoshirenai* in the sense that it also involves one's uncertainty. In contrast, *daroo* does not specifically involve one's uncertainty, hence there is no problem with its co-occurrence with *ka*, as illustrated in (19a).

Daroo 'Refraining from Asserting the Speaker's Certainty' and *Wa*

Having reached this point, the connection of *daroo* with the certainty is that it indicates the speaker's attitude of 'refraining from asserting' his/her certainty. This feature of *daroo* becomes clearer when compared with *da*, which is *dantei no hyoogen* 'assertive expression', i.e. the speaker asserts his/her certainty about the propositional information straightforwardly. Compared to this, *daroo* is referred to as *sonomama danteishinai* 'the speaker does not assert his/her certainty of the proposition being true as it is' (Moriyama, 1989: 112) or as *dantei o horyuusuru* 'the speaker refrains from asserting his/her certainty of the proposition being true' (Morita, 1980, 222; Masuoka, 1991: 112). That is, with *daroo* the speaker is certain that the proposition is true, and yet he/she does not assert his/her certainty in a straightforward manner. Teramura (1984) notes that the use of *daroo* does not necessarily mean the low degree of the speaker's certainty, but it is useful for avoiding the *da*-like way of asserting the speaker's certainty thereby softening the assertive tone of *da*. Johnson (2003) also makes a similar claim, saying that *daroo* is typically used when the speaker wishes to avoid the tone of directness associated with the use of *da*. In short, while *(ni) chigainai* and *kamoshirenai* involve the speaker's uncertainty of the proposition being true, *daroo* does not involve such uncertainty. Further, it differs from the assertive expression *da* in that it denotes the speaker's attitude of refraining from asserting his/her certainty.

Keeping this feature of *daroo* in mind, let us return to our discussion of the co-occurrence restrictions of *wa* with modal expressions. Focusing first on the use of *wa* with *(ni)chigainai* 'must (be)' and *kamoshirenai* 'may (be)', their co-occurrence is a well predicted one. Consider (20) below.

(20) a. *Hanako   wa   gakusei   ni chigainai   wa.*
      Hanako   TOP   student   must   WA
      'Hanako must be a student.'

    b. *Hanako   wa   gakusei   kamoshirenai   wa.*
      Hanako   TOP   student   may   WA
      'Hanako may be a student.'

As noted earlier, *(ni)chigainai* in (20a) indicates a high degree of the speaker's certainty, and thus it indicates the speaker strongly believes that Hanako is a student. By adding *wa* here, the speaker is committed to deliver her strong belief in a firm manner, which can be paraphrased as 'I strongly believe that Hanako is a student, and I am firmly stating my belief to you'. Similarly, *kamoshirenai* in (20b) indicates a low degree of the speaker's certainty. By using *wa* here, the speaker attempts to deliver her judgement, Hanako may or may not be a student, in a firm manner.

In contrast, the impossible use of *wa* with *deshoo* 'suppose' is due to the fact that the nature of *deshoo* does not match with the speaker's intention conveyed by the use of the particle.

(21) **Hanako   wa   gakusei   deshoo   wa.*
      Hanako   TOP   student   suppose   WA
      'I think Hanako is a student.'

The use of *deshoo* here indicates that the speaker is committed to refraining from asserting her certainty of Hanako being a student. This speaker's attitude with *deshoo* reflects her feeling that she needs (or wants) to speak with deliberation, as also pointed out by Morita (1980). This means that by using *deshoo*, while the speaker judges Hanako to be a student, she wants to avoid showing her definite attitude. The use of *wa* would add her firm attitude in delivering the judgment, and this firm attitude would accompany the speaker's feeling that she wants to state her judgment in a definite manner with full confidence. This speaker's attitude and feeling associated with the use of *wa* directly conflicts with the characteristic of *deshoo* of avoiding to show her definite attitude. This is the reason for the incompatibility of *wa* with *deshoo*.

Finally, we noted in 3.1 that *wa* can co-occur with the evidentials which indicate the fact that the speaker has gained the information from a secondary source. (22) below provides extended examples of this, in which *wa* is used with *rashii* 'it seems' in (22a), *yoo(da)* 'apparently' in (22b) and *soo(da)* '(hearsay)' in (22c).

(22) a. *Hanako   wa   gakusei   rashii   wa.*
      Hanako   TOP   student   seem   WA
      'It seems that Hanako is a student.'

b. *Hanako wa gakusei no yooda wa*
   Hanako TOP student BE apparently WA
   'It looks like Hanako is a student.'

c. *Hanako wa gakusei da sooda wa.*
   Hanako TOP student BE hear WA
   'I hear that Hanako is a student.'

Hanako wa gakusei rashii in (22a) and *Hanako wa gakusei no yooda* in (22b) indicate the fact that the speaker is not one hundred percent sure what Hanako does, but for instance, she saw the picture of Hanako wearing a school uniform and has judged Hanako as being a student.[14] *Hanako wa gakusei da sooda* in (22c) indicates the fact that the speaker has heard from somebody that Hanako is a student. These facts signified by the given evidentialities can be delivered in a firm manner without any problem. With *wa*, these utterances are interpreted as 'I have gained the information that Hanako is a student from what I saw, heard or felt, and I am firmly stating this to you'.

Considering the Hearer's Side

Thus far we have demonstrated how the speaker's attitude of firm delivery is expressed through the use of *wa* in close connection with its co-occurrence possibility/impossibility with modal expressions. Next, we would like to add a further point that the speaker's firm delivery indicated by *wa* does not denote the speaker's particular consideration of the hearer's side. Rather, it denotes that the speaker focuses on her side only, as shown in the interpretation of the particle, 'Listen. I am firmly stating this to you'. It has been noted in section "Previous Studies" that this feature of the particle is also acknowledged in Cheng's (1987) statement, *aite ni nattokushite morau* 'convince the hearer of it for the speaker's benefit'. This means that with *wa* the speaker does not show her particular commitment to make the hearer understand what she says. This aspect of *wa* can be confirmed by the fact that *wa* cannot co-occur with commands, requests and proposals, as shown earlier. Examples are re-presented below.

(9)' a. * *Ima ike wa.*
        now go WA
     'Go now.'

   b. * *Ima ikinasai wa.*
         now go WA
      'Go now.'

(10)' a. * *Ima itte wa.*
          now please.go WA
       'Please go now.'

---

[14] For details of the difference between *rashii* 'it seems' and *yooda* 'apparently', see Teramura (1984), Tanomura (1991), Johnson (2003) and Narrog (2009).

      b.   * *Ima   itte kudasai   wa.*
                now   please.go   WA
         'Please go now.'

(11)' a.   * *Ima   ikoo   wa.*
                now   let's.go   WA
         'Let's go now.'

      b.   * *Ima   ikimashoo   wa.*
                now   let's.go   WA
         'Let's go now.'

Ike and *ikinasai* in (9)' are commands, *itte* and *itte kudasai* in (10)' are requests, and *ikoo* and *ikimashoo* in (11)' are proposals. As illustrated in these examples, *wa* is compatible with none of these sentences. What commonly underlies these three types of utterances is the speaker's intention of controlling the hearer's future action. For example, with *ike* in (9a)', *itte* in (10a)' and *ikoo* in (11a)', all the utterances convey the speaker's intention of making the hearer go. Naturally, these utterances presuppose that the hearer completely understands what he/she is supposed to do, and otherwise he/she would be unable to correctly respond to the speaker's intention. From the speaker's point of view, this means that these utterances require the speaker's strong commitment to make the hearer understand what to do. In other words, the speaker needs to 'consider the hearer's side' in order to make sure that the hearer does act as he/she (the speaker) commands, requests or proposes.

    This point of 'considering the hearer's side' in these three types of utterances can be seen more clearly by comparing them with a simple descriptive statement, for example, *Daigaku ni iku* 'I will go to the university'. Although this descriptive statement can still be informative for the hearer, it does not in particular require the speaker's strong commitment to make the hearer understand the conveyed information, and hence the speaker's 'consideration of the hearer's side' is not specifically expected. Compared to this, commands, requests and proposals involve a high level of the speaker's 'consideration of the hearer's side', since, as noted above, the success of the speaker's intended goal with these utterances depends on whether or not the hearer understands and acts as the speaker says. The incompatibility of *wa* with these three types of utterances suggests that the particle lacks the speaker's consideration of the hearer's side. In short, *wa* is characterised as a particle which signals that the speaker delivers the utterance in a firm manner without indicating her specific consideration of the hearer's side.

Expressive Effects of Wa

As noted in the section "Previous Studies", the effect of *wa* is often seen as 'softening' the tone of the utterance (Oda, 1964; Suzuki, 1976; Kuwayama, 1981; Ide, 1982; Chino, 1991; Masuoka and Takubo, 1994; Usami, 2006). On the other hand, some studies view that the particle indicates the speaker's 'insistence'

(Uyeno, 1971; Nihongo Kyooiku Gakkai, 1987; Tanaka, 1989), or 'strong emotional feeling' (McGloin, 1990), which is opposite to the effect of softening the tone of the utterance. These two contrasting views for the single particle *wa* are due to the fact that each account sees only one aspect of the use of the particle, and comprehensively explainable from the perspective of involvement and the monopolistic nature of *wa*. Look at (23) and (24) below.

(23) *Hora, mada   yogoreteru   wa.*
     look   still become.dirty-PROG   WA
     Look, (your clothes) are still dirty.'   (HD2)

(24) A: *A,   Kirishima san   gobusata   shitemasu.*
        oh, Mr. Kirishima   long.silence   do-PROG

        Kaisha   setsuritsu   omedetoo gozaimasu.   Waga
        company   foundation   congratulations   my

        Raioneru Guruupu   no   hokori   desu   wa.
        Lionel.Group   LK   pride   BE   WA
        'Oh, Mr. Kirishima, long time no see. Congratulations on establishing your company. Our Lionel Group is proud of your achievement.'

    B: *Yamete kudasai   yo.   Chichi   kara   kogaisha*
       please.stop   YO   father   from   subsidiary

       o   uketsuida   dake   na   n   da   kara.
       OBJ   took.over   only   BE   NOM   BE   since
       'Please stop it. I only took over a subsidiary from my father.'
                                                                 (HD2)

In (23) the speaker states that the hearer's clothes are still dirty. *Wa* is deployed here. What underlies the use of *wa* here is the speaker's commitment to deliver the information in a firm manner, which denotes her feeling that she is very confident in judging the hearer's clothes still being dirty. (24) is a conversation between A, whose father owns the Lionel Group, and B, Mr. Kirishima, who established his company which is under the umbrella of the Lionel Group. At a party of the Lionel Group, A congratulates B on establishing his company and states that she is proud of him. A's use of *wa* here further adds a nuance that she is very firm about her feeling of being proud of B. What we can easily observe from these examples is that *wa* delivers the speaker's confidence in what she says and how she feels, without indicating her consideration of the hearer's side. This invokes a 'self-assured' tone, which is also interpreted as 'insistence', or as strengthening the tone of the utterance.

However, this does not necessarily mean that the statement with *wa* carries a higher degree of the declarative tone compared to a normal declarative statement without the particle. For example, compare A's utterance *Waga Raioneru Guruupu no hokori desu wa* 'Our Lionel Group is proud of your achievement' in

(24) with (25) below which is a duplication of A's utterance in (24), but with *wa* omitted.

(25)   *Waga*   *Raioneru Guruupu*   *no*   *hokori*   *desu*
       my   Lionel.Group   LK   pride   be
       'Our Lionel Group is proud of your achievement.'

Example (25) without *wa* unilaterally states the speaker's feeling, thereby the assertiveness of its declarative tone is straightforwardly expressed. This results in delivering the statement in an 'official' tone, implying 'I am definitely certain that our Lionel Group is proud of your achievement, and have no more to say'. Compared to this, (24)' with *wa* markedly indicates the speaker's invitation of the hearer's involvement, by which it explicitly shows the speaker's recognition of the hearer as her conversation partner and her willingness to continue the conversation with the hearer. This aspect of the use of *wa* gives us the feeling that the assertiveness of the declarative tone would be moderated, which will in turn be seen as softening the tone of the utterance. In short, *wa* has dual aspects with respect to its expressive effects, i.e. strengthening and softening. With the speaker's recognition of the hearer as the conversation partner and her willingness to continue the conversation, rather than terminate it, the statement would be interpreted as softening the tone of the utterance. Yet with a strong tone of voice, the monopolistic nature of the particle, i.e. 'You should listen to me. I am very confident in what I am saying', would prominently be expressed and the statement would be perceived as indicating the speaker's strong self-assured tone.

Finally, the attitudinal and expressive effect of *wa* is also closely related to the level of formality involved; more specifically, the particle is not normally used in a formal situation. As discussed above, *wa* indicates the speaker's monopolistic-firm attitude, 'Listen. I am firmly stating this to you', as well as her feeling, 'I am willing to continue the conversation with you'. Thus, with *wa* the utterance strongly indicates the speaker's firm and self-assured tone as well as their friendly feelings towards the hearer. Note that formality/informality is generally ensured not only by verbal forms, e.g. the polite *desu-masu* forms *vs.* the casual *da-ru* forms, but also by the different restrictions on the way the speaker expresses his/her attitude and feeling/emotion towards the hearer. For example, Lee (2002) points out that a direct and strong display of the speaker's attitude and feelings/emotions is generally acceptable in informal situations where the speaker has a close relationship with the hearer. This provides a straightforward explanation for the use of *wa* in informal situations, i.e. this is the situation where the speaker is allowed to expose her attitude and feelings/emotions in a direct and strong fashion. This also explains why the particle is rarely used in formal situation, i.e. this is the situation where such a direct exposure of the speaker's attitude and feelings/emotions is not normally allowed.

For example, (26) below is a conversation between a teacher, A, and her student, B, and B's use of *wa* is seen as inappropriate here.

(26) A: *B-san,   natsuyasumi   wa   dokoka   ni*
       Miss. B   summer.holidays TOP   somewhere   to

   ikimashita   ka.
   went   QUE
   'Miss. B, did you go somewhere during your summer holidays?'

   B: a. *Hai, Okinawa ni   ikimashita.*
          yes   Okinawa to   went
       'Yes, I went to Okinawa.'

      b. ? *Hai, Okinawa ni   ikimashita   wa.*
             yes   Okinawa to   went   WA
       'Yes, I went to Okinawa.'

In (26), teacher A asks student B if she went somewhere during her summer holidays, and B answers that she went to Okinawa. In the given situation, B's answer with *wa* in (26b) sounds inappropriate, while (26a) without the particle is not problematic at all. In this case, B is required simply to answer A's question whether or not she went somewhere. However, in (26b) by using *wa* B expresses her confidence in what she says, firmly with a self-assured tone. This makes the utterance sound as if she is very proud of the fact that she went to Okinawa, and imparts an overbearing nuance. As noted above, such an expression of the speaker's strong attitude and feelings/emotions would be acceptable when the speaker has a close relationship with the hearer. However, in a Japanese context, students are in general presumed to keep a formal relationship with teachers, hence they are not allowed to directly and strongly indicate their attitudes and feelings/emotions towards teachers. Thus, B's use of *wa* in (26b) is interpreted as inappropriate and impolite. This is the reason for the fact that *wa* is not, in principle, used in a situation where a high level of formality is required.

Wa and Gender Specification

Gender and Language

It has widely been acknowledged that in many societies men and women use language differently (Coates, 1993; McCormick, 1998). The Japanese language is not an exception of this, and many studies have pointed out a number of linguistic features used differently by Japanese men and women, which include personal pronouns, SFPs, honorifics, pitch heights and intonation (e.g. Oda, 1964; Jugaku, 1979; Ide, 1982; 1990; Reynolds, 1985; Shibamoto Smith, 1985, 2004; Mizutani and Mizutani, 1987; Ide and McGloin, 1990; Oota, 1992; Suzuki, 1993; Masuoka and Takubo, 1994; Maynard, 1997; Aizawa, 2003; Kawasaki and McDougall, 2003; Okamoto and Shibamoto Smith, 2004; Kashiwagi, 2006). Further, the gender-distinction in the Japanese language has often been discussed in relation to the notion of *-rashii* '-like, -ly' such as *otoko-rashii* 'manly' and *onna-rashii* 'womanly' (Jugaku, 1979; Falconer, 1984; Ide and McGloin, 1990; Reynolds,

1990), and a considerable amount of attention has been paid to the female speech called *onna-kotoba* or *josei-go* 'women's language' which is associated with the notion of *onna-rashisa* 'womanliness' (e.g. Jugaku, 1979; Ide, 1982, 1990; Reynolds, 1985, 1990; Shibamoto Smith, 1985; Suzuki, 1993; Endo, 1997; Inoue, 2002; Aizawa, 2003; Okamoto, 2004; Yukawa and Saito, 2004; Endo, 2006; Nakamura, 2006; Matsumoto, 2007). In the remainder of the current study we will explore how the particle came to indicate the speaker's gender being a female and what this implies in light of its function and expressive effects of *wa* as discussed in the previous sections. Below, however, we will first briefly outline the general trend of the researches on the relationship between gender and language in Western societies.

Many studies acknowledge that the following three approaches are major research streams of the relationship between gender and language in Western societies (Kendall and Tannen, 2001; McIlvenny, 2002; Eckert and McConnell-Ginet, 2003; Yukawa and Saito, 2004): (i) Dominance approach (e.g. Trudgill, 1972; Lakoff, 1975; Zimmerman and West, 1975), (ii) Difference approach (e.g. Maltz and Borker, 1982; Tannen, 1990, 1993, 1996), and (iii) Social construction approach (e.g. McElhinny, 1995; Eckert and McConnell-Ginet, 2003; Holmes and Stubbe, 2003).

The 'dominance' approach empirically investigates differences between male and female speeches and identifies the role of language as creating and maintaining social inequality between men and women. For instance, Zimmerman and West (1975: 125) report that men interrupt women more often in conversations, and conclude that "just as male dominance is exhibited through male control of macro-institutions in society, it is also exhibited through control of at least a part of one micro-institution". Lakoff (1975: 54) also links women's use of hedges with unassertiveness, and argues that this is because women "are socialised to believe that asserting themselves strongly isn't nice or ladylike, or even feminine". Within this approach the difference in using language between men and women reflects the unequal gender relations (or power relations) in society in the way that men dominate women.

The 'difference' approach argues that sex-separate socialisation is the source of different language use between men and women. Tannen (1990), for example, claims that while all speakers must find a balance between seeking connection and negotiating relative status, conversational rituals learned by boys and maintained by men tend to focus on the status dimension, and those learned by girls and maintained by women do more on the connection dimension. This approach does not deny either the existence of dominance relations in general or the dominance of women by men in particular. Rather, it questions the notion that the source of the different use of language between men and women is simply located in male domination over women. Crawford (1995) notes that within the difference approach, male and female talks are equally limiting for their users in cross-sex interaction, and thus the speech style attributed to men is no longer powerful, but merely one way of negotiating the social landscape.

The 'social construction' approach considers diverse language forms and gender meaning mediated by cultural ideologies,[15] and attempts to overcome the essentialism[16] of the earlier studies. Within this approach, gender is not seen as an identity someone just 'has' or 'is', but rather as a product of people's social interaction. More specifically, this approach assumes that gender does not just exist, but is continually produced, reproduced, and changed through people's performance in social interaction, recognising that such performances are related to both conventional gendered identities and identities that in one way or another challenge such conventional gendered norms. For example, Holmes and Stubbe (2003) provide a summary of the most widely cited features of 'feminine' and 'masculine' interactional styles[17] and examine data produced by two female managers from New Zealand at different business meetings. Holmes and Stubbe (2003) find that both managers skilfully mixed a variety of features typically associated with the feminine and masculine speech styles in the way that is appropriate to the norms of their workgroup, and to the specific situation at the given time. Holmes and Stubbe (2003: 595) conclude that "individual women and men construct their gender identities and balance these with their professional roles within the parameters established as acceptable by the group with which they work".

As such, the major approaches of Western societies show that gendered socio-cultural constraints influence different language use by men and women to some extent, while individuals accommodate, resist or contest such gendered socio-cultural norms and strategically choose appropriate linguistic performance to suit a given situation. Needless to say, the use of gender-specific language in Japanese can also be influenced by and explained in terms of the performative aspect of gendered socio-cultural norms to indicate or emphasise their gender identity in conversation. However, what is special for the gender-language relationship in Japanese is that the male/female language dichotomy in the Japanese language has a close connection with the notion of *-rashii* '-like, -ly'. For example, Falconer (1984) remarks that the difference between Japanese male and female speeches is induced by much greater significance of *-rashii* '-like,

---

[15] The term 'ideology' refers to "the system of beliefs by which people explain, account for, and justify their behaviour, and interpret and assess that of others" (Eckert and McConnell, 2003: 35).

[16] According to McIlvenny (2002: 2), the perspective of essentialism is that "gender has tended to be seen as a variable attribute or essence of a speaker that is expressed in, or causes, certain linguistic behaviours, practices and/or actions in particular social contexts. Talk is simply a vehicle for the display of what are essentially independent, internal properties: one talks the way one does because one is a man or a woman, and talk is reflective of that essential difference".

[17] Feminine interactional styles are characterised as indirect, conciliatory, facilitative, collaborative, giving minor contribution (in public), supportive feedback, person/process-oriented and affectively oriented. Masculine styles are characterised as direct, confrontational, competitive, autonomous, dominating (public) talking time, aggressive interruptions, task/outcome-oriented and referentially oriented (Holmes and Stubbe, 2003: 574).

-ly'[18] such as *otoko-rashii* 'manly' and *onna-rashii* 'womanly' in Japanese society, which carries much stronger connotations of expectations and conforms to rules, than in the West. Ide and McGloin (1990) also point out that gender exercised in the Japanese language cannot be reduced to questions of power and status alone, as has been one of the central issues in Western societies, and state that

> "…among highly developed industrial countries Japan is unique in that feminism has not revolutionised people's ways of thinking and living. Though it has had a certain influence, most people stick to old ways. The reasons might lie in assumptions about what it is to be a man or a woman in Japanese society. In Western societies interaction is carried out on the basis of individualism and egalitarianism. Instead of claiming the same status and role as men, Japanese women prefer a complementary vision of status and role differences, giving them equal dignity, despite differences in form". (Ide and McGloin, 1990: i-ii)

In the next section, we will further explore the notion *onna-rashisa* 'womanliness', which plays a crucial role in development of the gender-specific language expressions in Japanese.

Development of the Notion Onna-Rashisa *'Womanliness'*

The emergence of the notion of *onna-rashisa* 'womanliness' as well as *onna-kotoba* 'women's language' including our target particle *wa* is closely related to the Japan's modern nation-state formation pursued from the late 19th century to the early 20th century during the Meiji era. It was the time when Japanese society rapidly moved from its old feudalism to a modern form, which brought fundamental changes in a wide range of fields including its social structure, economy, politics, education, science, and so forth. While language played a significant role for building a nation-state by importing and simulating Western science and technology and achieving national integration, language itself has also undergone the reform of the modernization. In the language reform during this period, two events are particularly important to note for the establishment of the notion of *onna-rashisa* 'womanliness' and *onna-kotoba* 'women's language'.

The first event is the reinforcement of the *ryoosai-kenbo* 'a good wife and wise mother' education by the government. In 1879, the Meiji government enforced the educational system in which males and females were forbidden to learn at the same school. What underlies the enforcement of this educational system was the government's reinforcement of the *ryoosai-kenbo* education (Nakamura, 2006). The idea of *ryoosai-kenbo* was derived from Confucianism, and required women to take on a critical gendered role in Japanese modern society, which included an emphasis on motherhood, rational and scientific management, and saving (Inoue, 2002). This means that the educational reform during that time was based on the principle of Confucianism, as also well indicated in the following notes made by Tanaka (1987: 226):

---

[18] Falconer (1984) uses the term '-*rashii*' as attributes, activities and behaviours which one is expected to have in Japanese society.

"Education at the time of the expansion of the educational system was linked to the general societal drive to 'Westernise' and the individualism and practically of the West's educational philosophy was reflected therein. However, the Education Ordinance and the 'Reformed Education Ordinance' issued the following year focused on Confucian thought as the conservatives attempted to place moral and behavioural education in a central position".

It is rather ironical that the conservative Confucianism-based education was a key ideology of the educational reform which moved towards modernization or Westernization. The Meiji government needed to unify and train its people as *kokumin* 'nation members' who would become faithful labour and a force to build up modern Japan. Needless to say, women also took part in this modernization of Japan, but with a different role from men. While men had a more direct role of a labour and force for the modernization, women were expected to have a role of wife to internally support their husbands, as well as a role of mother to raise the next generation. For this, the government had to limit the role of women to the faithful wife and mother in order to avoid the situation in which women become independent and deny the control of the government (Nakamura, 2005, 2006).

Importantly for our discussion, it was widely recognised among people that a woman had to use good language as well as show a good behaviour and manner in order to be a *ryoosai-kenbo* 'a good wife and wise mother' and support her husband and children. This point was, for example, overtly stated in a textbook published in 1900 in which women were urged to be gentle and graceful in all things, not only in manners but also in speech (Shinpen Shuushin Kyooten, 1962: 650, via Endo, 2006: 61). Similarly, according to Nakamura (2005, 2006), books that were used for the *ryoosai-kenbo* education included strict norms about women's language use such as *Onna wa otonashiku, shitoyakani hanasu bekide aru* 'Women must speak gently and politely' or *Josei wa muyoo no kuchi wa kikazu, shizukanishite okuyukashiku iru bekide aru* 'Women should not say unnecessary things, staying calm and quiet'. Likewise, through the education reform, the Meiji government established the social norm that Japanese women must be *onna-rashii* 'womanly' with the ideal role of *ryoosai-kenbo* 'a good wife and wise mother'. Japanese women's language was seen as an important means to express *onna-rashisa* 'womanliness' and women were expected to behave and speak gently, quietly and gracefully.

The second event that directly influenced the establishment of *onna-rashisa* 'womanliness' and *onna-kotoba* 'women's language' was *genbunitchi undoo* 'the movement of the unification of spoken and written language styles' by Meiji writers. Up until the late 19th century, written Japanese had been based on the sentence style of the classic Japanese, and there was a huge gap in sentence styles between what people wrote and what people actually spoke in daily conversations.[19] From the late 19th century, a movement took place among writers of novels to write conversations of their characters in the style of actual spoken Japanese. What was behind this movement was the need at the time to translate Western realist novels into Japanese. They were required to develop the

---

[19] For further details, see Okuda (1957).

linguistic forms of dialogue and report in order to translate and appropriate the Western realist novels, and hence manipulated the verb-ending forms such as the *desu-masu* forms and various sentence-final particles (Inoue, 2002). Our target particle *wa* and other particles such as *zo* and *ze* were also developed to indicate a particular gender of speakers in their novels. The development of these particles can be observed, for example, through the comparison of sentence-final particles used in the fiction *Ukiyoburo* written by Sanba Shikitei in 1813 and the novel *Sanshiro* written by Soseki Natsume in 1909. According to Inoue (2002: 405), *wa, zo* and *ze* were gender-neutral and found to be used by both genders in *Ukiyoburo*, but had become gendered into either male- or female-specific particles and *wa* was used exclusively by female speakers whereas *zo* and *ze* were used by male speakers only in *Sanshiro*.

In relation to our discussion of *wa*, it is interesting to note that *wa* and some other particles such as *teyo* and *noyo* have begun to be used by *jogakusei* 'schoolgirls' since *danjo-betsugaku* 'gender-segregated school system' was adopted in the educational system in 1879 (Nakamura, 2006). Around that time, these particles were in fact associated with neither gentleness nor femininity. Quite on the contrary, educators and intellectuals considered those particles as a 'vulgar' speech form adopted by daughters from the low-rank families and strongly advised parents and teachers not to let their daughters and students use those particles (Inoue, 2002; Nakamura, 2006). A famous writer, Koyo Ozaki, also noted that "Strange verb endings such as *dawa*,[20] *teyo* and *noyo* occurred among elementary schoolgirls between close friends and seemed to be spreading among high school girls and even adult women", and warned that sensible ladies should not use these verb endings (quoted from Ooka, 1994). Meiji writers, or *genbunitchi* writers, initially limited the use of these particles in the speech of *keihakuna* 'indiscreet' schoolgirl's characters in their novels (Ishikawa, 1972, cited in Inoue, 2002: 406).

However, in 1899, *Kootoojogakkoorei* 'Women's School Act' was officially announced by the government and there was a dramatic increase in the number of young women who wanted to be educated (Nakamura, 2006). This increase of educated women in turn brought the increase of women readers of novels, whereby writers' attention to women's language had become ever higher. Influenced also from the government's reinforcement of the *ryoosai-kenbo* 'a good wife and wise mother' education at that time, writers eventually revised these particles and started using them to *indexicalise* the speech of female characters, as also noted in Inoue (2002: 406).

> "[i]n early 20th-century writing, these particles were resignified and elevated to women's language, through the process of writers actively indexicalising the speech of female characters as generic and universal yet increasingly feminised".

With continuous use in novels over time, the particles *dawa, teyo* and *noyo* were eventually recognised as not only the language of schoolgirls, but also the language of women of the middle and upper classes (Inoue, 2002; Endo, 2006).

---

[20] '*Dawa*' involves a combination between the declarative *da* and the particle *wa*, which is a different way of representing *wa*.

To summarise, we have discussed the establishment of *onna-rashisa* 'womanliness' in connection with the historical events in the Meiji era. The Confucianism-based *ryoosai-kenbo* 'a good wife and wise mother' was promoted by the government as an ideal Japanese woman, for which Japanese women were educated and expected to be *onna-rashii* 'womanly', and behave and speak in a gentle and graceful manner. Further, writers' *genbunitchi undoo* 'the movement of the unification of spoken and written language styles' played a key role in developing and promoting the women's language which was one of the significant tools to represent the notion of *onna-rashisa* 'womanliness'. The particle *wa* had been established and developed along with these historical needs in the Meiji era, and further widely spread among female speakers.

Wa *and* Onna-Rashisa *'Womanliness'*

The issue of *wa* shows an interesting aspect of how a linguistic form can be associated with a particular gender-specific value. *Onna-kotoba* 'women's language' that is associated with *onna-rashisa* has been characterised as polite, soft, non-assertive and indirect in a number of researches (e.g. Suzuki, 1976; Falconer, 1984; Reynolds, 1990; Suzuki, 1993; Masuoka and Takubo, 1994; Okamoto, 1997; Aizawa, 2003). For instance, Falconer (1984: 105) notes that "[women's language] is less direct, more polite, and generally softer than men's. Women are expected to use honorific and self-depreciating words and expressions more frequently than men, and to use them with a precisely-defined *onna-rashii* voicing which is clear, high-pitched, and whispery, in contrast to *otoko-rashii* back-of-the-throat, growl-like gruff enunciation." Similarly, Suzuki (1993) focuses on the level of politeness in female speech and points out that polite speech is interpreted as an index of femininity because the essence of Japanese women's language is their concern with politeness.

Recall that the use of *wa* indicates the speaker's commitment to deliver the content and feeling conveyed in the utterance in a firm manner, and it invokes a self-assured tone which is often interpreted as indicating the strong tone of the utterance or the speaker's insistent attitude. This attitudinal and expressive aspect of *wa* does not seem to match well with *onna-rashisa* 'womanliness', which has been characterised as gentle and graceful. However, it should be noted that these gentle and graceful features for *wa*, or more generally, polite, indirect, soft and non-assertive features of women language, are the 'image' that has socially been created. In other words, the soft and non-assertive nuance by the *onna-rashisa* 'womanliness' indicates the soft and non-assertive imaginary ideal of a woman (or *ryoosai-kenbo* 'a good wife and wise mother'), and does not necessarily mean the linguistically defined soft or non-assertive expressions — for example, *kamoshirenai* with a lower degree of the speaker's certainty can be seen as a non-direct or non-assertive expression, compared to the assertive/declarative *da* (cf. The Function of *Wa*).

As discussed in the section "Expressive Effects of *Wa*", the use of *wa* is often perceived as impolite in a formal situation. This also confirms that the particle does not necessarily make the utterance linguistically and attitudinally soft or non-assertive. The impoliteness of *wa* is caused by its function to indicate the speaker's attitude of firm delivery, which is interpreted as the direct indication of her attitude and feeling, while in a formal situation such a direct display of her attitude and feeling is not readily allowed.

What the above discussions suggest is that the primary function of *wa* is ambivalent. That is, on the one hand, the particle indicates the speaker's firm attitude in delivering the utterance, which is sometimes seen as strengthening the tone of the utterance. On the other hand, it is associated with a socially indexicalised value of *onna-rashisa* 'womanliness', which is seen as polite, gentle and graceful. These ambivalent functions of the particle are easily observed in utterances in which *wa* is used. For example, in utterances below, the speaker asserts her willingness to go with the hearer in (27a), and her permission that the hearer may leave in (27b), respectively.

(27) a. *Chotto   matte,   Katchan.   Issho ni   iku   wa.*
a.little.bit   wait   Katchan   together   go   WA
'Please wait for me, Katchan. I will go with you.'   (T1)

b. *Kokode   ii,   wa   Arigatoo.*
here   fine   WA   thank.you
Here is fine (You may leave now). Thank you.'   (T3)

In both utterances, the use of *wa* further adds the speaker's firm attitude in conveying her willingness or permission. At the same time, the utterances further indicate the feeling of Japanese female-specific value, or *onna-rashisa* 'womanliness', of the feminised gentle and graceful tone. As a whole, from these utterances native speakers of Japanese perceive the mixed feeling of the feminised, yet firm tone of the speaker.

Conclusion

In this study, we have discussed the particle *wa* in Japanese, which indicates that the speaker is female. We have first clarified the linguistic property of the particle. Invoking the interactive nature of the particle, we have proposed that its linguistic property is to convey the speaker's firm tone within the monopolistic attitude. In this connection, we have accounted for the linguistic distributions which include its co-occurrence restrictions with modal expressions as well as with certain sentence types.

Further, in exploring the gender issue of the particle, we have shown that its female-specific value is the notion *onna-rashisa* 'womanliness', the ideal goal of which is the *ryoosai-kenbo* 'a good wife and wise mother'. It was also shown that the notion was established during the Meiji era in response to the need at the time, and promoted and widely spread through the Meiji writers who adopted *genbunitchi* 'the unification of spoken and written language styles' in their novels. These facts suggest that the adoption of *wa* to the female-speech for the notion *onna-rashisa* 'womanliness' was arbitrary in nature; that is, its adoption was not directly motivated by the linguistic property of the particle, but rather it was deliberately established in order to differentiate female speech from male speech.

Social groups organise and conceptualise men and women in culturally specific and meaningful ways (Ochs, 1992: 339). Through the case of *wa,* we have witnessed how gender-specific values can be conceptualised by, and adapted into, members of the society. In short, *wa* was arbitrarily and intentionally associated with the ideological notion *onna-rashisa* 'womanliness' to represent the female-specific values of gentleness and gracefulness. The particle also functions to signal the speaker's firm attitude which is sometimes seen as an insistent tone of the speaker. With this ambivalent functionality, *wa* plays an important role of a pragmatic strategy which conveys the speaker's firm attitude towards the hearer, and at the same time, indicates the gentle and graceful value of womanliness in Japanese society.

References

Aizawa, Manami. 2003. Shoojo manga ni miru onna kotoba [Women's language in girls' comics]. *Meikai Nihongo* [Miekai Japanese Language Journal, Meikai University] 8: 85-99.

Arndt, Horst and Richard Wayne Janney. 1987. *InterGrammar: Toward an Integrated Model of Verbal, Prosodic and Kinesic Choices in Speech.* Berlin: Mouton de Gruyter.

Asano, Yuko. 2003. *A Semantic Analysis of Epistemic Modality in Japanese.* PhD Dissertation. The Australian National University, Canberra.

Asano, Yuko. 2009. A semantic analysis of Japanese epistemic markers: Chigainai and hazuda. *Language Sciences* 31: 837-852.

Besnier, Niko. 1994. Involvement in linguistic practice: An ethnographic appraisal. *Journal of Pragmatics* 22: 279-299.

ChengChanghao. 1987. Shuujoshi: Hanashite to kikite no ninshiki no gyappu o umeru tame no bunsetsuji [Sentence-final particles: Sentence-final particles for closing the gap between the speaker's and the hearer's recognition]. *Nihongogaku* [Japanese Linguistics] 6 (10): 93-109.

Chino, Naoko. 1991. *All About Particles.* Tokyo: Koodansha International.

Coates, Jennifer. 1993. *Women, Men and Language.* London: Longman.

Crawford, Mary. 1995. *Talking Difference: On Gender and Language.* London, Thousand Oaks and New Delhi: SAGE Publications.

Daneš, František. 1994. Involvement with language and in language. *Journal of Pragmatics* 22: 251-264.

Eckert, Penelope and Sally McConnell-Ginet. 2003. *Language and Gender.* Cambridge: Cambridge University Press.

Endo, Orie. 1997. *Onna no Kotoba no Bunkashi* [Cultural History of Women's Language]. Tokyo: Gakuyo Shobo.

Endo, Orie. 2006. *A Cultural History of Japanese Women's Language.* Ann Arbor: Centre for Japanese Studies, the University of Michigan.

Falconer, Elizabeth. 1984. Considering onna-rashii: Its importance, enforcement, and effects. *Bulletin of Graduate School of International Relations, International University of Japan* 2: 91-103.

Hasunuma, Akiko. 1998. Zoku: Nihongo wan pointo ressun [One point lesson in Japanese, Part II]. *Gekkan Gengo* [Language Monthly] 17 (6): 94-95.

Hattori, Tadashi. 1992. Hanseigo no shuujoshi 'wa' ni tsuite [On the function of the general sentence-final particle *wa*]. *Dooshisha Joshi Daigaku Gakujutsu Kenkyuu Nenpoo* [Annual Reports of Studies, Doshisha Women's College of Liberal Arts] 43 (4): 1-15.

Hayashi, Asako. 2000. Shuujoshi 'yo' ga motsu 'shitsureisa' no doai [The degree of impoliteness the sentence-final particle *yo* indicates]. *Mie Daigaku Ryuugakusee Sentaa Kiyoo* [Bulletin of Centre for International Students, Mie University] 2: 39-51.

Holmes, Janet and Maria Stubbe. 2003. 'Feminine' workplaces: Stereotype and reality. In: Janet Holmes and Miriam Meyerhoff (eds.) *The Handbook of Language and Gender*. MA (USA), Oxford (UK), Victoria (AUS) and Berlin (GER): Blackwell Publishing, 573-599.

Ide, Sachiko. 1982. Japanese sociolinguistics: Politeness and women's language. *Lingua* 57: 357-385.

Ide, Sachiko. 1990. How and why do women speak more politely in Japanese? In: Sachiko Ide and Naomi Hanaoka McGloin (eds.) *Aspects of Japanese Women's Language*. Tokyo: Kuroshio Shuppn, 63-79.

Ide, Sachiko and Naomi Hanaoka McGloin. 1990. Preface. In: Sachiko Ide and Naomi Hanaoka McGloin (eds.) *Aspects of Japanese Women's Language*. Tokyo: Kuroshio Shuppan, i-iv.

Ide, Sachiko and Chikako Sakurai. 1997. Shiten to modaritii no gengo koodoo [Viewpoint and speech act of modality]. In: Yukinori Takubo (ed.) *Shiten to Gengo Koodoo* [Viewpoint and Speech Act]. Tokyo: Kuroshio Shuppan, 119-153.

Inoue, Miyako. 2002. Gender, language, and modernity: Toward an effective history of Japanese women's language. *American Ethnologist* 29 (2): 392-422.

Ishikawa, Sadayuki. 1972. Kindai-go no "teyo, dawa, noyo" ["Teyo, dawa, noyo" in modern Japanese]. *Kaishaku* [The Journal of Interpretation] 18 (10): 22-27.

Izuhara, Eiko. 1996. Shuujoshi 'na (naa)' no ichi koosatsu: Kikite ni nani o tsutaeteiru no ka [A study of the sentence-final particle *na* (*naa*): What does it deliver to the listener? —]. *Nagoya Daigaku Nihongo, Nihonbunka Ronshuu* [Nagoya University Working Papers on Japanese Language and Culture] 4: 65-82.

Izuhara, Eiko. 2008. Kantoojoshi, shuujoshi no danwa kanri kinoo bunseki: 'Ne', 'yone', 'yo' no baai [An analysis of the discourse management function of sentence-medial and sentence-final particles: In the cases of *ne*, *yone* and *yo*]. *Aichi Gakuin Daigaku Kyooyoobu Kiyoo* [The Journal of Aichi Gakuin University, Humanities & Sciences] 56 (1): 67-82.

Johnson, Yuki. 2003. *Modality and the Japanese Language.* Michigan: The Centre for Japanese Studies, the University of Michigan.

Jugaku, Akiko. 1979. *Nihongo to Onna* [The Japanese Language and Women]. Tokyo: Iwanami Shoten.

Kabashima, Tadao. 1990. *Nihongo no Sutairu Bukku* [Book for Japanese Styles]. Tokyo: Taishuukan.

Kashiwagi, Shigeaki. 2006. Shuujoshiron (Zoku) [Theory of sentence-final particles, Part II]. *Gaikokugo Gakkaishi* [Foreign Language Journal] 36: 107-114.
Katagiri, Yasuhiro. 2007. Dialogue functions of Japanese sentence-final particles 'yo' and 'ne'. *Journal of Pragmatics* 39: 1313-1323.
Kawasaki, Kyoko and Kristy McDougall. 2003. Implication of representations of casual conversation: A case study in gender-associated sentence-final particles. *Sekai no Nihongo Kyooiku* [Japanese-Language Education Around the Globe] 13: 41-55.
Kendall, Shari and Deborah Tannen. 2001. Discourse and gender. In: Deborah Schiffrin, Deborah Tannen and Heidi E. Hamilton (eds.) *The Handbook of Discourse Analysis*. Oxford: Blackwell Publishers, 548-567.
Kose, Yuriko Suzuki. 1996. Japanese sentence-final particle 'ne': A unified account. *ICU Nihongo Kyooiku Kenkyuu Sentaa Kiyoo* [The Research Centre for Japanese Language Education Annual Bulletin] 6: 71-109.
Kose, Yuriko Suzuki. 1997. Sentence-final particles in Japanese: An alternative to scalar analysis. *Studies in the Linguistic Sciences* 25 (1): 119-136.
Koyama, Wataru. 2004. The linguistic ideologies of modern Japanese honorifics and the historic reality of modernity. *Language & Communication* 24: 413-435.
Kuwayama, Toshihiko. 1981. Joshi no shurui [Types of particles]. In: Yasuo Kitahara, Tanjiro Suzuki, Ko Takeda, Tsunekichi Nasubuchi and Yoshinori Yamaguchi (eds.) *Nihon Bunpoo Jiten* [Dictionary of Japanese Grammar]. Tokyo: Yuuseido Shuppan, 220-240.
Lakoff, Robin. 1975. *Language and Women's Place*. New York: Harper and Row.
Lee Duck-Young. 2002. The function of the zero particle with special reference to spoken Japanese. *Journal of Pragmatics* 34: 645-682.
Lee, Duck-Young. 2007. Involvement and Japanese interactive particles 'ne' and 'yo'. *Journal of Pragmatics* 39: 363-388.
Maltz, Daniel N. and Ruth A. Borker. 1982. A cultural approach to male-female miscommunication. In: John J. Gumperz (ed.) *Language and Social Identity*. Cambridge: Cambridge University Press, 196-216.
Masuoka, Takashi. 1991. *Modaritii no Bunpoo* [Grammar of Modality]. Tokyo: Kuroshio Shuppan.
Masuoka, Takashi and Yukinori Takubo. 1994. *Kiso Nihongo Bunpoo* [Basic Japanese Grammar]. Tokyo: Kuroshio Shuppan.
Matsumoto, Yoshiko. 2007. Kaiwa no naka no iwayuru 'joseigo' [So-called 'women's language' in conversation]. *Gengo* [Language] 36 (3): 62-69.
Maynard, Senko K. 1989. *Japanese Conversation: Self-contextualisation Through Structure and Interactional Management*. New Jersey: Ablex Publishing Corporation.
Maynard, Senko K. 1997. *Japanese Communication: Language and Thought in Context*. Honolulu: University of Hawaii Press.
McCormick, Michael K. 1998. Gender and language. In: Jacob L. Mey (ed.) *Concise of Encyclopedia of Pragmatics*. Amsterdam, Lausanne, New York, Oxford, Shannon, Singapore and Tokyo: Elsevier, 316-325.

McElhinny, Bonnie S. 1995. Challenging hegemonic masculinities: Female and male police officers handling domestic violence. In: Kira Hall and Mary Bucholtz (eds.) *Gender Articulated: Language and the Socially Constructed Self.* New York: Routledge, 217-243.
McGloin, Naomi Hanaoka. 1990. Sex differences and sentence-final particles. In: Sachiko Ide and Naomi Hanaoka McGloin. *Aspects of Japanese Women's Language.* Tokyo: Kuroshio Shuppan, 23-41.
McIlvenny, Paul. 2002. *Talking Gender and Sexuality.* Amsterdam and Philadelphia: John Benjamins Publishing Company.
Miyazaki, Kazuhito. 1993. '-Daroo' no danwa kinoo ni tsuite [On the function of *daroo* in discourse]. *Kokugogaku* [Studies in the Japanese Language] 175: 40-53.
Miyazaki, Kazuhito, Taro Adachi, Harumi Noda and Shino Takanashi. 2002. *Modaritii* [Modality]. Tokyo: Kuroshio Shuppan.
Mizutani, Osamu and Nobuko Mizutani. 1987. *How to Be Polite in Japanese.* Tokyo: The Japan Times.
Morita, Yoshiyuki. 1980. *Kiso Nihongo 2: Imi to tsukaikata* [Basic Japanese 2: Meanings and usages]. Tokyo: Kadokawa Shoten.
Moriyama, Takuro. 1989. Ninshiki no muudo to sono shuuhen [Epistemic mood and its surroundings]. In: Yoshio Nitta and Takashi Masuoka (eds.) *Nihongo no Modaritii* [Japanese Modality]. Tokyo: Kuroshio Shuppan, 57-120.
Moriyama Takuro, Yoshio Nitta and Hiroshi Kudo. 2000. *Nihongo no Bunpoo 3: Modaritii* [Japanese Grammar 3: Modality]. Tokyo: Iwanami Shoten.
Nakamura, Momoko, 2005. Gengo ideorogii to shite no 'onna kotoba' ['Women's language' as a linguistic ideology]. *Goyooron Kenkyuu* [Studies in Pragmatics] 7: 109-122.
Nakamura, Momoko. 2006. Gengo ideorogii toshite no onna kotoba: Meijiki 'jogakusei kotoba' no seiritsu [Women's language as a linguistic ideology: The formation of 'schoolgirls' language' in the Meiji era]. In: Nihon Jendaa Gakkai (ed.) *Nihongo to Jendaa* [Japanese and Gender]. Tokyo: Hituzi Shobo, 121-138.
Nakazaki, Takashi. 2004. Shuujoshi 'wa' no kinoo ni tsuite no oboegaki [Notes on the function of the Japanese sentence-final form *wa* especially in monologue]. *STUDIUM* 32: 8-19.
Narrog, Heiko. 2009. *Modality in Japanese: The Layered Structure of the Clause and Hierarchies of Functional Categories.* Amsterdam and Philadelphia: John Benjamins Publishing Company.
Nihongo Kyooiku Gakkai. 1987. *Nihongo Kyooiku Jiten* [The Dictionary of Japanese Language Teaching]. Tokyo: Taishukan Shoten.
Nitta, Yoshio. 1991. *Nihongo no Modaritii to Ninshoo* [Modality and Personal Pronouns in Japanese]. Tokyo: Hituzi Shobo.
Ochs, Elinor. 1992. Indexing gender. In: Alessandro Duranti and Charles Goodwin (eds.) *Rethinking Context.* New York: Cambridge University Press, 335-358.
Oda, Toyoko. 1964. Josei no kotoba: Bunmatsu bubun no hyoogen o chuushin ni [Women's language: Focusing on sentence-final expressions]. *Rikkyoo*

Daigaku Nihon Bungaku [JapaneseLiterature, Rikkyo University] 13: 66-77.

Ogi, Naomi. 2011. *Involvement and Attitudes in Spoken Discourse: So-called Sentence-final Particles in Japanese*. PhD Dissertation. The Australian National University, Canberra.

Oishi, Toshio. 1985. A Description of Japanese Final Particles in Context. PhD Dissertation. UMI Dissertation Information Science, Michigan.

Okamoto, Shigeko. 1997. Social context, linguistic ideology Japanese. *Journal of Pragmatics* 28 (6): 795-817.

Okamoto, Shigeko. 2004. Ideology in linguistic practice and analysis: Gender and politeness in Japanese revisited. In: Shigeko Okamoto and Janet S. Shibamoto Smith (eds.) *Japanese Language, Gender and Ideology: Cultural Models and Real People*. New York: Oxford University Press, 38-56.

Okamoto, Shigeko and Janet S. Shibamoto Smith. 2004. Introduction. In: Shigeko Okamoto and Janet S. Shibamoto Smith (eds.) *Japanese Language, Gender, and Ideology: Cultural Models and Real People*. New York: Oxford University Press, 3-20.

Okuda, Yasuo. 1957. Hyoojungo ni tsuite [About standard language *Kyooiku* [The Journal of Education] 77: 61-74.

Ooka, Makoto. 1994. *Koyo Zenshu* [Collection of Koyo] Vol. 10. Tokyo: Iwanami Shoten.

Oota, Yoshiko. 1992. Danwa ni miru seisa no yoosoo: Shuujoshi o chuushin to shite [The difference between male and female speeches in the modern Japanese: Focusing on sentence-final particles]. *Yokohama Kokuritsu Daigaku Kyooiku Kiyoo* [The Educational Sciences, Journal of the Yokohama National University] 32: 329-342.

Reynolds, Katsue Akiba. 1985. Female speakers of Japanese. *Feminist Issues* 5: 13-46.

Reynolds, Katsue Akiba. 1990. Female speakers of Japanese in transition. In: Sachiko Ide and Naomi Hanaoka McGloin (eds.) *Aspects of Japanese Women's Language*. Tokyo: Kuroshio Shuppan, 129-146.

Sakuma, Kanae. 1983. *Gendai Nihongo no Kenkyuu* [Research on the Modern Japanese]. Tokyo: Kuroshio Shuppan.

Shibamoto Smith, Janet S. 1985. *Japanese Women's Language*. Florida: Academic Press Inc.

Shibamoto Smith, Janet S. 2004. Language and gender in the (hetero) romance: 'reading' the ideal hero/ine through lovers' dialogue in Japanese romance fiction. In: Shigeko Okamoto and Janet S. Shibamoto Smith (eds.) *Japanese Language, Gender, and Ideology: Cultural Models and Real People*. New York: Oxford University Press, 113-130.

Shinpen Shuushin Kyooten. 1962. *Nihon Kyookasho Taikei Kindaihen Shuushin 2* [Japanese Textbook System of Modern Ethics 2]. Tokyo: Kodansha.

Suzuki, Hideo. 1976. Gendai nihongo ni okeru shuujoshi no hataraki to sono soogoo shoosetsu ni tsuite [On the functions of sentence-final particles in the modern Japanese and explications of their correlations]. *Tokyo Daigaku Kokugo Kokubun Gakkai Kokugo to Kokubungaku* [Japanese

Language and Literature, Society for Japanese Language and Literature, University of Tokyo] 11: 58-70.
Suzuki, Mutsumi. 1993. Joseigo no honshitsu: Teineisa, hatsuwa kooi no shiten kara [The nature of women's language: Viewing from politeness and speech act]. *Nihongogaku* [Japanese Linguistics] 12 (6): 148-155.
Tanaka, Akio. 1977. Bunmatsu, kumatsu no hyoogen to gohoo [Sentence-final and phrase-final expressions and their usages]. *Nihongo, Nihonbunka* [Japanese, Japanese Culture, Osaka University of Foreign Studies] 6: 37-71.
Tanaka, Katsuyoshi. 1987. *Kyooikushi* [History of Education]. Tokyo: Kawashima Shoten.
Tanaka, Toshihiko. 1989. Modaritii kara mita shuujoshi [Sentence-final particles from a modal point of view]. *Tohoku Daigaku Nihongo Kyooiku Kenkyuu Ronshuu* [Journal of Japanese Language Teaching, Tohoku University] 4: 84-97.
Tannen, Deborah. 1990. *You Just Don't Understand: Women and Men in Conversation*. New York: Ballantine.
Tannen, Deborah. 1993. The relativity of linguistic strategies: Rethinking power and solidarity in gender and dominance. In: Deborah Tannen (ed.) *Gender and Conversational Interaction*. New York and Oxford: Oxford University Press, 165-188.
Tannen, Deborah, 1996. *Gender and Discourse*. New York and Oxford: Oxford University Press.
Tanomura, Tadaharu. 1991. 'Rashii' to 'yooda' no imi no sooi ni tsuite [On the semantic difference between *rashii* and *yooda*]. *Kooto Daigaku Gengogaku Kenkyuu* [Linguistic Research, University of Kyoto] 10: 62-78.
Teramura, Hideo. 1984. *Nihongo no Shintakkusu to Imi II* [Syntax and Semantics in Japanese II]. Tokyo: Kuroshio Shuppan.
Trudgill, Peter. 1972. Sex, covert prestige and linguistic change in the urban British English of Norwich. *Language in Society* 1: 179-195.
Usami, Mayumi. 2006. Jendaa to poraitonesu: Josei wa dansei yori porito na no ka? [Gender and politeness: Are women more polite than men?]. In: Nihon Jendaa Gakkai (ed.) *Nihongo to Jendaa* [Japanese and Gender]. Tokyo: Hituzi Shobo, 21-37.
Uyeno, Tazuko. 1971. *A Study of Japanese Modality: A Performative Analysis of Sentence Particles*. Ph. D. Dissertation. The University of Michigan, Michigan.
Washi, Rumi. 1997. Shuujoshi to hatsuwa ruikei: Tookyoogo shuujoshi 'wa' to 'na' no danwa ni okeru hataraki [Sentence-final particles and utterance types: The functions of the sentence-final particles *wa* and *na* of Tokyo dialect in discourse]. *Nihongo Nihon Bunka Kenkyuu* [Studies in Japanese Language and Culture, Osaka University of Foreign Languages] 7: 65-79.
Yonezawa, Masako. 2005. Shuujoshi no shiyoo hindo to seisa keikoo: Shinario o shiryoo to shite [A study of the relationship between the frequency of using sentence-final particles and gender: Using film scenarios as data].

Dooshisha Daigaku Ryuugakusei Bekka Kiyoo [Bulletin of the Centre for Japanese Language, Doshisha University] 5: 49-60.

Yukawa, Sumiyuki and Masumi Saito. 2004. Cultural ideologies in Japanese language and gender studies: A theoretical review. In: Shigeko Okamoto and Janet S. Shibamoto Smith (eds.) *Japanese Language, Gender, and Ideology: Cultural Models and Real People*. New York: Oxford University Press, 23-37.

Zimmerman, Don H. and Candace, West. 1975. Sex roles, interruptions and silences in conversation. In: Barrie Thorne and Nancy Henley (eds.) *Language and Sex: Difference and Dominance*. Rowley, MA: Newbury House, 105-129.

Chapter 5: Gender Variation in Compliment Responses: A Case of the Malaysian Tamil Community

Jariah Mohd Jan and Prabhalini Thevendiraraj, University of Malaya

Abstract: This study examines Malaysian Tamil males' and females' compliment responses. The purpose of this study is to determine the extent to which gender affects choice of strategy which these respondents use to respond to compliments. The study also aims to discover similarities and differences in the politeness strategies used between the groups. The data was gathered from 20 Malaysian Tamil professionals: ten men and ten women. Each respondent was required to orally respond to six compliment situations in the Discourse Completion Test (DCT), which was then accompanied by a semi-structured interview. The date revealed thirteen types of compliment response strategies which were employed to resolve the conflict between agreement and avoidance of self-praise. The findings revealed that there were no marked differences between the genders in the choices of their overall strategies. Men accepted and deflected compliments more, whilst women rejected more than men. Yet, a more thorough investigation relating gender to age provided evidence that the older female subjects deflected and rejected more compliments than they accepted. Thus, it was proposed from the findings that the compliment responses are assigned along a continuum in tandem with Pomerantz' Conversational Principles and Leech's Politeness Principle. The men and younger women in this study at large were motivated by Leech's Agreement Maxim whilst the older women's responses were motivated primarily by the Modesty Maxim. These differences are then related to the values of the Malaysian Tamil culture.

Introduction

Sociolinguistic variation associated with speaker's gender is a widely researched topic with a considerable amount of research carried out over the last decade. One of the main aspects investigated is gender variation in the expression of linguistic politeness. Findings from these studies reflect that men and women may differ in the strategies they use for constructing conversation in specific circumstances. This suggests that they may also differ in the language they use to perform various social functions through speech acts such as compliments, apologies or expressions of gratitude.

To date many empirical studies conducted on speech acts give evidence that particular speech acts are very likely to be realised quite differently across cultures. The compliment event is one such example. Researchers on compliment behaviour acknowledge that, although compliment and compliment responses are cultural universals, they vary from one society to another (Herbert, 1989; Holmes, 1986; Manes, 1983; Farghal and Al-Khatib, 2001). The study of the compliment speech act contributes valuable information not only about the context of when, how and to whom one proffers a compliment but also how to interpret implicit social and cultural meanings, as well as how to respond appropriately when one receives a compliment.

Research in the area of compliment events provides ample evidence that the complimenting speech act varies according to social variables such as power, distance (Wolfson, 1983, 1989; Nelson et al. 1996b; Gajaseni, 1995), gender (Herbert, 1989; Herbert and Straight, 1989; Holmes, 1989; Johnson and Roen, 1992) and culturally determined factors such as directness, politeness and culture (Pomerantz, 1978; Mursy and Wilson, 2001; David, 2002; Shanmuganathan, 2003; Ramazanoglu, 2003), topic (Manes and Wolfson, 1981; Baba, 1999), intensity of the compliment (Holmes, 1990; Lorenzo-Dus, 2001), and pragmatic norms (Han, 1992; Urano, 2000; Farghal and Al-Khatib, 2001; Yuan, 2001; Golato, 2002). Compliment responses (henceforth CRs) are also said to "provide an invaluable but underutilized insight into speakers' reactions to external appraisals of their personal and social identity" (Lorenzo-Dus, 2001: 108). Thus just like compliments, CRs act as a "mirror of cultural values" (Manes, 1983:96).

This research focuses on the subject of gender variation in compliment responses between Malaysian Tamil men and women, in order to gain insight into potential gender variation in terms of politeness strategies and the cultural norms underlying the language behaviour of Malaysian Tamil men and women. The researcher echoes David's (2002) line of argument that in order for effective communication and goodwill to be maintained in our country, Malaysians must be made aware of the cultural norms and values of a particular community, and this can be done by "researching/investigating and becoming sensitive to speech acts" (ibid.:111-112).

Literature Review

Theoretical Issues – Overview

Most researchers agree that compliments fall within the framework of some form of politeness theory, as in the often-cited theory of Brown and Levinson (1987). This theory claims that there are certain social principles that guide human communication. They argue that, as we communicate with others, we are constantly showing concern for people's *face* and responding to the need to maintain each other's *face*. Since *face* can be lost, maintained or enhanced through interaction, everyone attends to it consciously or unconsciously in all forms of communication.

Basically, politeness involves showing concern for two different kinds of *face* needs: negative *face* needs, or the need not to be imposed upon, and positive *face* needs, the need to be liked and admired. The former is evidence of negative politeness whilst the latter concerns positive politeness behaviour.

However, Mursy and Wilson (2001) argue that the concepts of *face* and 'politeness' that underpin Brown and Levinson's model may not characterise compliment events across cultures. Examples of exceptions to this are the Chinese or Japanese cultures. Mursy and Wilson (ibid.:134) further argue for a more culturally sensitive perspective to account for complimenting behaviours in those cultures where the needs of the groups take precedence in comparison to the individual's needs.

Chen (1993) also argues that although Brown and Levinson's theory is meant to be a framework for politeness strategies cross-linguistically, it does not offer a complete account of the CRs strategies employed by both the American English and Chinese speakers in his study. He states that the most adequate model is Leech's (1983*) Politeness Principle* as described below:

Agreement Maxim: maximise agreement between self and others and minimise disagreements between self and others.

Modesty Maxim: minimise praise of self and maximise dispraise of self.

Leech (1983), in his explanatory analysis of politeness, states that the *Modesty Maxim* basically puts pressure on the recipient of the compliment to reject it, thus disagreeing with the complimenter. Leech's *Politeness Principle* with reference to the two maxims, namely *Agreement* and *Modesty,* will be used for the purposes of this analysis.

Politeness Revisited

In Malaysia, there have been several sociolinguistic studies which have been conducted thus far in this definitionally fuzzy and empirically difficult area of politeness. Some of the findings in the local context are discussed in this section.

Jamaliah (1995b) observes that the three major cultures of Malaysia place a high value on humility and modesty, and thus it is considered inappropriate to accept or acknowledge complimentary remarks. Malaysians' general tendency, according to her, is "to play down their abilities and competence when confronted with complimentary remarks" (ibid: 119). To do otherwise would not be in good taste as it would reflect conceit and arrogance.

Since this study revolves centrally around Malaysian Tamils, a perspective on this group is taken from Jariah Mohd Jan (1999). In her view, South Asian groups include Tamils, Malayalees, Punjabis, Telegus and Ceylonese, who take on various faiths and are said to be relatively less flexible in terms of culture and social stratification. Clearly, there is a great deal of diversity among these groups, and generalizations will not apply to all individuals. However, speaking generally, it can be said that some common values found amongst them are those listed in Table 1.

Table 1: Common Values Among Indians in Malaysia (Jariah Mohd. Jan, 1999:103)

Indian Values			
Brotherhood	Championship of Cause	Face	Fear of God
Modesty	Security	Industriousness	Harmony
Karma	Loyalty	Participation	Sense of Belonging

Jariah Mohd Jan emphasises there is a need to be aware of different norms of speaking/speech styles of various ethno-linguistic group since Malaysia is a "potpourri of cultures" (ibid: 99) set against a multi racial, multi ethnic and multi lingual background. She further adds that ignorance and insensitivity can result in miscommunication or misunderstanding in cross cultural encounters (ibid.:99). Hence, Malaysians have to adhere to certain politeness features in their interaction, if the intentions are to establish and maintain good rapport and solidarity in the community they live in.

The various definitions of politeness which have been put forth by linguists world-wide provide evidence that politeness is multi-faceted. Since politeness is a highly significant element in interaction, one has to adhere to certain set rules of politeness if s/he desires to be in a 'win-win' situation.

Compliment Responses (CRs)

Pomerantz (1978) was the first to study compliment responses from a pragmatic perspective. She states that in American English, the recipient of a compliment faces two conflicting universal conversational principles which create a dilemma when responding. These principles are the following:

> Principle I: Agree with the speaker and/or accept compliment
> Principle II: Avoid self-praise

Pomerantz noted that when one accepts a compliment one indirectly praises oneself, thus violating Principle II, whereas when one rejects a compliment, one expresses disagreement with the complimenter, thus violating Principle I. In order to mediate this conflict, recipients of compliments use various solutions to contribute to the social solidarity of the relationship, which Pomerantz categorises as acceptance, rejection and self-praise avoidance.

Research in the area of CRs show that the above dilemma hinges upon varying politeness principles which are at work within and across societies (Brown and Levinson, 1978), indicating that CRs are far from being universal. Different cultures seem to have different ways of complying with Pomerantz's two constraints. In Arabic and South African English, there is a strong preference for acceptance of compliments compared to rejection, in comparison to American English (Herbert, 1989; Herbert and Straight, 1989; Nelson et al., 1996). However, according to some researchers, Asian speakers of English (Chinese,

Japanese, Malay, Thai and Turkish) tend to reject compliments and avoid any form of acceptance (Baba, 1999; Holmes, 1986; Chen, 1993; Gajaseni, 1995; Azman, 1986; Arifin, 2000; Ye, 1995; Ramazanoglu, 2003).

Studies on compliments, CRs and other politeness formulae in the Malaysian scenario are not plentiful. The commonly cited study of compliments in Malaysia is that of Azman (1986), who states that compliments are more often rejected than accepted amongst Malaysians. Norvita Zainal Arifin (2000) makes similar observations and claims that Malaysians feel rather uncomfortable saying "thank you" to compliments.

A recent study conducted by David (2002), however, shows that Malaysians' CRs include acceptance of the compliment, deflecting and even ignoring the compliments. Shanmuganathan's (2003) study on the influence of culture on CRs gives evidence that urban Malaysians are more inclined towards accepting compliments, although there are attempts to scale down the compliments.

Gender Differences in Compliment Responses

Research in the area of gender and CRs is scarce, as most linguistic studies seem to give minor attention to social variables such as gender. Nevertheless, gender is an aspect which cannot be ignored in the study of compliment events; hence, it is an area of concern which sociolinguists are presently delving into. Both Holmes (1990) and Herbert (1990) carried out research to gain insights on how the different genders responded to compliments. Generally, westerners accept compliments, albeit with some qualifications in certain instances. According to Holmes (1995:141-142), men and women in her New Zealand corpus employ CRs in largely similar ways. Compliments are readily accepted and unlikely to be rejected. However in the case of disagreement CRs, women adopt this strategy more than men in her data. She reasons that women are under strong pressure to be modest; hence, disagreement to CRs is considered a polite response and consistent with the view that women are relatively cooperative partners in conversation.

A more thorough examination of the preferred strategies within the three broad categories, namely *accept*, *deflect* and *reject*, indicates that New Zealand males were more likely to ignore or legitimately evade a compliment compared to their female counterparts. Holmes (1988) argues that these strategies are also used to change the topic or focus when the compliment given is found to be embarrassing.

Herbert's very detailed and thorough analysis (1990) of his American data gives a breakdown on CRs from males to males; males to females; females to females and females to males. He finds that women accept more compliments from their male counterparts than from other women. He states that women are also more likely than men to agree with the semantic content of the compliment. This however was not evident in Holmes' (1995:142) New Zealand data, where gender differences were "relatively minor".

Moreover, in the incidence of *non acceptance agreement* or *non agreement*, Herbert (1990) found that women resort to employing strategies in these categories more than men. They do so by progressing into a series of comments on the topic of the compliment, which is rarely done by men (ibid.:213-214).

Herbert asserts that both men and women in his study participate in conversational work "by not accepting" females' compliments (ibid.: 222).

In examining the relationship between CRs and the gender of the complimenter and complimentees, Farghal and Al-Khatib (2001) observed in their study of Jordanian Arabic that there was a clear-cut correlation between the gender of the subject and the CRs used by the subject. Male complimentees tended to use simple responses when they were complimented by males rather than females. These males also opted for exclusively non-verbal responses when complimented by their female counterparts. In addition, they found that a number of other elements were pivotal in the choice of CRs, such as the relationship of the complimenter to the complimentee.

Even though Holmes (1985,1988); Herbert (1990) and Farghal and Al-Khatib (2001) reported that gender-related variations in CRs exist, Gajaseni's (1994) study found that gender of the complimenter and receiver had minor effects on CRs. He attributes the differences in the findings to the topics of the compliment, which were exclusively about ability and performance. Gajaseni (1994) suggests that a topic such as appearance may have shown significant variation in terms of gender.

In the Asian context, Baba (1999) states that Fukushima (1990) is perhaps the sole researcher to have studied gender variation in CRs. Fukushima found that Japanese women refuse compliments more than the men. He found his women subjects "passive, subordinate, dependent, shy, polite and obedient to social principles" (cited in Baba, 1999:20). Baba argues that Japanese females refuse CRs in order to comply with the Japanese norm of humbleness. He concludes that "women's language is more reflective of the cultural norms than men's language" (ibid.:20).

Research Design and Methodology

Methodology

The sample in this study comprises twenty Malaysian Tamil professionals, born and bred in Kuala Lumpur, ten men and ten women between the ages of 33 and 42. In line with ethnographic research and to ensure triangulation is achieved, two methods of data collection, the DCT (see Appendix A) and a semi-structured interview, were employed, constituting a combination of qualitative and quantitative methods.

Prior to the data collection, a pilot study was carried out. The pilot study served as a yardstick by which the researcher could measure the validity and reliability of the primary instrument, the DCT adapted from Lorenzo-Dus (2001) and Chen (1993). The adapted DCT consisted of six compliment situations. The subjects were required to read and orally respond to the compliment event found in the situations. This was then followed by a semi-structured interview. The data was audio-recorded and subsequently transcribed. Basic frequency counts and percentages were tabulated for easy reference.

The analyses of the CRs were then interpreted in the light of the universal conversational principle put forth by Pomerantz (1978), an adaptation of Holmes (1988), Herbert (1989) and David's (2002) categorisation of CRs, set against

Leech's (1983) Politeness Principle. With reference to the Agreement and Modesty Maxims, the CRs used by men and women will be characterized.

Coding of Compliment Responses

Based on the framework developed by Holmes (1988), Herbert (1989) and David (2002), there are thirteen response types found in the data of this study, which have been classified into three broad categories: *Accept*, *Deflect* and *Reject*. The framework used in the analysis of data comprising CR strategies, illustrated with examples gathered from the current study, is presented in Table 2.

Table 2 Coding of Compliment Response Strategies

Category	Response Type	Examples
ACCEPT	Appreciation Token	Thanks/[smile]
	Praise Upgrade	I thought I always looked young.
	Bald Acceptance With/without explanation	Yeah, I did the right thing.
	Return Compliment	Thanks, you look great too.
	Acceptance and Concern	Well, thanks, shall I buy a drink?
	Acceptance and Scale Down	Thank you, just gave it a shot.
DEFLECT	Shift Credit	My husband gave it to me.
	Doubting/Seeking for Reassurance	You really think so?
	Offering	You can wear it for a while, but make sure you return it.
	Sarcasm	Didn't you go to school?
REJECT	Disagreement	No, I have small eyes.
	Challenge Complimenter's Sincerity	Don't joke.
	Downgrading	Nothing*lah*, okay*lah*.

Analysis and Discussion

The following discussion has three parts. In the first phase, a detailed analysis of the sample in terms of their age is presented. Then in the second phase, a generic analysis of the CRs proffered by the male and female respondents is presented. This is then followed by a more refined and in-depth analysis of the CRs, based on variables such as gender and age, of the respondents in the study. Finally, in the last phase, the CRs are discussed in the light of Pomerantz' (1978) *Conversational Principles* and Leech's *Politeness Principle* (1983) and also set against the cultural values of the Malaysian Tamil community.

Age Classification of Respondents

The sample in this study comprises Malaysian Tamil males and females ranging from 33 to 42 years of age as mentioned earlier. The respondents were classified into three age groups and will be referred to as follows:
33-35 years: the early 30's group
36-38 years: the mid 30's group
39-42 years: the late 30's group

Analysis of CRs and Genders

In totality, 120 compliment-responses were compiled from the 20 subjects multiplied by the six situations in the DCT. The CRs have been categorised into thirteen strategies, yielding a total of 128 tokens of response types.

As the respondents were given three to ten minutes to respond to each situation in the DCT, there were instances where the respondents utilised a combination of two different types of response strategies to a single compliment situation. The following section will report on each response type in the three broad categories, *Accept, Deflect* and *Reject*. Each response type will be dealt with in connection with the results of the data in the study.

Analysis of Accept Compliment Responses and Gender

The analysis reveals that the most preferred *Accept* response type, which was the *Bald Acceptance* strategy, was the same for both the males and females. Nevertheless, the females used it considerably more (26.4%) than the males (20.3%). Both preferred this strategy, as the overriding factor was to sound affirmative in receiving the praise in the compliment. There were no playful connotations tied to this response type. In terms of Leech's (1983) *Politeness Principle*, the respondents give more emphasis to the *Agreement Maxim* than to the *Modesty Maxim* when employing the *Bald Acceptance* strategy. Figure 1 summarises the Accept CRs and speaker gender as found in the data.

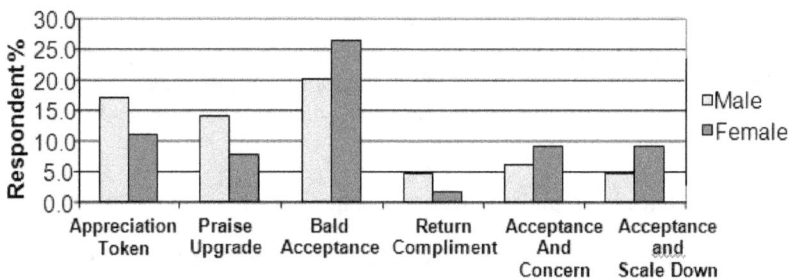

Figure 1 Compliment-Responses and Gender (Acceptance)

The least preferred *Accept* response strategy was both the *Return Compliment* and *Acceptance and Scale Down* compliment for the men, whilst for the women, the least preferred strategy was the *Return Compliment*, which only one respondent used. The returning of the compliment shifts the focus of the conversation back to the complimenter, in other words demonstrating more regard for the complimenter's needs. Hence, the *Agreement Maxim* is not given much weight in comparison to the *Modesty Maxim* when this strategy is employed. In the case of the *Acceptance and Scale Down* response type, the respondents strike a happy balance between the two maxims.

Analysis of Deflect Compliment Responses and Gender

It appears that both men and women in this study had very similar inclinations in the *Deflect* category. This can be clearly observed in Figure 2.

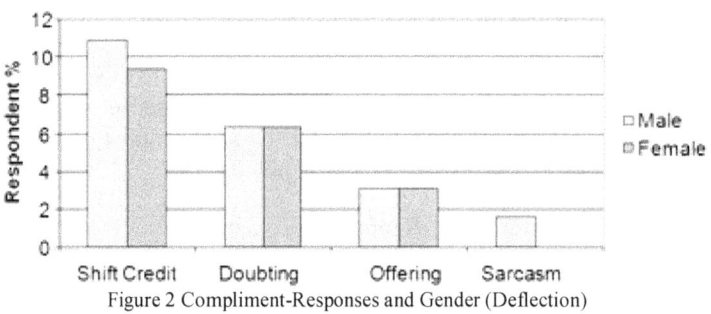

Figure 2 Compliment-Responses and Gender (Deflection)

The most preferred response type in this category for both men and women was the *Shift Credit* strategy. However men (10.9%) used it slightly more than the women (9.4%). In tandem with Leech's (1983) *Politeness Principle*, the respondents in using this strategy consider not only the *Agreement Maxim* but also the *Modesty Maxim*. By shifting the credit to someone else, the respondents attempt to solve the conflict between being cooperative and avoiding self-praise. Hence, in this case both maxims are given due consideration.

The least preferred response type for the men was the *Sarcasm* strategy, which was used by a sole respondent. The respondent demonstrates that he is well aware of the compliment content and avoids explicit self praise by using sarcasm to ward off the credit attributed. For the women, *Offering* was the least preferred strategy (3.1%); by this strategy the respondents do not directly agree with the content of the compliment and deflect the praise by offering the item/service being praised to the complimenter. Here, both the *Agreement* and *Modesty Maxim* are given equal priority.

Analysis of Reject Compliment Responses and Gender

It is evident that the most preferred strategy in the *Reject* category for the women was the *Disagreement* strategy (6.3%) whilst for the men it was the *Downgrading* strategy (4.7%). The least preferred strategy for the women was the *Downgrading* (3.1%). On the other hand, for the men it was *Disagreement* (1.6%).Figure 3 presents the analysis of the Reject Compliment Responses and Gender.

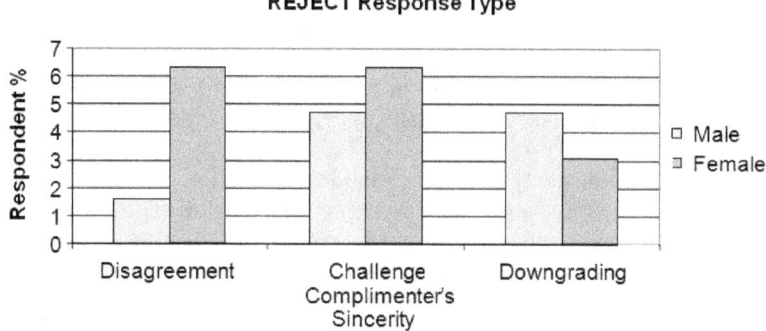

Figure 3 Compliment-Responses and Gender (Rejection)

The findings reveal that it was simply a case of mirror images in terms of the strategies preferred and least preferred between the two groups for this particular category. In essence, in employing the strategies mentioned above the respondents evidently downplay the *Agreement Maxim* by giving more emphasis to the *Modesty Maxim*.

Analysis of Compliment-Responses by Gender and Age

In order to gain more in-depth insight of compliment responses and gender, the age factor, categorised in three sub age brackets, is considered in the analysis of variance. The results of the analysis show rather vividly that the females (31.3%) in their early 30's are most inclined to accept compliments rather than deflect (4.7%) or reject (3.1%). The males (26.6%) in their early 30's also show an inclination to accept compliments, but more of them deflect (9.4%) and reject (4.7%) compared to their female counterparts (see Figure 4).

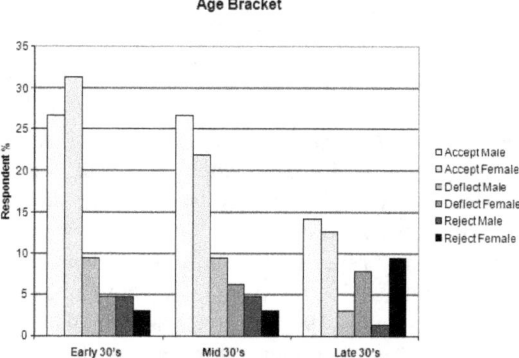

Figure 4 Analysis of CRs by Gender and Age

The males (26.6%) and females (21.9%) in their mid 30's seem to have similar inclinations. Most of the CRs fall in the *Acceptance* category, indicating once again that this is the preferred strategy amongst the three response types. In the

Deflection and *Rejection* category, the trend seems to be in the same vein as for the early 30's age group.

In the late 30's age group, there are more distinct differences, especially in the *Rejection* and *Deflection* category, where more women reject (9.4%) and deflect (7.8%) compared to the males in this sub grouping. An interesting feature worth noting is that the *Acceptance* category remains the most preferred strategy amongst the males (14.1%).

On the whole, the analysis reveals significant variation between the genders. The males in all the three age groups were more inclined to accept compliments. The emergent patterns in these groups demonstrate that acceptance is the preferred norm, which accords with findings in most western cultures.

In contrast, within the intra-group of females, it is found that the younger women accept more compliments whilst employing minimal deflection and rejection strategies. The women in the early 30's indicate through their response strategies that the *Agreement Maxim* is their primary consideration when responding to compliments.

The women in their late 30's, on the other hand, tend to reject or deflect compliments rather than accepting them. This reflects the avoidance of self-praise and is in line with the findings put forth by Azman (1986) and Arifin (2000) that Malaysians generally reject compliments due to the pressure of being modest and giving prominence to humility when responding to compliments, which they argue is a significant virtue in the Asian culture. Chen (1993) asserts that those who fall in the *Reject* and *Deflect* category treat the *Modesty Maxim* as the overriding motivation in employing these strategies.

Politeness Strategies

In this section the overall analysis will be viewed in the light of Pomerantz (1978) and Leech's (1983) *Politeness Principle,* particularly the *Agreement* and *Modesty Maxim* set against the cultural values of the Tamil community, to understand the politeness strategies employed by the subjects in this study. Since both men and women largely accept their compliments, then according to Leech, the respondents' primary consideration is adhering to the *Agreement Maxim*, which is clearly found in the two most preferred strategies employed by both men and women, which are *Bald Acceptance* and *Appreciation Tokens*. This supports Wolfson's (1989) belief that *thank you* remains the most appropriate response for most compliment situations. However, when faced with the conflict of wanting to agree and accept the compliment whilst warding off the self-praise, the respondents resort to various strategies.

In essence, the study revealed that the respondents resorted to a variety of responses to resolve the tension between agreement and avoidance of self-praise. As put forth by Pomerantz (1978) and Gajaseni (1994), the researchers also propose that there is a continuum that ranges from *Bald Acceptance* to *Disagreement* and the other strategies fall in between.

The men and younger women in this study gave more prominence to the *Agreement Maxim* than to the *Modesty Maxim*. Nevertheless, this does not mean that the Tamils do not value humility. It must be understood, as pointed out by Schiffman (2002), that the well-educated Tamils in Malaysia are becoming

"English speakers" (ibid.:164), and this group has relaxed its guard against English. Further, there is more knowledge of English and less of Tamil, to the point of being not committed to Tamil (ibid.:166). This line of argument probably stands true for this group of Tamil professionals who have assimilated the Western influences into their language.

In addition, similar to the Malaysian Chinese in Shanmuganathan's study, the majority of these Tamil career-oriented professionals were found to be direct in accepting compliments, as they recognised these "compliments to represent positive appreciation" (2003:139). Hence, their inclinations show clearly that they are working towards being solidarity partners in conversation or perhaps, as one of the respondents (AJ) put it, "it's best not to rock the boat, just accept the compliment and move on to more important matters in life".

In the case of the Malaysian Tamil women in their late 30's, their inclinations were more towards deflecting and rejecting compliments rather than accepting compliments. Hence, the *Modesty Maxim* was given more emphasis in comparison to the *Agreement Maxim*. Studies from Asian cultures with similar patterns regard this response strategy, which is not the mainstream norm, as an expression of humility. Yu (2003) asserts that when the Chinese disagree with a compliment, they are of the impression that it denotes modest behavior, as they are lowering themselves to maintain their image and, more importantly, attending to the others' needs and in turn protecting their own. This can be related to the older group of Malaysian Tamil women (late 30's), since humility is manifested in their CRs, which is also in line with Azman (1986) and Arifin's (2000) findings concerning Malaysians.

Conclusion

In conclusion, the findings in this study reveal that the Malaysian Tamil men were more prone to accept and deflect compliments than to reject them; hence, the *Agreement Maxim* was their primary consideration. The women in this study also accepted and deflected compliments just like the men. However, they rejected compliments more than the men. This was even more evident amongst the Malaysian Tamil women in their late 30's, who gave the *Modesty Maxim* more prominence than the *Agreement Maxim*, as they deflected and rejected compliments more than accepting them. According to Poynton (1989:79), "the greater the equality between interactants, the more likely they are to behave linguistically in parallel or symmetrical ways" (cited in Johnson and Roen, 1992:52). The findings of this study are consistent with Poynton's (1989) claim, since the Malaysian Tamil men and women at large demonstrated similarities in their linguistic choices, perhaps because of the equality that has been achieved between the two groups. As further social changes occur, corresponding changes in gendered variation may also be observable.

References

Azman, A. (1986). *Malaysian students' compliment responses*. Unpublished term paper. Wellington: Victoria University of Wellington.
Baba, J. (1999). *Interlanguage pragmatics: Compliment responses by learners of*

Japanese and English as a second language, Newcastle: LINCOM Europa.

Brown, P. and Levinson, S. (1978). Universals in language usage: Politeness phenomena. In Goody, E. (Ed.) *Questions and Politeness* (pp. 56-289). Cambridge: Cambridge University Press.

Brown, P. and Levinson, S. (1987). *Politeness: Some universals in language usage*. Cambridge: Cambridge University Press.

Chen, R. (1993). Responding to compliments: A contrastive study of politeness strategies between American English and Chinese speakers. *Journal of Pragmatics, 20:* 49-75.

David, M. K. (1999). Acquiring communicative competence in the reading classroom. *Literacy Across Cultures, 3(1)*, 16-19.

David, M. K. (2002). "You look good" - responses of Malaysians to compliments.In Talif, R. et al. (Eds.). *Diverse Voices 2* (pp. 111-119). UPM Serdang, Faculty of Modern Language and Communication,

Farghal, M. and Al-Khatib, M. (2001). Jordanian college students's responses to compliments: A pilot study. *Journal of Pragmatics*, 33:1485-1502.

Fukushima, N. (1990). *A study of Japanese communication: Compliment-rejection, production and second language instruction.* Dissertation. University of Southern California, Los Angeles.

Gajaseni, C. (1994). How Americans and Thais respond to compliments. Paper presented at the annual meeting of the International Conference on Pragmatics and Language Learning (8th, Urbana, IL, March 31-April 2, 1994).(ERIC Document Reproduction Service No. ED 378840).

Gajaseni, C. (1995). A constrative study of compliment responses in American English and Thai including the effect of gender and social status. Dissertation. University of Illinois at Urbana-Champaign.

Gu, Y. (1990). Politeness phenomena in modern Chinese. *Journal of Pragmatics*, 14: 237-257.

Herbert, R. K. (1989). The ethnography of English compliments and compliment responses: A contrastive sketch. In W. Oleksy (Ed.), *Contrastive Pragmatics* (pp. 3-35). .Amsterdam: John Benjamins.

Herbert, R. K. (1990). Sex-based differences in compliment behaviour. *Language in Society*, 19, 2, June, 201-224.

Herbert, R. K. (1991). The sociology of compliment work: An ethnocontrastive study of Polish and English compliments. *Multilingual* 10(4), 381-402.

Herbert, R. K. and Straight, H. S. (1989). Compliment-rejection versus compliment avoidance: Listener-based versus speaker-based pragmatic strategies. *Language and Communication,* 9: 35-47.

Holmes, J. (1984). 'Women's language': a functional approach. *General Linguistics*, 24, 3: 149-178.

Holmes, J. (1985). Sex Differences and miscommunication: Some data from New Zealand. In J.B. Pride (Ed.) *Cross-Cultural encounters: Communication* and *Miscommunication*. Melbourne, River Seine: 24-43.

Holmes, J. (1986). Compliments and compliment responses in New Zealand. English. *Anthropological Linguistics,* 28, 4: 485-508.

Holmes, J.. (1988). Paying compliments- a sex-preferential politeness strategy. *Journal of Pragmatics,* 12: 445-465.

Holmes, J. (1989). Sex differences and apologies: one aspect of communicative competence. *Applied Linguistics*, 10, 2: 194-213.
Holmes, J. (1990). Apologies in New Zealand English. *Language in Society*, 19, 2: 155-199.
Holmes, J. (1993). New Zealand women are good to talk to: An analysis of politeness strategies in interaction. *Journal of Pragmatics*, 20: 91-116.
Holmes, J. (1995). *Women, men and politeness*. London: Longman.
Holmes, J. & Brown, D. (1987). Teachers and students learning about compliments. *TESOL Quarterly*, 21/3: 445-465.
Jamaliah Mohd. Ali (1995a). *Malaysian student seminar: A study of pragmatic features in verbal interaction*. Unpublished Ph.D Thesis, University of Malaya, Kuala Lumpur.
Jamaliah Mohd. Ali. (1995b). The pragmatics of cross-cultural communications in a Malaysian context. In Majid, Z.A. and Baskaran, L. M. (Eds.). *Rules of speaking: Verbal interactions at play*. Petaling Jaya: Pelanduk Publications.
Jariah Mohd. Jan (1999). *Malaysian talk Shows: A study of power and solidarity in inter-gender verbal interaction*. Unpublished Ph.D Thesis, University of Malaya, Kuala Lumpur.
Johnson, D. M. and D. H. Roen (1992). Complimenting and involvement in peer reviews: Gender variation. *Language in Society*, 21:27-57.
Jung, Y. (2002). *The Korean face revisited: An application of Brown and Levinson's politeness theory. LEL Postgraduate Conference Archives.* http.//www.ling.ed.ac.uk/pgc/archive2000/lets/kwon.doc.
Knapp, M. L., Hopper, R., and Bell, R.A. (1984). Compliments: A descriptive taxonomy. *Journal of Communication*, 34(4): 12-31.
Leech, G. (1983). *Principles of pragmatics*. London, Longman.
Lorenzo-Dus, N. (2001). Compliment responses among British and Spanish university students: A contrastive study. *Journal of Pragmatics*, 33(1): 107-135.
Manes, J. (1983). Compliments: A mirror of cultural values. In Wolfson, N. and Judd, E. (Eds.), *Sociolinguistics and language acquisition* (pp. 96-102). Rowley: Newbury House.
Manes, J. and Wolfson, N. (1981). The compliment formula. In Coulmas, F. (Ed.), *Conversational Routine* (pp. 115-132). The Hague: Mouton.
Mao, L. R. (1994). Beyond politeness theory: Face revisited and reviewed. *Journal of Pragmatics*, 21: 451-486.
Mursy, A. and Wilson, J. (2001). Towards a definition of Egyptian complimenting. *Multilingua*, 20/2: 133-154.
Arifin, N. Z. (2000). *Creativity in Malaysian English*. Unpublished Term Paper for Varieties of English, University of Malaya.
Pomerantz, A. (1978). Compliment responses: Notes on the co-operation of multiple constraints. In Schenkein, J. (Ed.), *Studies in the organisation of conversational interaction*. New York: Academic Press: 79-112.
Poynton, C. (1989). *Language and gender: Making the difference*. Oxford: Oxford University Press.
Schiffman, H. (2002). Malaysian Tamils and Tamil linguistic culture. *Language and Communication*, 22: 159-169.

Shanmuganathan, T. (2003). The influence of culture on compliment responses. *Issues in language and cognition: Selected papers from the International Conference on Language and Cognition,* 127-142. Wolfson, Nessa and Joan Manes (1980) The compliment as a social strategy. *Papers in Linguistics: International Journal of Communication,* 13/3: 391-410.

Wolfson, N. (1981). Compliments in cross-cultural perspective. *TESOL Quarterly,* 15(2): 117-124.

Wolfson, N. (1983). An empirically based analysis of complimenting in American English. In N. Wolfson and E Judd (Eds.), *Sociolinguistics and language acquisition* (pp. 82-95). Rowley Massachusetts: Newbury House. Wolfson, N. (1984) Pretty is as pretty does. *Applied Linguistics,* 5/3: 236-244.

Wolfson, N. (1988). The Bulge: A theory of speech behaviour and social distance. In Fine, J. (Ed.) *Second language discourse: A textbook of current research* (pp. 21-38). Norwood, NJ: ABLEX.

Wolfson, N. (1989). Miscommunication. In Wolfson, N. (Ed.) *Perspectives: Sociolinguistics and TESOL.* Boston: Heinle and Heinle. Yu, M. (2003) On the Universality of Face: Evidence from Chinese Compliment Response Behaviour. *Journal of Pragmatics* 35: 1679-1710.

Yuan, Y. (2001). An inquiry into empirical pragmatics data gathering methods: Written DCTs, oral DCTs, field notes and natural Conversations. *Journal of Pragmatics,* 33: 271-292.

Yuan, Y. (2002). Compliments and compliment responses in Kunming Chinese. *Pragmatics,* 12(2): 183-226.

Appendix

Revised Discourse Completion Test

Instructions: This questionnaire consists of six compliment situations. You will be requested to respond to each situation at a time.

The test procedure is as follows: First, I will hand you a card which describes the situation in which the compliment occurs. You should read it carefully. When you finish, you are to respond to the compliment orally.

Please state the first thing that comes to your mind. There are no right or wrong answers. You may give more than one answer. Your responses will be tape recorded.

Situation 1 (Hair Cut)
You've just had your hair cut in a different style. You bump into your friend and after saying hello s/he says: "That haircut is really great. You are looking much younger!"

Situation 2 (Beautiful Eyes)
You're out for coffee with a group of friends from work. One of your male/female friends who has known you for a long time says to you: "You've got beautiful eyes."

Situation 3 (Singing)
You've invited your friends over for dinner. Just after the meal, you sing a song to entertain them. One of your male/friends says; "I didn't know that you could sing so well. Your voice is excellent."

Situation 4 (Watch)
You're wearing an original Rolex. One of your male/female friends sees it and says to you: "WOW! What a watch! I wish I had one like that."

Situation 5 (Interpersonal Skills)
Over the past week, you've been helping to organize a charity food fair for the temple. A male/female friend, who has been helping you, says "You're the right person for this type of job. You're ever so nice and diplomatic with the others."

Situation 6 (Writing)
A friend asks you to show him/her an article that you had written for a computer magazine, for which you had received very good reviews. When s/he returns it s/he says: "It's an excellent piece. You've structured it so well. If only I could write like that."

Chapter 6: Gender Variances in Chinese and Korean Requests: A Continuum Rather than Polarity

Yong-Ju Rue[1] and Grace Zhang[2]

Abstract: This paper examines connections between gender and request strategies in Mandarin Chinese and Korean, a topic of relatively limited past research. Data was collected through role-plays, and data analysis was based on the coding system of the Cross-Cultural Speech Act Realization Project (Blum-Kulka, House and Kasper 1989). In terms of interactional styles (direct or indirect), both genders chose indirect head acts and downgrading supportive moves (external modifications) as the most preferred, to lessen the impositional force of a request. They differed in their degree of directness: men were somewhat more direct than women, and more adaptable in responding to power status (Chinese men) and social distance (Korean men). Women were more consistent in choosing an indirect approach regardless of variances in social factors. In using supportive moves, men were proactive, which helped them to mitigate the impact of a direct request; women were more defensive and passive. An important implication of this study is that gender variance is not categorically polarised, but there is a continuum between the two gender groups. With this understanding of a continuum rather than polarity, a better understanding of gender issues can be obtained.

Keywords: Request, gender variance, speech act, Korean, Chinese

---

[1] *University of New South Wales*
[2] *Curtin University*

Introduction[3]

Requesting is something everyone does every day; it plays a significant role in terms of effective communication. However, requests may be moderated by gender, which is 'a salient dimension in everyday life ... . Our discourse is drenched in gender' (Holmes 2006, 26). Investigations of connections between requesting and gender will enhance current request research. There have been fruitful studies on requests such as speech acts[4] (e.g. Blum-Kulka, House and Kasper 1989, among others), but less work has been done on the linkage between requesting and gender variance, and even fewer works based on East Asian languages. This study aims to explore how the speech act of requesting is conducted in Mandarin Chinese and Korean, with special attention to gender variance.

Requests: The working definition of a request in this study is taken from Rue and Zhang (2008, 1): 'A request is to ask someone to do/not do something or to express the need or desire for something.' Requests may carry a certain degree of imposition on the addressee; therefore, they are potentially 'Face-Threatening Acts' (Brown and Levinson 1987, 70-71). This view is supported by Holmes (1995, 5) who states that 'any utterances which could be interpreted as making a demand or intruding on another person's autonomy can be regarded as a potential face-threatening act. This even included suggestions, advice and requests, which can be regarded as face threatening acts since they potentially impede the other person's freedom of action.' In order to minimise the imposition, we tend to make requests using various strategies, which are the focus of this study.

Gender variance: This study takes the view that gender is a 'socially constructed' category (Talbot 1998, 7) from which linguistic behaviour can be studied; it concerns 'differences between women and men being socially or culturally *learned, mediated* or *constructed*' (Sunderland 2004, 14). Gender variance in this study refers to the cultural and social differences between women and men manifested through their linguistic behaviours. Exploring the speech act of request in relation to gender is useful because (1) while requests have often been studied in relation to cross-cultural pragmatics, gender variance has been overlooked, and (2) gender is a 'pervasive social category' (Weatherall 2000, 287), 'potentially relevant in every social interaction' (Holmes 2006, 2).

The purpose of this study is to explore gender variances in the making of requests, namely the way in which gender contributes to requesting variations. There are two research questions: (1) Do men and women make requests differently in and between Chinese and Korean? (2) If so, what are the linguistic realizations of the gender variances in the two languages?

This study employs role-play data, with two types of spoken interactions, male/male and female/female, so that differences between same-gender groups

---

[3] We thank the role-play participants, without whose help this research would not have been possible, and for which we are extremely grateful. The authors acknowledge with gratitude the research grant awarded by Curtin University (Humanities).
[4] A speech act refers to an act of utterance that accomplishes an action, i.e. we do things with words rather than merely use them for descriptive purposes (Austin 1962). For example, John may ask, 'Mary, could you please turn down the music?', which is a speech act of requesting.

can be examined. To investigate the requesting strategies in the realization of request speech acts in cross-cultural pragmatics, this study adapts the framework of the Cross-Cultural Speech Act Realization Project (CCSARP, Blum-Kulka *et al*. 1989); see Section 3 for details. This study shows that women use requesting language differently from men, particularly in terms of direct and indirect approaches. We hope to gain an understanding of how gender interacts with requests in Chinese and Korean, and add an important dimension to the field of request research in general.

Theoretical Backgrounds

Request speech acts is a significant subject for research because such acts entail an imposition on the requestee: the purpose of a request is to get the requestee to do something (Levelt 1989, 60). Making a request involves asking the requestee to perform some kind of action which often is of benefit to the speaker and at a cost to the requestee. Because of this, the speaker tends to employ strategies that can minimize potential imposition in order to achieve an effective outcome. There have been studies of request speech acts in interlanguage/variational pragmatics and cross-cultural research projects (Blum-Kulka *et al*. 1989, Blum-Kulka and Olshtain 1984, Schneider and Barron 2008, Trosborg 1995). There are also works on requests in relation to particularly the degree of directness in various languages (Blum-Kulka and Olshtain 1987, Economidou-Kogetsidis 2002, García 1993, Meyer 2002, Owen 2001, Pair 1996, Umar 2004, Van Mulken 1996). However, the issue of gender variances in relation to requesting has attracted little attention.

In terms of works that consider Chinese and Korean languages, some studies show that Chinese speakers tend to use more direct request acts, under the effect of different social and cultural variables, than do Western language speakers (Hong 1998, Lee-Wong 2000, Zhang 1995a, 1995b). Studies of Korean request speech acts in comparison with English find that Koreans tend to be less direct than English speakers in their requesting behaviour (Byon 2001, Kim 1994). Comparing Chinese with Korean, Rue and Zhang (2008) show that Chinese speakers are more indirect than Korean speakers.[5] In choosing request strategies, Chinese speakers are more influenced by the degree of familiarity between interlocutors than by perceived differences in power status, while in contrast, Korean speakers are more attuned to status than familiarity. However, this study does not take gender differences into account; we intend to pursue this important issue here in the present study.

The biological differences between men and women excite less controversy than their non-biological differences. It is argued that gender differences are a myth, and there is no evidence to indicate that men and women talk differently. For example, Cameron (2007, 163) finds 'a great deal of similarity between men

---

[5]The extensive structure of honorifics in Korean may make it appropriate to make a request that is seemingly direct but polite. Comparatively, Chinese seems more indirect as far as employed relevant requesting strategies go, but this does not mean that they are more polite, or Korean speakers less polite.

and women, and the differences within each gender-group are typically as great as or greater than the difference between the two.' Other studies (e.g. Canary and Hause 1993, Wilkins and Andersen 1991) suggest that gender differences in social interaction are inconsistent, and that there is no significant difference in communication styles between males and females.

Against this, Holmes (2006, 2) stresses that,

> [G]ender is always potentially relevant to understanding what is going on in face-to-face interaction. Ignoring it will not make it less relevant. Gender is always there – a latent, omnipresent, background factor in every communicative encounter, with the potential to move into the foreground at any moment, to creep into our talk in subtle and not-so-subtle ways.

Studies on language and gender have attempted to identify differences between male and female speech behaviour (Bucholtz 1999, Holmes 1995, 2006; Mills 2002, Rubin and Greene 1992, Zimmerman and West 1975). The general finding is that female speech is more polite than male, and male speech is coarser and more direct. Male speech is characterized as competition-oriented and adversarial; female speech is characterized as more supportive, collaboration-oriented and affiliative. Holmes (1995) shows that females are more likely to use mitigating strategies to avoid or minimise threats to their interlocutor's face; specifically, females tend to interrupt less in conversation and to be more attentive than males. Moreover, studies which have examined the features of powerlessness and politeness in female language find males to be more strongly influenced by social status than females (Holtgraves and Yang 1990).

Previous studies show some controversies and inconsistencies in terms of gender variance and request strategies (direct or indirect) associated with particular languages and cultural groups. This is not exclusive to these lines of research, and should not be a surprise because controversy and inconsistency are part of research endeavours. This study takes the view that the issues are complex and multifaceted. It is important that we do not over-claim or overgeneralise beyond what our findings can support. It should be made clear that the findings in this study are tendencies situated in 'specific contexts of interaction', not 'laws and general principles' but 'clues and guidelines' (Cheng and Tsui 2009, 2367).

While previous studies shed light on the topics of requests and gender variance, there are some questions left to be answered. Our main objective is to see if gender variance exists in making Chinese and Korean requests, and if so to find out the ways in which the variances are realised in the two languages.

Method

This study examines request behaviour of male and female speakers of Chinese and Korean. Video data was obtained of role-plays conducted by office workers.

Data

There are two basic types of role-play: closed and open (Kasper and Dahl 1991). In a closed role-play, participants act individually in response to a given situation, and there are no interactions between participants. In an open role-play, participants interact, and a fully developed speech production can be obtained. The role-play data in this study is of the open type, to provide a full picture of request realization with information on speech sequences of negotiation in the process of completing a request (Trosborg 1995). While role-play data are not as authentic as naturally occurring data, they may be more useful in showing the impact of social variables (e.g. gender and power status) because they can be directed via prepared scenarios. Natural conversations may prove less helpful in providing sufficient data to study gender variance, because of gaps in some configurations of social variables. To be as natural as possible, this study used the method of role-enactment (McDonough 1981, 80), where the participants play out a role that is the same or similar to their real-life role. For example, a real-life boss plays a boss of some kind in the role-play. This allows more close-to-life data to emerge, as participants are able to act more naturally and confidently.

The original data were designed to study three social variables: power, distance, and gender. We have published a book on requests in relation to power status and social distance. This current study focuses on requests and gender variances. Nine situations were envisaged in which social status (power) operated at three levels: +Power (the requestee has a higher social status than the speaker), =Power (the interlocutors have parallel status) and -Power (the requestee has a lower social status than the speaker). Familiarity (distance) also operated at three levels: +D (the interlocutors are unfamiliar with each other), =D (the interlocutors are merely acquaintances) and -D (the interlocutors are very familiar with each other). An English version of the nine scenarios appears in the Appendix; the Chinese and Korean versions are available in Rue and Zhang (2008, 299-303).

The scenarios were based on the context of the workplace. The requests are types of speech acts that take place in everyday interactions, particularly in offices where requests are high frequency. It is essential to investigate the language of social institutions, and the workplace is a good source of linguistic strategies and gender issues (McElhinny 2003, 32).

Participants and Procedure

The data collection was conducted in two medium-sized companies each, in Korea and China. For each language, there were nine pairs of males and females each: that is, one male pair and one female pair for each of the nine situations (9 male pairs + 9 female pairs = 18 pairs). For one language, a total of 36 participants produced 18 role-plays, for both languages a total of 72 participants and 36 role-plays. This same-gender organization was designed to reveal the impact of gender between the male and female groups. Using the role-enactment method, participants were matched to their real-life positions (power and social distance) as much as possible to achieve naturalness in speech production.

Before conducting the data collection, informed consent was sought from the participants. They were given detailed explanations of the role-plays before recording began, to ensure the quality of the data. Before the role-play, participants did not discuss the situations, or compare notes about how they would behave in a given situation, to preserve maximum spontaneity. The 36 role-play sessions took between thirty seconds and five minutes each.

Data Coding

Data were coded by adapting the request coding system developed in CCSARP (Blum-Kulka *et al.* 1989), which is often used by researchers in coding requests and apologies across languages. This study used a modified version of CCSARP to fit Chinese and Korean speech acts (Rue and Zhang, 2008), as CCSARP was developed to analyse Western languages. The coding was done by the researchers, and an inter-rater (a postgraduate student and native speaker) for each language was asked to code 10% of the data. The item-to-item agreement was 100% for both Chinese and Korean languages.

According to CCSARP, the level of directness in the choices of request head acts (the main part of a request where the request is made) can be assessed in combination with other devices of the request (opener, internal, and external modifications); therefore, in addition to the use of head acts, an observation of how participants utilize external modifications is beneficial. Due to length constraints, this study focuses on two CCSARP categories: head acts and external modifications. The category of request head acts were grouped into three levels of directness and further classified into eight strategies: direct head acts (mood derivable, performative statement, obligation statement, want statement), conventionally indirect head acts (suggestory formula, query preparatory), and non-conventionally indirect head acts (strong hint, mild hint). The external modifications (supportive moves) are not part of head acts; they precede or follow a head act, to mitigate or aggravate a request act. External modifications were divided into downgrading external modifications (used to minimize the extent of face threat) and upgrading external modifications (used to intensify the extent of face threat). For example:

Chinese request:	我想借一下,	用一会儿。
	Wo xiang jie yixia,	*yong yihuar.*
	'I want to borrow it,	just for a while.'
	(Head act)	(External modification)
Korean request:	아 ...저도 급한 회의가 있는데,	제가 먼저 하면 안될까요?
	A... ce-to kupha-n hoywuy-ka iss-nun-tey,	*cey-ka mence ha-myen an toy-lkka-yo?*
	'Well...... I also have an urgent meeting,	can I copy it first?'
	(External modification)	(Head act)

Table 3.1 Head acts in Chinese requests (quoted from Rue and Zhang 2008, 40-41)

| *Direct strategies (Impositives)* | *Descriptions and examples* |

Mood derivable	Imperatives are the grammatical form of the utterances of this type. For example, *Bu yao gaosu ta!* 不要告诉他! ('Don't tell him!')
Performatives	The speaker conveys the illocutionary intent by using relevant performative verbs, making the utterance an order, a plea, or begging. For example, *Wo mingling nimen mashang chufa.* 我命令你们马上出发. ('I order you to set out at once.')
Obligation statement	The speaker conveys the illocutionary intent by denoting moral obligation directly. For example, *Ni yinggai zao dianr huilai.* 你应该早点回来. ('You should come back early.')
Want statement	The speaker conveys the illocutionary intent by asserting a particular want, desire, or wish. For example, *Wo xiang gen ni jie qian.* 我想跟你借钱. ('I want to borrow your money.')
Conventionally indirect strategies	*Descriptions and Examples*
Suggestory formula	The speaker conveys the illocutionary intent that is phrased as a suggestion, usually in the interest of both interactants. For example, 今天不去怎么样? *Jintian bu qu zenmeyang?* ('How about not going there today?')
Query preparatory	The utterance of this strategy contains preparatory conditions referring to asking the requestee's ability, willingness, permission, possibility, or convenience to perform an act. For examples, 你能不能快点儿做? *Ni neng bu neng kuaidianr zuo?* ('Can you do it quickly?') 你可以借我手机用吗? *Ni keyi jie wo shouji yong ma?* ('Can you lend me your mobile?')
Non-conventionally indirect strategies (Hints)	*Descriptions and Examples*
Strong hint	The speaker conveys the illocutionary intent by referring to partially relevant statements of the request act. For example, 这个房间很热. *Zhege fangjian hen re.* ('This room is very hot.') (Clue: The speaker intends to ask the requestee to open the window.)
Mild hint	The speaker conveys the illocutionary intent without referring to the request proper, but which is interpretable as request by context. For example, 你怎么了? *Ni zenme le?* ('What's the matter with you?') (Clue: The speaker intends to ask the requestee to stop touching his umbrella.)

Table 3.2 External modifications in Chinese requests (quoted from Rue and Zhang, 2008: 44-46)

Downgrading external modifications	*Descriptions and examples*
Preparator	The speaker prepares for the ensuing request by asking or announcing potential availability or permission of the requestee for carrying out the request. For example, 我有句话跟你说. *Wo you ju hua gen ni shuo.* ('I have something to talk to you about.')

Grounder	The speaker gives reasons, explanations, and justifications for the request. For example, 我丢了钱包. *Wo diu le qianbao.* ('I lost my purse.')	
Cost minimizer	The speaker tries to minimize the burden of the potential request on the requestee. For example, 我明天就还你. *Wo mingtian jiu huan ni.* ('I will return it to you tomorrow.')	
Promise of reward	To increase the likelihood of the requestee's compliance with the speaker's request, a reward due on fulfilment of the request is announced. For example, 这次给我面子，我请客吧. *Zheci gei wo mianzi, wo qingke ba.* ('Please allow me to treat you this time.')	
Apology	The speaker apologizes for the problem that the potential request might bring about. For example, 对不起. *Duibuqi.* ('Sorry.')	
Joking	The speaker makes jokes to elicit compliance for the request. For example, 我不想让你离开... 哈哈, *Wo bu xiang rang ni likai ... hehe* ('I don't want to make you move... (laugh)')	
Humble oneself	The speaker blames and lowers him/herself to elicit the requestee's sympathy. For example, 我做得不好，你能帮我吗？ *Wo zuo de bu hao, ni neng bang wo ma*? ('I couldn't handle this well, can you help me?')	
Gratitude	The speaker expresses gratitude for the expected compliance with the request. For example, 谢谢你的合作. *Xiexie ni de hezuo.* ('Thank you for your cooperation.')	
Begging help	The speaker tries to elicit compliance with the request by making an obvious appeal. For example, 求求你. (*Qiuqiu ni.* 'I beg you.')	
Sweetener	The speaker compliments the requestee's ability regarding the potential request. For example, 我知道你很会赚钱的. (*Wo zhidao ni hen hui zhuanqian de.* 'I know you are very good at making money.')	
Disarmer	The speaker tries to remove any potential refusal whereby the requestee might disagree with the potential request. For example, 我知道你没有时间，但是... *Wo zhi dao ni meiyou shijian, danshi...*('I know you don't have time, but ...')	
Asking requestee's opinion	These forms, *Zenmeyang*? 怎么样? ('How about it?'), *Ni kan xing ma?* 你看行吗? ('Is that OK to you?'), are used in the end of a request to elicit the requestee's opinion, but ultimately they ask for compliance with the request.	
Upgrading external modifications	*Descriptions and Examples*	
Reprimanding	The speaker uses criticizing statements which increase the impositive force of the request. For example, 你怎么只会做这些啊？ *Ni zenme zhi hui zuo zhexie a*? ('Why can you only do these?')	
Confirmation of request	In order to obtain compliance from the requestee, the speaker highlights a request by checking at the end of the request. For example, 再确认那个文件. 你明白我的意思吗？ *Zai queren nage wenjian. Ni mingbai wo de yisi ma*? ('Check that document again. Do you understand me?')	
Moralizing	By stating general moral maxims, the speaker triggers the requestee's intention for the potential request. For example, 你这样做对吗？ *Ni zheyang zuo dui ma*? ('Is your behaviour acceptable?')	

Table 3.3 Head acts in Korean requests (quoted from Rue and Zhang 2008, 47-48)

Direct strategies (Impositives)	Descriptions and examples
Mood derivable	Imperatives are the grammatical form of the utterances of this type. For example, 그쪽 연락처를 남겨줘요. *Kuccok yenlakche-lul namky-e-cwu-e-yo*. ('Leave your address.')
Performatives	The speaker conveys the illocutionary intent by using relevant performative verbs, making the utterance an order, a plea, or begging. For example, 내가 부탁하는데 꼭 좀 돌려줘. *Nayka pwuthak-ha-nun-tey kkok com toly-e-cwu-e*. ('I beg you to give it back to me.')
Obligation statement	The speaker conveys the illocutionary intent by denoting moral obligation directly. For example, 내일 까지는 꼭 제출을 해야 해요. *Nayil kkaci-nun kkok ceychwul-ul hay-ya hay-yo*. ('You must submit it tomorrow.')
Want statement	The speaker conveys the illocutionary intent by asserting a particular want, desire, or wish. For example, 다해 연락처를 좀 알고 싶습니다. *Dahay yenlakche-lul com al-ko sip-sup-ni-ta*. ('I want to know Dahay's address.')
Conventionally indirect strategies	Descriptions and Examples
Suggestory formula	The speaker conveys the illocutionary intent that is phrased as a suggestion that usually is in the interest of both interactants. For example, 휴가를 좀 연기하면 어떨까요? *Hyuka-lul com yenki-ha-myen ette-lkka-yo?* ('How about postponing your holiday?')
Query preparatory	The utterance of this strategy contains preparatory conditions referring to asking the requestee's ability, willingness, permission, possibility, or convenience to perform an act. For examples, 지금 녹음 해 줄 수 있어? *Cikum nokum hay cwu-l swu iss-e?* ('Can you record that right now?')
Non-conventionally indirect strategies (Hints)	Descriptions and Examples
Strong hint	The speaker conveys the illocutionary intent by referring to partially relevant statements of the request act. For example, 왜 남의 물건을 만지고 그래? *Way nam-uy mwulken-ul manci-ko kulay?* ('Why do you touch my things without asking me?') (Clue: The speaker intends to ask the requestee not to take his books.)
Mild hint	The speaker conveys the illocutionary intent without reference to the request proper, but which is interpretable as a request by context. For example, 이것 쓰는것 있잖아, 이거. *Ikes ssu-nun-kes iss-canh-a, ike*. ('This is the one we usually use.') (Clue: The speaker intends to ask the requestee to bring the stamp for him.)

Table 3.4 External modifications in Korean requests (quoted from Rue and Zhang 2008, 52-54)

Downgrading external modifications	Descriptions and Examples
Preparator	The speaker prepares for an ensuing request by asking or announcing potential availability or permission of the requestee for carrying out the request. For example, 뭣 좀 여쭤봐도 돼요? *Mwes com yeccwu-e-po-a-to tway-yo?* ('May I ask you something?')
Grounder	The speaker gives reasons, explanations, and justifications for the request. For example, 3 시에 웨딩있으니까 11 시까지 와. *3-si-ey weyting-iss-u-nikka 11-si-kkaci wa.* ('There is a wedding at 3 o'clock, so come by 11 o'clock.')
Cost minimizer	The speaker tries to minimize the burden of the potential request on the requestee. For example, 오래 걸리지는 않을 거예요. *Olay kelli-ci-nun anh-ul ke-yey-yo.* ('It won't take long.')
Promise of reward	To increase the likelihood of the requestee's compliance with the speaker's request, a reward due on fulfilment of the request is announced. For example, 내가 밥 살게요. *Nay-ka pap sal-key-yo.* ('I will treat you.')
Apology	The speaker apologizes for the problem that the potential request might bring about. These include *Mian-hay* (미안해) /*Mian-ha-ci-man*...(미안하지만...) /*Coysong-ha-ci man*...(죄송하지만...) ('I am sorry./ I am sorry, but...').
Joking	The speaker makes jokes to elicit compliance for the. For example, 나는 Y 씨 보내주기 싫은데,허허... *Na-nun Y-ssi ponay-cwu-ki silh-un-tey,* (hehe) ('I don't want to make you move... (laugh)')
Gratitude	The speaker expresses gratitude for the expected compliance with the request. For example, 도와주면 참 고맙겠어요. *Towacwu-myen cham komap-keyss-e-yo.* ('I'd appreciate it if you could help me.')
Begging help	The speaker tries to elicit compliance for the request by denoting obvious appeal. For example, 도와줘. *Towa-cwu-e.* ('I beg you.')
Sweetener	The speaker compliments the requestee's ability regarding the potential request. For example, 너 밖에 이일을 잘 할 사람이 없어. *Ne pakey i-il-ul cal ha-l salam-i eps-e.* ('No one can do this work very well, except you.')
Disarmer	The speaker tries to remove any potential refusal in case the requestee rejects the potential request. For example, 힘드신 줄 압니다만... *Himtu-si-n cwu-l apnita-man ...* ('I know it is very difficult, but...')
Self introduction	The speaker introduces him/herself to provide some background information. For example, 저 관리부에서 왔는데요. *Ce kwuanlipwu-eyse o-ass-nun-tey-yo.* ('I am from the Management Department.')
Asking requestee's opinion	The form *Ettehkey sayngkak-hay?* (어떻게 생각해? 'What do you think?'), is used at the end of a request to elicit the requestee's opinion, but ultimately it asks for compliance with the request.

Humble oneself	The speaker blames and lowers him/herself to elicit the requestee's sympathy. For example, 제가 또 이 업무에 능력도 없는 것 같고… . *Ceyka tto i epmwu-ey nunglyek-to epsnun kes kath-ko…*'(I think that) I don't have enough ability for this work task… .')
Upgrading external modifications	*Descriptions and Examples*
Reprimanding	The speaker uses criticizing statements which increase the impositive force of the request. For example, 이거 틀렸잖아요. 모르겠어요? *Ike thully-ess-canh-a-yo. Molu-keyss-e-yo?* ('This one is wrong. Don't you know?')
Confirmation of request	In order to obtain compliance of the requestee, the speaker highlights a request by checking at the end of the request. For example, 내일까지 제출하셔야 해요. 언제까지 가능하겠어요? *Nayil-kkaci ceychwul-ha-sy-e-ya hay-yo. Encey-kkaci kanung-ha-keyss-e-yo?* ('You should hand it in by tomorrow. When can you do it?')
Moralizing	By stating general moral maxims, the speaker triggers the requestee's intention for the potential request. For example, 좋은게 좋잖아요. 그러니까… *Coh-un-key coh-canh-a-yo. Kule-nikka … .* ('This is good for everyone. Take it easy, so … .')

Request Strategies and Gender

Requests are expected to manifest in ways that gender appropriateness is followed, as Holmes (2006, 5) states:

> In any conversation, people bring to bear their expectations about appropriate ways of talking, including appropriately gendered ways of talking. These expectations derive from our extensive experience of the diverse meanings conveyed by language in context. Gender is one particular type of meaning or social identity conveyed by particular linguistic choices, which may also concurrently convey other meanings as well.

This can be shown in the various ways there are, for example, of asking someone to open the window: (1) Open the window please. (2) If you don't mind, could you please open the window for me? The former is obviously more direct than the latter. Would more women prefer to use the latter than men? The answer is probably positive if we take the view that women are more indirect than men, according to widely accepted perceptions (Holmes 2006, 6). In this section, we examine how directly or indirectly Chinese and Korean male and female speakers use head acts (main request acts) and external modifications (supportive moves) when making requests.

Head Acts in Chinese

According to the data, six types of request strategies were chosen by Chinese speakers: direct head acts (mood derivable, performative statement, obligation statement, want statement) and conventionally indirect head acts (suggestory formula, query preparatory), shown in Figure 4.1.

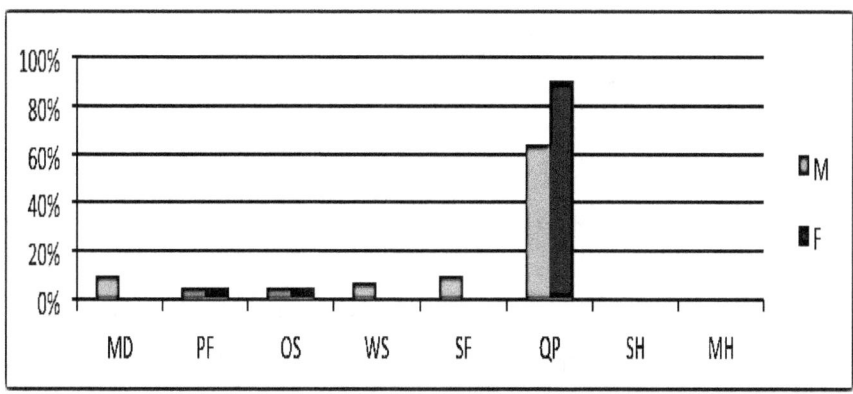

MD (Mood derivable), PF (Performative), OS (Obligation statement), WS (Want statement), SF (Suggestory formula), QP (Query preparatory), SH (Strong hint), MH (Mild hint)

Figure 4.1 Head acts used by Chinese speakers in all nine situations

Both genders used more 'query preparatory' than other strategies, exemplified in (4.1):

(4.1)
Chinese male (CM):
您看，能不能您给我帮忙协调一下？
Nin kan, neng bu neng nin gei wo bangmang xietiao yixia?
'Could you help me to coordinate this please?'
Chinese female (CF):
我想能不能等您出差之后我再把这个东西给您交过来？
Wo xiang neng bu neng deng nin chuchai zhizhou wo zai ba zhege dongxi gei nin jiao guo lai?
'Could I please submit this after you come back from your business trip?'

Figure 4.1 is an overall picture of the head acts used by Chinese speakers, showing that across all nine situations both male and female groups preferred the use of conventionally indirect requests. This indicates that the choice of request head acts in Chinese may not be greatly affected by gender overall. However, we should also note that while the general trend is indeed similar, there are gender differences shown: males used about 20% fewer 'query preparatory' than females. This means that men were to some extent more direct than women, employing more direct head acts.

While both male and female speakers showed a similar general trend, there were two request situations, Situation 1 [+P, +D, +R][6] and Situation 2 [+P, =D, +R], where distinctive gender differences were found.

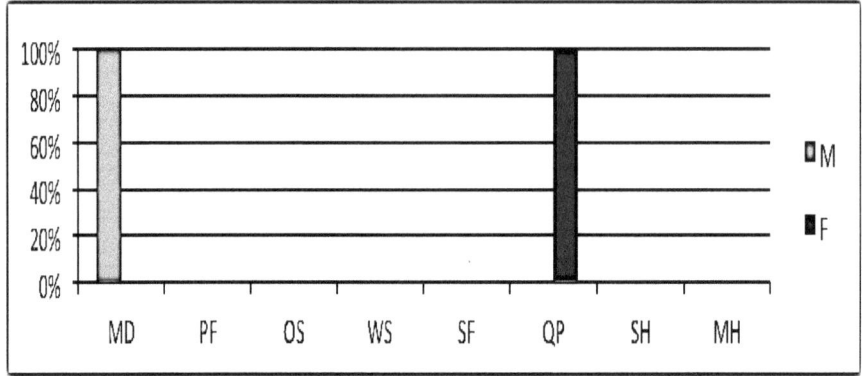

Figure 4.2 Head acts used by Chinese speakers in Situation 1

The Situation 1 role-play was an employee being interviewed by a boss for a promotion; they did not know each other. The employee needed to ask the boss for an extension to submit additional documents requested by the boss during the interview. As shown in Figure 4.2, the male used the most direct language in making the request, whereas the female used the opposite conventionally indirect strategy. This indicates that the Chinese female felt that there was a need to be less direct to an unfamiliar boss, while the male did not.

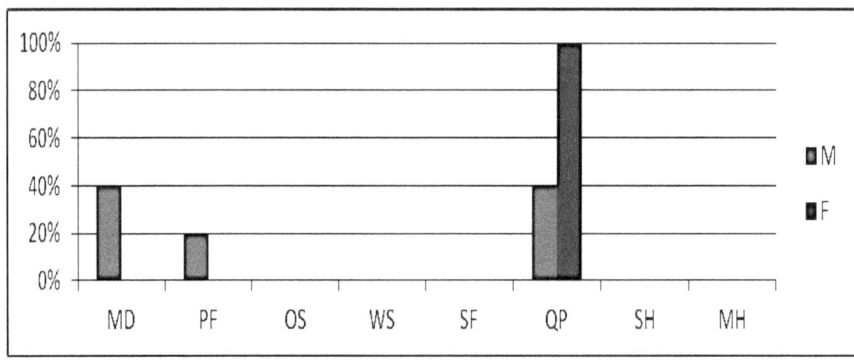

Figure 4.3 Head acts used by Chinese speakers in Situation 2

The Situation 2 role-play was that the addressor needed to ask their immediate supervisor at work for a job change, which would be a problem to the supervisor due to the shortage of staff in the unit. Figure 4.3 shows that the female chose a conventionally indirect strategy again, which suggests that females do not distinguish between requests made to an unfamiliar boss and those made to an acquainted supervisor. However this was not the case for male speakers, who in

---

[6] R refers to the rating of imposition. Making requests is imposing, hence represented by +R here.'

this case used a less direct approach; this could have been an effect of the acquaintance relationship, or the different content of requests (see Appendix for details).

Figures 4.2 and 4.3 show that the female speakers were prone to use conventionally indirect strategies (query preparatory) as the most appropriate way to realize requests in situations in which the requestees had higher social status and there was no (Situation 1) or minimal (Situation 2) familiarity between the interlocutors. The male speakers displayed a strong preference for the use of direct head acts when they made requests to requestees who held higher social status. For example:

>(4.2)
>CM: 嗯，那就麻烦您, 那个在同事里头然后安排一下.
>   *En, na jiu mafan nin, nage zai tongshi litou ranhou anpai yixia*
>   'Well, please help to arrange this among colleagues.' (Direct head act: Mood derivable)
>CF: 你能不能招一些新的员工？
>   *Ni neng bu neng zhao yixie xin de yuangong*
>   'Could you employ new work members?' (Conventionally indirect head act: Query preparatory)

Gender is our focus here, but we discuss it in the context of other relevant and contributing factors, including power status and social distance. Holmes (2006: 26) notes that while studying gender she looks at other 'intersecting and layered influences when they are relevant in contributing to an understanding of what is going on in an interaction.'

Head acts in Korean

Seven request head acts were chosen by Korean speakers: direct head acts (mood derivable, performative statement, obligation statement, want statement), conventionally indirect head acts (suggestory formula, query preparatory), and non-conventionally indirect head act (strong hint). Unlike their Chinese counterparts, the Korean speakers employed non-conventionally indirect head acts – hints, as shown in Figure 4.4.

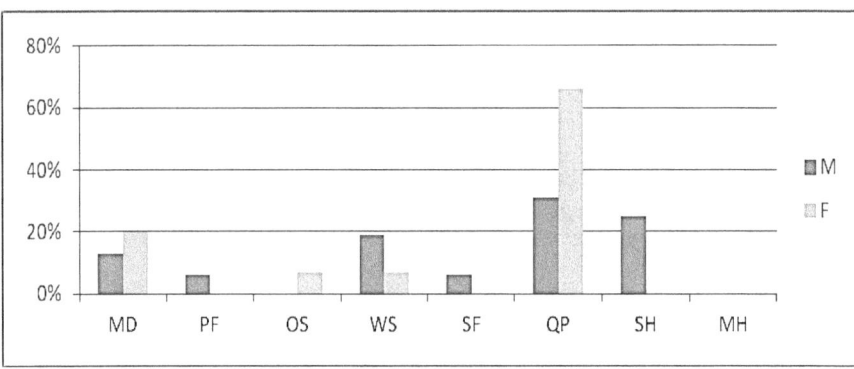

Figure 4.4 Head acts used by Korean speakers in all nine situations

The general trend was again a preference for indirect strategies, similar to the Chinese speakers in that there was no marked gender difference in the overall tendency, although males were slightly more direct than woman: 62% vs. 66% (the use of indirect strategy). Specifically, male speakers used 38% direct strategies, 37% conventionally indirect strategies, and 25% non-conventionally indirect strategies. Female speakers placed greater emphasis on the use of conventionally indirect strategies (66%), followed by direct strategies (34%). A striking gender variance is that female speakers displayed a strong tendency toward conventionally indirect head acts throughout all request situations: twice that of male speakers (female, 66% versus male, 37%). For example:

(4.3) Korean female (KF) :
조금만 시간을 더 주시면 안 될까요?
Cokum-man sikan-ul te cwu-si-myen an toy-lkka-yo?
'Could you give me a little more time?'(Conventionally indirect head act - Query preparatory)

Another salient difference between male and female speakers is a complete absence of non-conventionally indirect head acts (hints) in female speakers' requests, whereas male speakers used 25% hints. For example:

(4.4) Korean male (KM):
빨리 좀 바꿨으면...
Ppalli com pakkwu-ess-u-myen...
'If I could move quickly...' (Strong hint, intent: asking for transfer)

Male speakers showed a strong tendency to use hints, particularly in Situations 7 and 9, where requests were made to co-workers of equal social status.

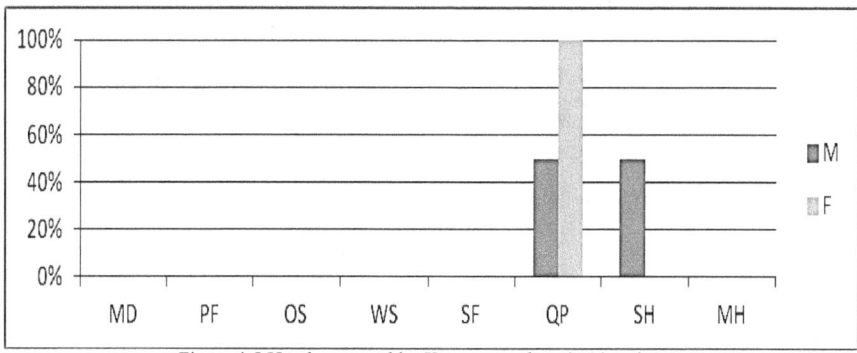

Figure 4.5 Head acts used by Korean speakers in Situation 7

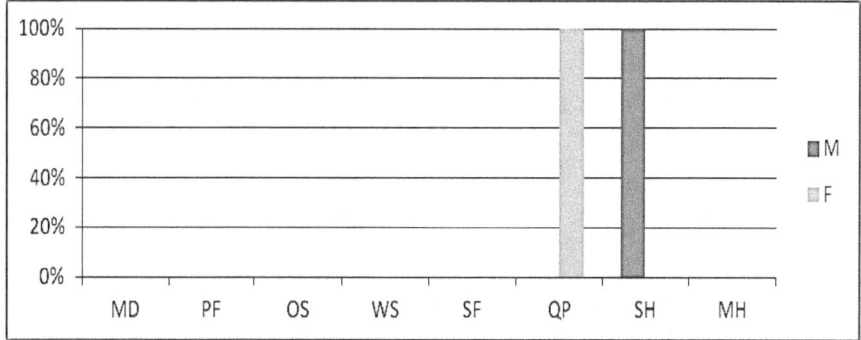

Figure 4.6 Head acts used by Korean speakers in Situation 9

Situation 7 [=P, +D, +R] is a request (to photocopy first) directed to an unfamiliar co-worker, and Situation 9 [=P, -D, +R] is the same situation except that the requestee is a good friend. Both are power-balanced situations, so there is no power issue here. In the former, the males used equally query preparatory and strong hint, but strong hint only was used when talking to a good friend. On the other hand, the female used the same strategy whether to an acquaintance or a good friend. It seems that the social distance factor had some effect on the Korean males' request making, but not on the females'.

External Modifications in Chinese

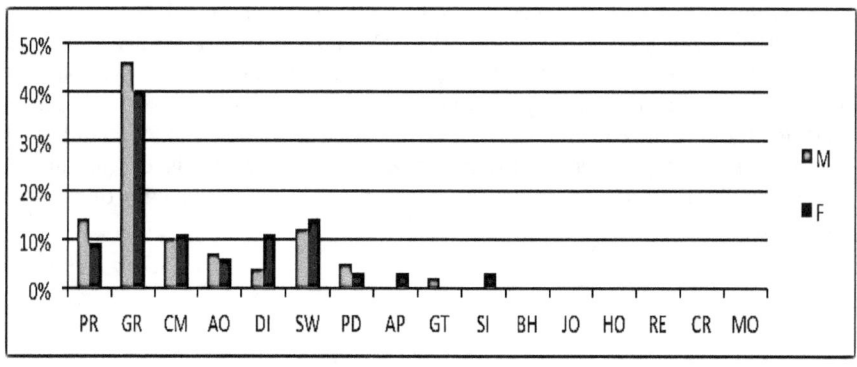

PR (Preparatory), GR (Grounder), CM (Cost minimizer), AO (Asking the requestee's opinion), DI (Disarmer), SW (Sweetener), PD (Promise of reward), AP (Apology), GT (Gratitude), SI (Self introduction), BH (Begging for help), JO (Joking), HO (Humbling oneself), RE (Reprimanding), CR (Confirmation of request), MO (Moralizing)

Figure 4.7 External modifications used by Chinese speakers in all nine situations

Generally speaking, both Chinese male and female speakers displayed a similar trend in their choices of external modifications: they all preferred downgrading external modifications across nine request situations. The grounder (background information that gives reasons for asking requests) was the most favoured for both groups to minimise the imposing force of head acts, followed by sweeteners, cost-minimizers, and preparatories. Examples are shown in 4.5.

(4.5)
 CM 啊, 那个, T 总, 您可能误解我了。我不是说马上就要走。这个可能就是说, 我只是想征 求 一下您的意见。您就这个时间的话, 看您来协调安排 。 然后这个交接工作, 也是 就请您监督一下 。

  A, nage, T zong, nin keneng wujie wo le. Wo bu shi shuo mashang jiu yao zou. Zhege keneng jiu shi shuo, wo zhishi xiang zhengqiu yixia nin de yijian. Nin jiu zhege shijian de hua, kan nin lai xietiao anpai. Ranhou zhege jiaojie gongzuo, ye shi jiu qing nin jiandu yixia.

  'Ah, Boss T. You have probably misunderstood me. I don't mean that I leave right now. Well, I merely seek your opinion. <u>As for my leave time, it is up to you. Also, please oversee the transfer.</u>

  (Underlined sentence: head act; non-underlined sentences: external modification-grounder)

 CF: 能让我先印吗? 我马上就开会了。

  Neng rang wo xian yin ma? Wo mashang jiu kaihui le.

  '<u>Could you let me photocopy first?</u> I have a meeting very soon.

A gender variance appears when we examine the use of individual strategies. It seems that men used more proactive strategies, such as preparatory, grounder, and promise of reward, whereas women used more defensive and passive methods, such as disarmer and apology. There was also a difference in the total number of external modifications produced per request throughout request situations. In particular this was seen in Situation 1 (+P, +D, +R) and Situation 2 (+P, =D, +R), where male speakers exhibited a higher frequency of external modifications per request head act than female speakers. Male speakers used more external modifications together with direct request head acts made to a requestee of higher social status. In similar situations, female speakers preferred to utilize conventionally indirect request head acts with a much lower frequency of external modifications.

External Modifications in Korean

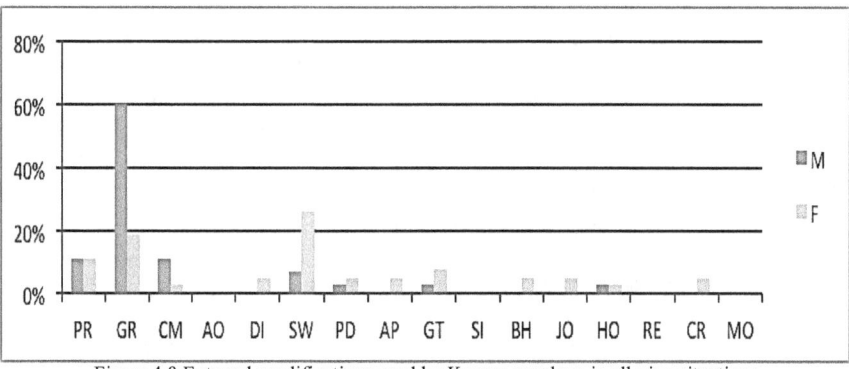

Figure 4.8 External modifications used by Korean speakers in all nine situations

The selection of external modifications by male and female speakers across nine request situations is less uniform than among the Chinese speakers, shown in Figure 4.7. There is more diversity in the types of external modifications here, and higher frequency in the female speakers' data. Grounder (60%) is the most favoured external modification for males. In contrast, sweetener is the favourite of female speakers (26%). For example:

(4.6)
KM: 나 급한 회의가 있는데 복사 좀 내가 먼저 하면 안될까?
Na kup-ha-n hoyuy-ka iss-nun-tey poksa com nay-ka mence ha-myen an-toy-lkka?
'I have an urgent meeting, <u>so can I copy first?</u>' (non-underlined: Grounder)

KF: 승진인데 축하해요. 한턱 쏴요.
Sungcin-in-tey chwukha-hay-yo. Han-thek sso-a-yo.
'Congratulations on your promotion. <u>Give us a treat</u>.' (non-underlined: Sweetener)

A gender variance in external modifications, similar to the Chinese, occurs, with males using more proactive strategies including grounder and cost minimiser, whereas females used more passive strategies such as sweetener. The use of external modifications by female speakers was frequent and wide-ranging (there was even a small number of upgrading strategies), compared to that of male speakers. It appears that Korean female speakers put more effort into using external modifications.

In examining individual request situations, we find that in Situations 7 and 9 Korean males frequently used external modifications, due to perhaps their use of strong hints as head acts in these situations. Hints do not explicitly convey the illocutionary act of a request on the surface, so perhaps more types and frequent use of external modifications were needed to provide adequate supporting information about the request.

General Discussion

According to Rue and Zhang (2008), Chinese speakers as a whole are more indirect than Korean speakers, and Korean speakers utilise more strategies and a greater frequency of external modifications than Chinese speakers in making requests. In choosing request strategies, Chinese speakers are more influenced by the degree of familiarity between interlocutors than by perceived differences in status, while in contrast Korean speakers appear more attuned to status than familiarity. However, the findings based on gender behaviours on request making in this study produce a somewhat different picture.

Most Preferred Request Strategy: No Striking Gender Variance

The data show that the general trend is a preference for indirect strategies in request making for both Chinese and Korean speakers, as shown in Table 5.1.

Table 5.1 Gender similarity in most preferred request strategies

	Head acts (most preferred)	External modifications (most preferred)
Chinese male	Indirect (CI_QP)	Grounder
Chinese female	Indirect (CI_QP)	Grounder
Korean male	Indirect (CI_QP)	Grounder
Korean female	Indirect (CI_QP)	Sweetener

Both genders prefer indirect strategies in making requests, a finding that does not support some of the existing literature. For example, Bradac, Mulac and Thompson (1995), examining data of problem-solving interactions between strangers in dyads, find that males use hedges (e.g. 'kind of' and 'sort of') more than women. One of the possible reasons is that men may 'experience more uncertainty in initial interactions than women do and accordingly hedge more' (112).

Table 5.1 shows that in the use of external modifications all groups except Korean females preferred grounders (the speaker gives reasons, explanations, and justifications for the request) to help smooth the execution of the head act of request; this seems a logical choice. Korean females went for sweeteners (the speaker compliments the requestee's ability regarding the potential request) instead, indicating a conciliatory approach (Holmes 2000).

Degree of Indirectness Corresponding to Specific Situations: Salient Gender Variance

The similar trend towards indirectness shown in Table 5.1 does not mean that there is no gender difference in other areas; there are, indeed, a number of gender variances revealed when role play situations are examined individually. For example, in terms of frequency of indirect strategies used, men were somewhat more direct than women, which supports the claim that male speech is more direct (Blum-Kulka and Olshtain 1987, García Gómez 2000, Holmes 1995, 2000;

Lakoff 1973b, Okamoto 2002). This result also confirms, to a certain extent, the validity of the claims of the relative tentativeness of women's language, manifested in using abundant polite language (e.g. Lakoff 1973a, 1975).

Table 5.2 Gender variance in individual situations

	Head acts (most preferred acts)	
	Chinese male	Chinese female
S1 (+P, +D, +R)	Direct (MD)	Indirect (QP)
S2 (+P, =D, +R)	Dir/Indirect(MD_QP)	Indirect (QP)
	Korean male	Korean female
S7 (=P, +D, +R)	Indirect (QP_SH)	Indirect (QP)
S9 (=P, -D, +R)	Indirect (SH)	Indirect (QP)

Table 5.2 shows some marked gender variance in Chinese. In Situations 1 and 2 males and females made different choices; men were somewhat more direct when talking to a boss they did not know. The result supports the claim that males are more strongly influenced by social status than females (Holtgraves and Yang 1990), and goes against the assumption that when dealing with superiors we tend to utilise indirect ways of speaking.

Unlike the Chinese, Korean speakers were all indirect; however, men used more strong hints when making request to someone of equal status that they were familiar with, showing that they are more prone to familiarity than Korean women. Given that hints do not explicitly convey the illocutionary act of requests, the requestee may need to rely on context, such as the background situation, to construe the request (Blum-Kulka and Olshtain 1987). This may explain why hints were used more between friends, who know each other quite well.

Both Chinese and Korean women stuck to query preparatory strategy for all situations, but men changed their tactics in responding to different situations.

Table 5.3 Gender variance in external modifications

	Proactive	Defensive/passive	More frequent	More diversified
Chinese male	yes		yes	
Chinese female		yes		
Korean male	yes			
Korean female		yes	yes	yes

While both groups of language users chose downgrading external strategies to mitigate the imposition of a request, men used more proactive strategies and women used more defensive and passive ones. Chinese men used more external modifications than Chinese women, because the Chinese men used more direct head acts, meaning that more supporting moves were needed to smooth things over. Compared with Korean males, Korean females used more frequent and diverse external modifications, behaviour consistent with their most preferred external move (sweetener). It seems that Korean females made greater efforts to ensure a well received and ultimately successful request.

There are similarities and differences between men and women's linguistic behaviours in making request. Mills rightly states that gender is a complex issue, and that we need 'to move beyond polarising women and men as distinct groups and concentrate more on the way that people "do gender" in particular communities of practice, hypothesising their own appropriate gender performance and set of interpretative frameworks from the stereotypes and actual performances that they think are available to them and to others' (2003, 198). It should be noted that gender differences in this study should not be regarded as absolute; they are 'tendencies' and 'variation', to borrow terms from Sunderland (2004, 14).

Conclusions and Implications

This study contributes to the literature of request speech acts, through presenting fresh insights and new resources. The findings of this study indicate that it is problematic to make a blanket statement about whether or not there is gender variance in Chinese and Koreans' request making. Gender variance is present in most aspects of request making, but is absent from some. As far as interactional styles (direct or indirect) are concerned, both genders chose similar indirect head acts and downgrading supportive moves; in particular they all chose indirect head acts as most preferred to lessen the imposing force of requests. This suggests that the participants wanted to be less confrontational in order to mitigate the face-threatening component of a request. The gender groups differed in their degree of directness, their choices of strategy, and their elasticity when dealing with the social variables of power status and social distance.

In using head acts in a request, Chinese men were more direct than Chinese women (about 20% more), while Korean men were merely 4% more direct than Korean women. Chinese men were more indirect (about 10% more) than Korean men, and Chinese women were more indirect (about 25%) than Korean women. Overall, men were more direct than women and Koreans were more direct than Chinese. The data demonstrate that men were more prone to power status (Chinese men) and social distance (Korean men, who used more strong hints). Women on the other hand were consistent in choosing indirect approaches regardless of changes in social factors (power status and social distance). Men changed their strategies according to different situations, while women remained relatively static. For example, when making a request to someone of a higher power status who was not familiar, Chinese men chose a direct strategy; when making a request to someone of equal power status who was more familiar, Korean men chose to use hints. In all nine situations, all women chose to be indirect. The use of hints by Korean speakers in this study is not found in any of previous studies of request speech acts. This outcome may stem from the data of talk-in-interactions in the contexts of workplace, unlike previous studies that mostly employed written questionnaires and interviews.

While both Chinese and Korean speakers most preferred the downgrading strategies of external modifications, men were more proactive and women more defensive and passive. This corresponds to our findings concerning head acts, that men were somewhat more direct than women. It is logical that in making a direct request, proactive external modifications would be used to explain why the requestee should comply. There is a positive relationship here between the use of head acts and external modification. Men used more direct head acts; they also used more proactive external strategies to make the impact of a direct request less unpleasant. Women were more indirect in using head acts; their preferred defensive and passive style of external modification was in line with this indirectness, in that there was no need to be as proactive as men, who needed to do more to mitigate their more direct requests.

Gender variances should not be stereotyped, for they are not fixed but dynamic, shifting constantly. As shown in this study, men and women behave similarly in some aspects and differently in others. An important implication here is that gender variance is perhaps not categorically polarised, but that there is a continuum between the two gender groups. In one situation men and women may be at the two ends of the continuum, but in another situation they may meet in the middle. This continuum metaphor may offer a clearer understanding of gender issues.

References

Austin, John L. 1962. *How to Do Things with Words*. London: Oxford University Press.

Blum-Kulka, Shoshana, Juliane House and Gabriel Kasper. 1989. *Cross-Cultural Pragmatics: Requests and Apologies*. Norwood, N. J.: Albex.

Blum-Kulka, Shoshana and Elite Olshtain, 1984. "Requests and apologies: A cross-cultural study of speech act realization patterns." *Applied Linguistics* 5(3): 196-213.

Blum-Kulka, Shoshana and Elite Olshtain. 1987. "Indirectness and politeness in requests: Same or different." *Journal of Pragmatics* 11(2): 131-46.

Bradac, James J., Anthony Mulac, and Sandra A. Thompson. 1995. "Men's and women's use of intensifiers and hedges in problem-solving interaction: Molar and molecular analyses." *Research on Language and Social Interaction* 28(2): 93 -116.

Brown, Penelope and Stephen Levinson. 1987. *Politeness: Some Universals in Language Use*. Cambridge: Cambridge University Press.

Bucholtz, Mary. 1999. "Transgression and progress in language and gender studies." In *Reinventing Identities: The Gendered Self in Discourse,* edited by Mary Bucholtz, A. C. Liang, and Laurel A. Sutton, 3-24. Oxford: Oxford University Press.

Byon, Andrew S. 2001. *The Communicative Act of Requests: Interlanguage Features of American KFL Learners,* PhD Thesis, The University of Hawaii at Manoa.

Cameron, Deborah. 2007. *The Myth of Mars and Venus*. Oxford: Oxford

University Press.
Canary, Daniel J. and Hause, Kimberley S. 1993. "Is there any reason to research sex differences in communication?" *Communication Quarterly* 41(2): 129-144.
Cheng, Winnie and Amy B.M. Tsui. 2009. " 'Ahh ((laugh)) well there is no comparison between the two I think': How do Hong Kong Chinese and native speakers of English disagree with each other?" *Journal of Pragmatics* 41(11): 2365–2380.
Economidou-Kogetsidis, Maria. 2002. "Requesting strategies in English and Greek: Observation from an airline's call centre." *Nottingham Linguistic Circular* 17: 17-32.
García, Carmen. 1993. "Making a request and responding to it: A case study of Peruvian Spanish speakers." *Journal of Pragmatics* 19 (2): 127-152.
García Gómez, Antonio 2000. "Discourse, politeness and gender roles: An exploratory investigation into British and Spanish talk show verbal conflicts." *Esudios Ingleses de la Universidad Complutense* 8: 97-125.
Holmes, Janet. 1995. *Women, Men and Politeness*. London: Longman.
Holmes, Janet. 2000. "Women at work: Analysing women's talk in New Zealand workplaces." *Australian Review of Applied Linguistics* (ARAL) 22(2): 1-17.
Holmes, Janet. 2006. *Gendered Talk at Work*. Oxford: Blackwell.
Holtgraves, Thomas and Joong-man Yang. 1990. "Politeness as universal: Cross-cultural perceptions of request strategies and inferences based on their use." *Journal of Personality and Social Psychology* 59(4): 719-729.
Hong, Wei. 1998. *Request Patterns in Chinese and German: A Cross-cultural study*. München: Lincom Europa.
Kasper, Gabriele and Merete Dahl. 1991. "Research methods in interlanguage pragmatics." *Studies in Second Language Acquisition* 13(2): 215-247.
Kim, Min-Sun. 1994. "Cross-cultural comparisons of the perceived importance of conversational constraints." *Human Communication Research* 2 (1): 128-151.
Lakoff, Robin. 1973a. "Language and woman's place." Language in Society 2, 45-80.
Lakoff, Robin. 1973b. "The logic of politeness; or minding your p's and q's." *Papers from the Regional Meeting of the Chicago Linguistic Society* 9: 292-305.
Lakoff, Robin. 1975. Language and Woman's Place. New York: Harper & Row.
Lee-Wong, Song Mei. 2000. *Politeness and Face in Chinese Culture: Cross Cultural Communication*. Melbourne: Monash University Press.
Levelt, Willem J.M. 1989. *Speaking: From Intention to Articulation*. Cambridge: MIT Press.
McElhinny, Bonnie. 2003. "Theorising gender in sociolinguistics and linguistic anthropology." In *The Handbook of Language and Gender*, edited by Janet Holmes and Mirian Meyerhoff, 21-42. Oxford: Blackwell.
Meyer, Janet R. 2002. "Contextual influences on the pursuit of secondary goals in request messages." *Communication Monographs* 69(3): 189-203.
Mills, Sara. 2002. "Rethinking politeness, impoliteness and gender identity." In *Gender Identity and Discourse Analysis*, edited by Lia Litosseliti and Jane

Sunderland, 69-89. Amsterdam: John Benjamins.
Mills, Sara. 2003. *Gender and Politeness.* Cambridge: Cambridge University Press.
Okamoto, Shigeko. 2002. "Ideology and social meanings: Rethinking the relationship between language *in Language*, edited by Sarah Benor, Mary Rose, Devyani Sharma, Julie Sweetland, and Qing Zhang, 91-113. Stanford, CA: CSLI Publication.
Owen, Jeanette S. 2001. *"Interlanguage Pragmatics in Russian: A Study of the Effects of Study Abroad and Proficiency Levels on Request Strategies."* PhD Diss., Bryn Mawr College.
Pair, Robert Le. 1996. "Spanish request strategies: A cross-cultural analysis from an intercultural perspective." *Language Sciences* 18(3-4): 651-70.
Rubin, Donald L. and Kathryn Greene. 1992. "Gender-typical style in written language." *Research in the Teaching of English* 26(1): 7-40.
Rue, Yong-Ju and Grace Zhang. 2008. *Request Strategies: A Comparative Study in Mandarin Chinese and Korean.* Amsterdam: John Benjamins.
Schneider, Klaus P. and Anne Barron. 2008. *Variational Pragmatics: A Focus on Regional Varieties in Pluricentric Languages.* Amsterdam: John Benjamins.
Sunderland, Jane. 2004. *Gendered Discourses.* New York, N.Y.: Palgrave Macmillan.
Talbot, Mary M. 1998. *Language and Gender: An Introduction.* Cambridge (U.K.): Polity Press.
Tannen, Deborah. 1984. *Conversational Style: Analysing Talk among Friends.* Norwood, N. J.: Albex.
Tannen, Deborah. 1990. *You Just Don't Understand: Women and Men in Conversation.* New York: William Morrow.
Trosborg, Anna. 1995. *Interlanguage Pragmatics: Requests, Complaints and Apologies.* Berlin: Mouton de Gruyter.
Umar, Abdul Majeed A. 2004. "Request strategies as used by advanced Arab learners of English as foreign language." *Umm Al-Qura University Journal of Educational, Social Sciences and Humanities* 16(1): 41-87.
Van Mulken, Margot. 1996. "Politeness markers in French and Dutch requests." *Language Sciences* 18(3-4): 689-702.
Weatherall, Ann. 2000. "Gender relevance in talk-in-interaction and discourse." *Discourse & Society* 11(2): 286-288.
Wilkins, Brenda M. and Andersen, Peter A. 1991. "Gender differences and similarities in management communication: A meta-analysis." *Management Communication Quarterly* 5(1): 6-35.
Zhang, Yanyin. 1995a. "Strategies in Chinese requesting." In *Pragmatics of Chinese as a Native and Target Language,* edited by Gabriele Kasper, 23-68. Honolulu, HI: University of Hawai'i Press.
Zhang, Yanyin. 1995b. "Indirectness in Chinese requesting." In *Pragmatics of Chinese as a Native and Target Language*, edited by Gabriele Kasper. 69-118. Honolulu, HI: University of Hawai'i Press.
Zimmerman, Don and Candace West. 1975. "Sex roles, interruptions and silences in conversation." In *Language, Gender and Society*, edited by Barrie Thorne, Cheris Kramarae and Nancy Henley, 89-101. Rowley, MA:

Newbury House.

Appendix

The role-plays (reproduced from Rue and Zhang 2008: 304-306)

Situation 1: [+P, +D, +R]
Imagine that: You are being interviewed for a promotion by your department head. You do not know this person, because s/he has been on leave due to illness and you have worked for the company for less than six months. During the interview, the interviewer is not satisfied with your documentation, and asks you to provide more information together with an additional reference letter from one of your previous employers. The interviewer wants to make a decision tomorrow because s/he is leaving to attend a conference the day after tomorrow, so s/he asks you to submit the additional information by tomorrow. However, you would like to extend the due date to give your former employer and yourself more time to prepare. Now you ask her/him to give you more time.

Situation 2: [+P, =D, +R]
Imagine that: You are talking with your immediate supervisor at work. S/he has only been with the company for a few months, so at this stage you don't know each other very well. You would like to change jobs within the same company, because you feel that you cannot cope with the responsibilities that your present position entails. However, if you change jobs, it would put your supervisor in a difficult situation, because unfortunately several of your team members are on leave and nobody is available to take over your current duties. Nonetheless, you ask your supervisor to consider your request.

Situation 3: [+P, -D, +R]
Imagine that: You are talking with your immediate supervisor at work. You and your supervisor have been close friends for quite a few years. You would like to change jobs, because you feel that you cannot cope with the responsibilities that your present position entails. However, if you change jobs, it would put the requestee in a difficult situation, because unfortunately several of your team members are on leave and nobody is available to take over your current duties. Nonetheless, you ask the requestee to consider your request.

Situation 4: [-P, +D, +R]
Imagine that: You are a department head conducting promotion interviews in your company. The requestee is one of the candidates coming for a promotion interview. You do not know him/her, because you have just come back from leave and the requestee began his/her job after you went on leave. During the interview, you are not happy with his/her documentation; you want more documentation and an additional reference letter from one of his/her previous employers. Because you want to make a decision tomorrow as you are leaving to attend a conference the day after tomorrow, you request her/him to submit the additional information by tomorrow. You know there probably won't be enough time for the requestee and his/her former employer to prepare the required

documentation. Nevertheless, you ask him/her to submit the documentation by tomorrow.

Situation 5: [-P, =D, +R]
Imagine that: You are in a supervisory position in your company, and the requestee is one of your employees and has only been with the company for a few months. You have heard that up to now the requestee has done a great job as a marketing manager. You have a big project coming up, which needs this capable person to manage it urgently. However, unfortunately the requestee is due to go on leave for a month the following week, which is a well-deserved and long overdue break, because the requestee was very busy and worked extra shifts. You believe that the requestee is the only person in the company who can take on this project and does it well, so you want him/her to postpone his/her leave until this project is finished. Now you ask him/her to consider your request.

Situation 6: [-P, -D, +R]
Imagine that: You are in a supervisory position in your company, and the requestee is one of your employees and has also been a close friend for several years. You have heard that up to now the requestee has done a great job as a marketing manager. You have a big project coming up, which needs this capable person to manage it urgently. However, unfortunately the requestee is due to go on leave for a month the following week, which is a well-deserved and long overdue break, because the requestee was very busy and worked extra shifts. You believe that the requestee is the only person in the company who can take on this project and does it well, so you want him/her to postpone his/her leave until this project is finished. Now you ask him/her to consider your request.

Situation 7: [=P, +D, +R]
Imagine that: You have a colleague, whom you do not know, because s/he has just joined the company. You need to photocopy a lot of documents for a meeting, and only have 15 minutes before the meeting starts. However, when you get to the photocopier, the requestee you have not met before is using the photocopier and s/he has many documents to finish too, and needs them for a meeting which also starts soon. Now you ask the requestee whether or not you can interrupt and do your photocopying first.

Situation 8: [=P, =D, +R]
Imagine that: You have a colleague, whom you know as an acquaintance. The requestee has just got a promotion. Now you ask him/her to treat the office members to a dinner.

Situation 9: [=P, -D, +R]
Imagine that: The requestee is your colleague, who is a good friend of yours. You need to photocopy a lot of documents for a meeting, and only have 15 minutes before the meeting starts. However, when you get to the photocopier, the requestee is using the photocopier and s/he has many documents to finish too, and needs them for a meeting which also starts soon. Now you ask the requestee whether or not you can interrupt and do your photocopying first.

Chapter 7: Topic Introduction Elements in Single-gender and Mixed-gender Social Club Business Meetings in the US

Theresa McGarry, East Tennessee State University

Abstract: This study compares the distributions of specific elements of topic introductions in an all-women and a mixed-gender context and demonstrates that the women's single-gender speech, women's mixed-gender speech, and men's speech pattern differently with regard to the various elements in ways that reflect the speakers' contextualized purposes. While differences in men's and women's topic introductions have been examined to a degree in previous research, systematic comparison of the frequencies of specific elements that appear in the introductions has so far been lacking. This analysis looks at six elements suggested by previous work on gender and/or topic introductions: pre-signals, connectors, directives, questions, declaratives, and justifications. Moreover, since previous studies of gendered speech have found that results differ according to not only the speaker gender but also the group gender composition, I examine two contexts closely matched but differing in gender composition: all-women and mixed-gender business meetings of the same social club in the Midwestern U.S.

The results indicate that both speaker gender and group gender composition affect the participants' speech, but the effect is not uniform across the various elements examined. The women produce a higher proportion of utterance-initial connectors than do the men in both contexts. However, they produce a lower proportion of directives and a lower proportion of directives referring to addressee action rather than joint action than do the men only in the single-gender meetings, while in the mixed-gender context men's and women's introductions are very similar in this regard. On the other hand, the frequencies of questions show an effect for both speaker gender and group composition; the women produce a higher proportion than the men, and a higher proportion in the single-gender than in the mixed-gender meetings. The frequencies of justifications, whereby the speaker provides a reason for introducing the topic, shows yet another pattern; the women produce a higher proportion than the men do in the mixed-gender meetings, but in the all-women speech the proportion is about the same as that of the men (in the mixed-gender meetings). Finally, the proportions of topic introduction pre-signals are about equal across speaker gender and group meeting type.

These results suggest that a) the women attach comparatively more importance to linking their topics to previous discussion and involving the other participants in developing the topic; b) the women may be less sure that their topics will be seen as valid or understood in the way the speaker intends; c) the women use directives differently in response to context, as indicated by earlier studies; and d) accommodation with regard to gender patterns is complex and must be examined in light of context and the situated functions of linguistic items. The analysis brings together previous findings on gender correlations relating to specific linguistic features such as directives, on differences in men's and women's topic introductions such as contrast in degree of abruptness, and on gender style accommodation such as the claim that men and women accommodate to the other gender's style with regard to certain features.

Introduction[1]

Previous discussions of gendered discourse have shown interesting ways in which interlocutor gender relates to topic flow (e.g. Fishman 1983, West and Garcia 1988, Murphy 1989). However, much about the interaction between gender and topic management still remains to be studied. This study investigates a particular aspect of topic introduction in the speech of women and men in business meetings of an outdoor sports club in Michigan. The aim is to contribute to the understanding of how women and men use topic introductions for their own purposes in single-gender and mixed-gender settings.

Previous research suggests that topic introduction, as well as other aspects of topic management, is linked both to speaker gender and to the gender composition of the interlocutor group. For example, researchers such as Tannen (1991), Zimmerman and West (1975), and Fishman (1978) have investigated whether men or women introduce more topics in mixed-gender conversation and for what purpose. The types and patterns of turns occurring in topic introductions are addressed by researches such as Geluykens (1991, 1993, 1999), and the relation of this issue to gender is addressed by Coates (1989) and Murphy (1989). Coates (1989) also addresses the coherence of topic introduction in all-women discourse, while Bublitz (1989) and Yabuuchi (2002) examine various types of coherence in conversation generally. A related aspect is interlocutor cooperation in topic transition, addressed in relation to gender by West and Garcia (1988) and Ainworth-Vaughn (1992). Still other aspects are the use of elements that signal the opening of a new topic (Geluykens 1991, 1993, 1999; Berthoud and Mondada 1991) and the presence of specific speech acts in topic introductions, e.g. questions, which are studied in relation to gender by Jones et al. (1999).

This summary is intended to represent not a complete list of either topic introduction aspects studied or research devoted to these issues, but rather a

---

[1] This paper is based on a presentation given at NWAV 2004. I would like to thank Laura Ahearn, Tracey Weldon, and Janina Fenigsen for help with this study and Edith Seier for help with statistics.

representative sample. The present study takes up a further possible way of investigating the issue, by examining patterns in topic introductionsjsutifcation, including the use of specific elements in specific introduction phases. The central research question is therefore whether the speech of the women and that of the men in the social club meetings under consideration differ in frequencies of topic introduction elements in single-gender and in mixed-gender conversation.

Data

The speakers are members of the Ladies Auxiliary and joint (men's and Auxiliary) board of an outdoor sports club in a small town in Michigan. The club is a men's group, which was started in the early 1940s for the purposes of socializing, recreation, and land conservation. The members of the Auxiliary, which was started in 1954, are wives (in certain, very limited cases, ex-wives), mothers, unmarried daughters, or sisters of members of the men's group. For a fuller description of the speakers, see McGarry (2004).

The data consist of audio recordings of meetings of the Ladies' Auxiliary and the joint board. The Auxiliary meets once a month, except during June, July, and August. All members may attend the meetings; attendance is typically 8-20 members. (The men's club also meets monthly; however, these meetings are not analyzed in the current study.) Joint board meetings, open to elected officers of the Auxiliary and the men's club, are held 3-4 times per year. Meetings of both types take place in the clubhouse and are routinely audio-taped by the secretary, for the purpose of preparing the minutes.

The Auxiliary meetings are chaired by the president, who is elected yearly. The joint board also elects a president at the beginning of the year. However, in two of the three joint board meetings studied, the president was absent and the meeting chair was chosen informally by brief discussion among the members.

In the Auxiliary meetings, the women share information and plan activities. The joint board meetings provide a forum for sharing information among the joint board members and often, by extension, between the Auxiliary and the men's group, and for planning events that require the cooperation of the two groups. Joint board meeting participants also discuss ways in which to improve the club and handle problems, and they carry out projects to further specific aims. For example, in the meetings studied here they discussed a recent lack of member participation in events, established a committee to draft a questionnaire on members' interests, and formulated plans for distributing the questionnaire.

In 1999, joint board meetings were held in February, May, and November. The data examined in this study are the audio-tapes of these three joint board meetings and the three Auxiliary meetings that took place the same months. In each case, the Auxiliary meeting preceded the joint board meeting on the same day. The number of attendees at each meeting is shown in Table 1.

Table 1. Number of Participants in Meetings Examined

	women	men	total
Feb. aux.	9		9
May aux.	11		11

Nov. aux.	13		13
Feb. joint	8	6	14
May joint	4	5	9
Nov. joint	7	5	12

Seventeen women attended one or more of the Auxiliary meetings, eight women attended one or more joint board meeting, and eight men attended one or more joint board meeting; thus, while the meetings did not include exactly the same speakers, there was a great deal of overlap. All of the female participants in each board meeting also participated in the immediately preceding Auxiliary meeting.

Topics and Introductions

A primary step in analyzing topic management in the meetings is to identify the topics discussed and the points in the interaction at which new topics are opened. The difficulties inherent in defining *topic* and identifying topics in naturally occurring discourse have been pointed out by many researchers; for a helpful discussion of these issues, see Ainsworth-Vaughn (1992). The issue is particularly problematic with regard to conversation such as the meeting data in which formal structure, instantiated in formulaic speech, is an important resource for speakers who introduce topics, but the topic introduction strategies and methods typical of casual conversation are also widely used. Space limitations preclude a full discussion of the method whereby topics are identified in the current study; for details, see McGarry (2004). Drawing on Bublitz (1989), *topic* is operationally defined as follows.

> Topic: a connection between a concept or set of concepts and a linguistic action, realized in interaction among participants by relatively unpredictable and non-formulaic exhange of information

Introduction Elements

This section describes some elements of topic introductions identified in previous research and suggested by preliminary examination of the data in this study. While introduction elements have been described in terms of both speech acts (e.g. statements) and grammatical constructions (e.g. existential phrases), the present study focuses on speech acts, specifically pre-signals, statements, questions, directives, and justifications.

Pre-signals

Geluykens (1999, 41-42) observes that speakers may facilitate negotiation of a topic by pre-signaling its proposal with a phrase such as 'anyway, what I was going to say', 'oh yes one thing too', or 'what else'. Similarly, Berthoud and Mondada's (1991) taxonomy of linguistic markers of topic introduction in French discourse includes phatic markers such as *écoute* 'listen', and *tu sais* 'you know', metalinguistic markers such as *à propos* 'by the way', or on the mode of speaking, as with *je voulais te dire* 'I wanted to tell you' or *je voulais te demander* 'I wanted to ask you', and markers intermediary between metalinguistic and linguistic, such as *pour en revenir à ce que je disais* 'to get back to what I was saying'. While distinctions among the uses of the various pre-signaling mechanisms may prove interesting for future research, the present analysis focuses on their common function of directing the hearers' attention to the topic introduction. Thus the questions pursued here are whether a different number of introduction pre-signals (of any type) appear in the speech of the women in the Auxiliary meetings, the women in the board meetings, and/or the men in the board meetings. Possibly the speaker's attempt to guide the hearers' attention will reflect less certainty on the part of the speaker that the introduction will be accepted. In a study of conversation between married couples, Fishman (1978) concludes that topics proposed by the men are nearly always accepted and developed by the women, while the converse is not true. For this reason, she argues, when introducing topics the women often use attention-getting devices such as 'Do you know?' when opening topics, to try to ensure that the men engage with and participate in developing the topic introduced. If the women and men in the meetings replicate these patterns, it seems likely that the women in either setting will use more pre-signals than the men do. Moreover, in the joint board meetings the women may use more pre-signals than in the Auxiliary meetings, to ensure that the men in the joint board meetings accept the topics proposed.

Introduction Utterance Types

Following any pre-signal that occurs, the speaker references the new topic. Geluykens (1993) observes a variety of first-mention utterance types, some corresponding to speech acts and others to grammatical structures. These are presented in Table 2, with examples from his study (following Geluykens' transcription conventions, the phrase representing the first mention of the topic is italicized).

Table 2. First-mention utterance types described in Geluykens (1993)

	Utterance form	Example
clausal NP (noun phrase)	1. simple declarative clause	Professor Worth asked me to get *some books* for him.
	2. existential 'there' construction	there was [u:] [ə:] *one other man* that I [ə:] wondered about ...
question	1. yes/no question	yes do you know *Malcolm Bowen* over at the computer unit
	2. wh- question	*how how* was *the wedding*
bare NP	1. left-dislocation construction	[ə:m]. about *[ði:] lexicology seminar*
	2. quasi-left-dislocation construction	as far as *the archaeology* is concerned ... I couldn't have a better centre
explicit topic announcement		m- ((good)) – I'll tell you something else if you see by any chance anywhere around *cheap geraniums*. [ə] in pots you know

This phase of the introduction largely corresponds to Berthoud and Mondada's (1991) fourth category of topic introduction markers, i.e. linguistic markers (see Figure 2, below). Berthoud and Mondada describe five sub-categories of linguistic markers: explicit markers such as *à propos de* 'about', *au sujet de* 'on the subject of', and *quant à* 'as to'; existence markers such as *il y a* 'there is/are', *prenons* 'let us take', *posons* 'let us suppose'; certain connectors such as *parce que* 'because', *alors* 'then/in that case/so', and *bon* 'right/okay'; deictic forms, defined in the study as personal pronouns; and topicalization by means of left or right dislocation.

This taxonomy overlaps considerably with that of Geluykens. Both include NP (quasi-) dislocation; that Geluykens mentions only left dislocation while for Berthoud and Mondada it can be in either direction is probably a reflection of a difference between French and English discourse. Similarly, Berthoud and Mondada's 'existence markers' correspond to Geluykens' sub-type of clausal NPs (noun phrases), the existential 'there' construction, although for Berthoud and Mondada this category goes beyond the direct translation of the existential 'there' construction to also include postulations such as those opening with *prenons* 'let us take', and *posons* 'let us suppose'. A third point of clear overlap is between Berthoud and Mondada's explicit markers and Geluykens' bare NPs, as shown by the example Geluykens provides, 'about the lexicology seminar'; 'about' is a translation of *à propos de*, given by Berthoud and Mondada as an instantiation of this category. While Geluykens refers to this example as left-dislocation, a sub-type of 'bare NPs', the term 'dislocation' more commonly refers to cases in which the NP is truly bare, not, for example, embedded in a prepositional phrase; an example would be 'The lexicology seminar, I think it's next month'. This explains why Berthoud and Mondada posit separate categories for explicit markers such as *à propos de* 'about' and dislocations. For the purposes of this study, the category will be referred to as 'focused NPs' and will include dislocated bare NPs, NPs preceded by explicit markers such as those described by Berthoud and Mondada, and constructions referred to by Geluykens as 'quasi-dislocations' such as 'as for London'.

A more complex intersection between the two studies concerns Geluykens' 'explicit topic announcements'. This category corresponds not to one of Berthoud and Mondada's sub-types of linguistic markers but rather to their metalinguistic markers that anchor on the mode of speaking, such as *je voulais te dire* 'I wanted to tell you' and to their metalinguistic-linguistic markers such as *pour en revenir à Pierre* 'to get back to Pierre', discussed above as topic introduction pre-signals rather than first-mention utterance types. The correspondence between the types of markers described by Berthoud and Mondada and the categories of first-mention utterances provided by Geluykens is illustrated in Figure 1.

pre-signals			first-mention utterances		
phatic markers	metalinguistic markers		linguistic markers		
	anchor on act	anchor on mode	metalinguistic-linguistic markers	explicit markers, dislocations, existence markers	connectors, deictics
	explicit topic announcements			*bare NPs, left-dislocations, existentials*	*questions, declaratives*

Figure 1. Intersection of taxonomies of Berthoud and Mondada (1991) and Geluykens (1993)
(Geluykens' categories in italics)

The figure shows a range of strategies for introducing topics; generally, though not in every case, those farther left make the topic introduction more salient than those farther right. For example, while it is debatable whether a phatic marker such as 'you know' is a more explicit topic introduction than an 'explicit topic announcement' such as 'I'll tell you something else', it is clear that each of those pre-signals is more explicit than a declarative clause containing the first mention of the topic referent. Therefore, it is not surprising that the most explicit form included by Geluykens in his categorization of first-mention utterances overlaps with a category in Berthoud and Mondada's classification of linguistic markers of introduction.

In fact, while Geluykens characterizes pre-signals and first-mention strategies as distinct, in functional terms the difference seems more gradient than discrete. For example, compare the explicit topic announcement provided by Geluykens and included in Table 2, above, '... I'll tell you something else if you see by any chance anywhere around *cheap geraniums* ...' with two examples (not from actual data) he gives of pre-signals, 'anyway, what I was going to say' and 'oh yes one thing too'. The basis for the distinction seems to be that 'I'll tell you something else' occurs in the same utterance as the first mention of the topic, while presumably the other two phrases do not. Functionally, however, they seem to have the same value in calling attention to the topic introduction, i.e.

substituting one for another in the topic introduction, whether included in the same utterance as the first mention or not, would not result in noticeably more or less attention being directed to the new topic introduction and would preserve the greater amount of attention compared to, for example, 'I'd like to find some cheap geraniums'.

Thus, in functional terms the distinction between pre-signals and first-mention strategies is unimportant. In the present study it is for methodological convenience only that the distinction is preserved and what Geluykens refers to as 'explicit topic announcements' are classified as pre-signals. That is, an operational way of looking at how often the men and women in the meetings draw attention to their topic introductions is by examining their use of the group of features listed in the figure under 'pre-signals'. Other information on their strategies of topic introductions may be gained by examining the strategies grouped under 'first-mention utterance types', e.g. by comparing how often men and women first mention their new topic referent in a question.

While the development of a complex taxonomy of topic introduction strategies is not a goal of this study, preliminary analysis indicates at least two additional categories needed to accommodate the meeting data. First, in the meetings, the first-mention phase is frequently instantiated in a directive, as in the following excerpt from the May Auxiliary meeting.[2]

Excerpt 1

AB: Why don't we make it for September?

AY: [Absolutely.]

...

NA: have to talk to the men about that.

GH: can't you

→HI: [LS did the showcase for me,]

GH: [decide that ( )]

---

[2] The transcription conventions are as follows.
- A sequence of two capital letters represents a speaker. Real initials are not used. "M" and "F" represent male and female speakers, respectively, whose identity I cannot determine.
- Italics indicate speech produced by men.
- Square brackets indicate overlap. Where necessary, double brackets distinguish one overlap from another. Some overlaps irrelevant to the current analysis are omitted.
- Periods indicate falling intonation and question marks indicate rising intonation. Hyphens indicate abruptly discontinued speech.
- Words in parentheses indicate uncertain transcriptions. Empty parentheses indicate words that can't be distinguished. Some indiscernible speech is omitted.
- Materials in double parentheses gives information about speakers' movements, gestures, or manner of speaking.
- The "=" sign indicates latching, i.e. a speaker beginning an utterace just as a previous utterance ends.

AY: [[Right.]]

→ HI: [[would you]] see that she's, thanked?

AB: [Uh-huh.]

HI: [I mean if]

GH: [Yes.] She helped you.

The utterances indicated by the arrows contain the first mention of the topic, a polite directive. AB's assent establishes the topic, which is then taken up by LH, and discussed further in the interaction following this excerpt. Examples like this suggest that directives appearing in first-mention utterances, like questions, tend to evoke a response that acknowledges and establishes the topic at the same time. While this directive is a request to a specific person (which is nevertheless taken up as a topic by the group), in other cases speakers suggest actions to be undertaken by all the participants present or by the Auxiliary or joint board as a whole, either at the time of suggestion or in the future. In this study I use the term 'directive' to refer to the range of utterances intended to elicit a specific action from the hearer(s), encompassing the categories provided by Ervin-Tripp (1976, 29).

The second additional category suggested by the data is justifications. What I intend this term to represent is cases in which speakers include in their first mention utterances clauses that explicitly indicate the reason for the introduction of the topic, as in this example from the November joint board meeting. (Italics indicate men's utterances.)

Excerpt 2

EF: Okay, that's the way it was written down.

RT: *Yeah, I um=*

EF: =Well he's up north, so ( ). ... ( )

AY: Seeing that was brought up about the illustrious, president, and

EF: [Sorry.]

AY: [because] he told women

AY: [[at the last meeting that there was]]

RT: *[[Oh it's not a problem with me,]] it's just*

AY: no [Halloween party,]

EF: [( ) (give it to me)]

EF: ( ) the way you want it,

AY: [Hunter's Ball,]

EF: [and I'll make sure ( )]

RT: *I'll make sure it goes in the next one.*

→AY: Who on the board, men's board can the women go to to get something straight <u>so we know if it's happening or it isn't</u>.

The underlined script represents two reasons AY explicitly provides for introducing the new topic before she actually does so in the utterance indicated by the arrow, and an additional one that occurs after she mentions the topic. Therefore, while the actual first mention appears in a question, remarks such as these that justify the topic introduction also constitute part of this and other topic introductions. The combination of these introduction form types observed in the data, Geluykens' proposed categories of forms, and the markers posited by Berthoud and Mondada yields the categories shown in Table 3, with examples from the meeting data. Following Geluykens' convention, the NP most closely connected to the topic is italicized.

Table 3. Introduction Phase Utterance Types in the Meeting Data

Utterance form	Example
statement[3]	Well anyway, I've got *the old Santa Claus suit* if anybody ever needs it.
question	Are you going to go to *the men's board meeting*?
directive	LS did *the showcase* for me, would you see that's she's thanked?
justification	Uh, we need to come up with some dates for like *the Easter party*, cause we got to get dates on the calendar.

More than one of these acts can be involved in the first-mention phase of the introduction, as the following example shows.

Excerpt 3

AB: So we've got a lot at stake, if we don't keep things current. And I don't, really believe, and and maybe it's a case of we just haven't educated him. I mean maybe that is absolutely the case. Maybe he doesn't realize.

→AY: Well he wasn't in charge of Vegas Night and that was a flop. What happened to that.

IM: *What happened to Vegas Night,*

AB: I think we were in competition with the ball game,

AY's introduction of the topic evaluating the last Vegas Night, indicated by the arrow, is composed of both a statement and a question. Both clauses seem integral to the introduction; the statement mentions the key referent, Vegas Night, while the question calls for other members' participation in developing the topic. Together, they serve to propose the topic, which is then established by other

---

[3] I use "statement" rather than Geluykens' "declarative clause" to match the other items in the taxonomy, which are clearly speech acts rather than clause types. While statements can clearly be made by means other than declarative clauses, all the cases in the data coincide.

members' answers to the question. Accordingly, in the analysis of the meeting data each first-mention utterance can be coded as embodying multiple topic introduction strategies.

The influence of participant gender on the form chosen for the first-mention phase of the introduction has so far not been studied as such. However, other research on gendered speech in various contexts is relevant to various degrees. Accordingly, I now consider previous findings that relate to the various forms given in Table 3.

While gender-related use of clausal noun phrases has been directly addressed in very little research, Fishman (1978, 402), in the above-mentioned study of the conversations of married couples, does find that men produce over twice as many statements as women. She interprets this difference as constituting part of the larger pattern in male-female interaction, in which women are supportive of men's speech but receive much less reciprocal support; 'statements display an assumption on the part of the speaker that the attempt will be successful as it is: it will be understood, the statement is of interest, there will be a response'. Thus, the men use more statements because they count on the women's being supportive, while the women tend to use other forms, such as questions, that have more power to evoke interlocutor response.

While her finding relates to conversation generally, not to topic introductions specifically, Fishman's interpretation has interesting implications for the use of declarative clauses in the introduction context. Geluykens (1993) considers these forms to be the least explicit of the topic-introducing mechanisms because the NP is not highlighted by any special marking. In this way, a speaker using a statement to introduce a topic shows relatively less concern for giving the hearer signals that will help process the introduction, and relatively more assurance that the topic will be accepted by the other participant. Therefore, if Fishman's findings can be extrapolated to the meeting context, it seems likely that the men will use this introduction form more than the women will.

For questions, there is reason to expect the opposite result. Hirschman (1994) reports that in an experimental setting, in mixed-sex dyads of people meeting for the first time, women ask more questions than men; similarly, Mulac et al. (1988)'s experimental study of same-sex and mixed-sex dyads of previously unacquainted speakers shows questions to be one of a cluster of features that predicts female gender of the speaker. Examining data from married couples, Fishman (1978, 400-401) finds that the women ask almost three times as many questions as the men.

More specific to topic introductions, Jones et al. (1999) find that, among dyads in an experimental setting discussing a broad topic given by the researchers, women ask more questions to change the topic; by doing so the women involve their partners in establishing the topic. This interpretation accords with Geluykens' (1993, 199) observation that when a topic is introduced by means of a question, 'since the hearer is expected to be cooperative and answer the questions, the referent is almost certain to be established. Similarly, Fishman (1978, 400-401) comments that questions are a way to ensure at least a minimal interaction; 'People respond to questions as "deserving" answers. The absence of an answer is noticeable and may be complained about.'

This argument is supported by the data from the meetings generally, and by one exchange in particular from the May joint board meeting.

> Excerpt 4
>
> AY: A question on the breakfastes[4].
>
> M *We'll try.*
>
> AY: Pardon?
>
> M *Said we'll try and answer it.*
>
> AY: Oh well, he's having a breakfast for mothers is he also gonna have one for fathers?
>
> OP: *He's made no arrangement for fathers, he's gonna have a Mother's Day breakfast,*
>
> AY: It was not mentioned?
>
> OP: *In uh, the information I received so far, there will be flowers available for the ladies as they come in, the mothers, [( )]*
>
> AY: [You did] not answer my question.
>
> DR: *No, nothing's been*
>
> AY: Nothing for fathers.
>
> DR: *Nothing for fathers.*
>
> AY: Okay.

This exchange constitutes one of the very few times in the meeting data where topic development can clearly be described as problematic for the participants. AY's complaint that her question has not been answered, while delivered in a manner teasing rather than angry, still indicates that she resists OP's attempt to introduce a different topic, *establishing understanding of Mother's Day breakfast arrangements*, rather than developing the topic she has proposed in response to her question on the topic, 'It was not mentioned?', and DR steps in to address the topic in the way she has requested. Therefore, there is clear support for the strength of the question-answer pair as described by these various researchers. Given these findings on the gendered prevalence and function of questions, the women in both types of meeting are likely to use more questions in the first-mention phase than do the men, in order to involve the other interlocutors in the topic establishment.

While the use of questions thus concerns their function as methods of evoking interlocutors' participation in the immediate discourse, predictions concerning directives relate instead to their function in construing the relationship between or among the interlocutors. Several studies (e.g. Stodtbeck and Mann

---

[4] The spelling "breakfastes" represents a non-standard pluralization using the syllabic variant of the plural morpheme.

1956; Mulac et al. 1988; Haas 1979) have found men to use more directives than women. However, Goodwin (1990, 136-137) finds a more pronounced difference not in the quantity of directives used but in their purpose. In Goodwin's study, girls tend to formulate directives as proposals for group action, in a way that avoids differentiation among participants and shares in decision making, and when using direct imperative forms they often "support their directives with explanations which justify their use, frequently in terms of benefits to the addressee" (136). Similarly, West (1998) finds that women doctors use directives, often proposals for joint action, that minimize the status difference between themselves and their patients, construing a more symmetrical relationship than do the directives used my men doctors. If these findings can be extrapolated to cases of topic introduction, it seems likely that the women in both meeting types will use fewer directives to introduce topics than do the men, and a higher proportion of their directives in this context will propose joint action, rather than attempt to elicit action from one or more other meeting participants, than is true for the men.

For the final category of first-reference markers, justifications, previous research is ambiguous and not specific to topic introductions. Mulac and Lundell (1986) find justifiers to be one of a cluster of features that predicts male gender among speakers describing photographs in an experimental setting. However, in another experimental study Mulac et al. (1988) find them to be linked to female speaker gender in dyadic conversation. While neither of these studies addresses the function of these clauses in the speech samples studied, Goodwin (1991), as mentioned above, finds that when girls give directives they often justify them with reference to potential benefit to the addressee, thus minimizing the status difference implied by the directive. If the women in the meetings also choose to justify their guiding the conversation in proposing new topics, their topic introductions may contain more justifications than those of the men.

Hypotheses

Pre-signals have been discussed in the research cited mainly without reference to gender. Based primarily on Fishman's (1987) finding that when talking to men women use more attention-getting devices to elicit the hearer's participation in the conversation, I hypothesize the following.

> 1. Pre-signals will occur in a higher proportion of the women's topic introductions in the joint board meetings than in the Auxiliary meetings, and a higher proportion will occur in the women's introductions in both contexts than in the men's.

The remaining hypotheses concern elements of the first-mention utterance. First, based on Fishman's (1978) claim that men produce more statements than women, reflecting greater assurance that their contributions will be accepted and developed, I predict the following:

> 2. A higher proportion of the men's utterances first referencing the topic will include statements than will the women's.

Similarly, several studies that find women to pose more questions than men, particularly Jones et al.'s (1999) finding that women involve their partners in establishing new topics by using questions to change the topic, lead to the third hypothesis:

> 3. A higher proportion of the women's utterances first referencing the topic will include questions than will the men's.

Directives, on the other hand, have been found to occur more often in men's speech than in women's. Moreover, Fishman (1978) and Jones et al. (1999) find that women's directives are more likely to minimize status differences; a key way in which they do so is by proposing joint action to undertaken by the speaker and the hearer(s). Therefore, the fourth hypothesis is this:

> 4. A lower proportion of the women's first-mention utterances will include directives than will the men's, and a higher proportion of the directives used by the women will propose joint action than is true for the men.

Finally, extrapolating from Fishman's (1978) finding that women tend to justify their directives, I predict the following:

> 5. The women's topic introductions in both meeting types will include more justifications than will the men's.

Results

Pre-signals

The first hypothesis concerns the occurrence of pre-signals. Geluykens (1999, 38) points out that topic preparation (elicitation) probably affects the introduction process; specifically, in cases where a new topic introduction is elicited and therefore expected, speakers are unlikely to pre-signal the introduction. In the meetings, topic elicitors are built into the structure of the meeting, occurring at pre-determined junctures in the meetings and taking forms such as 'Is there any new business?' The data indicate that pre-signals can occur even following these elicitors, as shown in the following example from the May joint board meeting.

> Excerpt 5
>
> AB: But uh, I should be able to do it next month without any problem because I got to, I can drive next month. ... Okay, is there anything else to come before this body?
>
> OP: *I just ( ) tell you the money ( ) spent here the last, we're doing here it's the, east side of the building and the peak, down, the roof and down the flat roof. Need to replace – should- should be done this month. That uh, fourt- eighteen four sixty wasn't it.*

Following AB's formulaic elicitor 'is there anything else to come before this body?', OP begins a topic introduction with a reference to the mode of speaking;

his utterance is very similar to the *je voulais te dire* 'I wanted to tell you' provided by Berthoud and Mondada as an example of a meta-linguistic marker of new topic introduction. This is, therefore, clearly a case of a topic pre-signal occurring after a topic elicitor.

On the other hand, while pre-signals can appear after elicitors, they may be less likely to, in which case an apparent difference in the number of pre-signals might be a reflection of the number of elicitors in the meeting instead of, or in addition to, an indication of the use of pre-signals per se. Moreover, the chair of the Auxiliary meetings and of two of the joint board meetings often follows her own invoking a meeting section heading (either by simply naming the section or in the more canonical elicitor form) by introducing a topic herself, in effect both eliciting and providing a topic. An example appears in this excerpt from the February Auxiliary meeting:

Excerpt 6

> AB: Okay, is there any other new business? ... Uh, we need to come up with some dates for like the Easter party, cause we got to get dates on the calendar. Uh, Easter is on the fourth of April, so, what are we looking at,=

While such conjunctions of elicitor and new topic introduction to all appearances go entirely unremarked in the meetings, it seems particularly unlikely, though not impossible, that a pre-signal would occur preceding the introduction, i.e. between the elicitor and introduction. Due to this uncertainty as to whether introductions that follow an elicitor are as conducive to pre-signals as those that do not, I first analyzed all introductions and then repeated the analysis excluding post-elicitor introductions. The results are shown in
Table 4.

Table 4. Proportions of pre-signals

	auxiliary	joint board women	joint board men
all introductions	9/39 (23.08%)	4/16 (25.00%)	7/24 (29.17%)
excluding post-elicitor	7/33 (21.21%)	3/13 (23.08%)	6/21 (28.57%)

The hypothesis is that the proportion of pre-signals will be higher in the joint board meetings than in the Auxiliary meetings and higher in the women's introductions than in the men's. In fact, the differences among the three groups is not statistically significant ($\chi^2 = 0.197$, $p = 0.906$ for all introductions). As the table shows, the proportion is higher for the women in the joint board meetings than in the Auxiliary meetings but still slightly lower than for the men. Even based on descriptive statistics, it would therefore be difficult to say that the women use more pre-signals in the mixed-gender context because such measures are necessary to engage the men in the topics introduced. Since the men use a slightly higher proportion of pre-signals than do the women in this context, it would seem logical that they were at least as unsure that their topics would be accepted and developed, or that the pre-signals serve a purpose other than engaging interlocutors' attention.

Moreover, the difference between the women's speech in the single-gender and mixed-gender context is smaller when introductions that follow elicitors are excluded from analysis ($\chi2 = 0.388$, $p = 0.824$). This is most likely due to the combination of the frequency of introductions in which the Auxiliary chair, as discussed above, follows an elicitor with a topic introduction in a way not conducive to new-topic pre-signals. Since the chair introduces a greater percent of the topics in the Auxiliary meetings than in the joint board meetings (see McGarry 2004), if many of her introductions follow elicitors it is logical that excluding post-elicitor cases affects the Auxiliary meetings more than the joint board meetings. When this constraint on pre-signals is removed from the analysis, the proportions for the women in both contexts and the men all fall within an even narrower range, less than seven percentage points apart. The overall picture, then, with pre-signals is one of similarity. The pre-signal analysis gives no evidence that women are less confident than men that their topics will be accepted or that the group gender composition affects their confidence.

Statements

The second hypothesis is that the proportion of statements first referencing the topic will be higher in the men's speech than that of the women's. Since justifications are examined separately, these clauses are not included in the count of statements. The numbers of introductions that include at least one statement is shown in Table 5.

Table 5 Statements

auxiliary	joint board women	joint board men	total
19/39 (48.72%)	6/16 (37.50%)	12/25 (48.00%)	37/80 (46.25%)

The numbers indicate great similarity between the speech of the women in the Auxiliary and the men in the joint board in this regard. The women in the Auxiliary show a lower proportion, but the difference among the three groups is not statistically significant ($\chi2 = 0.619$, $p = 0.734$).

A closer examination of the function of the statements in the introductions of the three groups shows both similarity and difference. First, speakers from all three groups report on or point out club events or situations. Some of these cases involve a report from a person closely concerned with the event, such as a committee chair's presenting the report in a way that is taken to be the opening of a topic for discussion (rather than in a way that elicits no participation, as is usually the case when a report is read, for example). These tend to be the longest introduction utterances. An example from the May Auxiliary meeting appears in this excerpt; statements in this and the following excerpts are underlined.

Excerpt 7

> AB: Report on any special committees? I think those are all in. Under old business, we do - I got the name of the - Darlene happens to be the name of the Pampered Chef representative. The option is 10% of sales on a product, in other words have a show and we get 10%=

HI: =What is Pampered Chef?

AB: Pampered Chef is a kitchen gadget

HI: Oh, I don't cook. ((laughs)) I'm sorry.

AB: I don't either, but I have all kinds of cooking - kitchen gadgets.

Here AB brings up a project discussed in a previous meeting, for which she has taken primary responsibility. The project is taken up as a topic discussion to which many members subsequently contribute.

In other cases of reporting, speakers describe or point out club events or situations based on their experience. For example, in the following excerpt from the November Auxiliary meeting, AY describes a problem with communication between the Auxiliary and the men's club.

Excerpt 8

AY: Well, <u>it's always on the</u> (   ), as always, <u>nothing ever happens</u>, can't we, find somebody to do this communication (   )? Is that going to be, everlasting, the same way as it always is?

F: Mm?

F: Probably.

As the two examples above illustrate, club events or situations reported on in introductions are often those calling for some type of action; the fund-raising party introduced in Excerpt 7 is open for adoption or rejection as an Auxiliary project and the communication problem in
Excerpt 8 will be taken up with the men in the joint board meeting later that day. Of the 19 introductions in the Auxiliary that include statements, 10 are of this type.

Similarly, men in the joint board meetings produce five introductions including statements that point out a problem and two in which the information provided by the statements constitutes background to a suggestion. (In one case the background information is not about club events but rather about a practice at another organization that the speaker suggests the club might emulate.) An example of statements preceding a suggestion appears in this excerpt from the February joint board meeting:

Excerpt 9

OP: *(   ) something else (   ) too. We had the family day- we had all kinds of snow the family day it was snow. (   ) coming back and the ice was nasty. It was ice, but was windy. The ones that were here seemed to have a good time. Didn't care what's (   ). Buy a hot dogs and chili, and dessert. We should look for a date, in the summer time some time. For another family day.*

AB: Another family day=

TOPIC INTRODUCTION ELEMENTS   145

>OP: =( ) *one set up on a, year, yearly rotation. ( ) The second week of February be a, winter family day and, whatever day we pick up in, June July or August, that- that way see, we have it so's, rolls over year to year.*
>
>DR: Yeah. Gets to be repetitious [( )]

As the example shows, OP's report on the difficulties and success of the family day provides support for his suggestion that another one be held in the summer. In addition to the introductions such as this, in which the report precedes a suggestion, in one case a speaker's report of information he has heard from other members on a discontinued activity that they would like to see revived can be seen as an indirect suggestion, as evidenced by the following discussion on the possibility of reviving the activity. Therefore, nine of the twelve introductions in which men use statements concern problems or suggestions, as is also true for a majority of the introductions of this type in the Auxiliary meetings. In two other cases, a male speaker uses statements to inform the women, and possibly the other men, about an event or plan that does not require action by the joint board or the Auxiliary, although it is well within the norm for the women to give input, as the following example demonstrates.

>Excerpt 10
>
>OP: *And he's talking about seeing uh, ( ) a couple times. ((phone rings))*
>
>RT: *Is that possible? Pick it up.*
>
>OP: *One day a ( ). ( ) some kind of dinner. Which I thought it () nice. For either a Friday or Saturday.*
>
>IJ: Just don't-
>
>NA: in a way that ( ).
>
>IJ: Just don't conflict with these,
>
>F   ( )
>
>IJ: routine things that
>
>F: [Yeah.]
>
>IJ: [you're]
>
>F   [[Yeah.]]
>
>IJ: [[trying]] to have. ...
>
>M   *Oh that's right we,*
>
>KL: *Well Mark said you*
>
>KL: *[have a calendar]*
>
>F: [( ) your calendar]

KL: *with the routine things on it*

OP's topic introduction and the following discussion indicate that no approval or planning is required. Thus, the evidence shows one purpose of the joint board to be a forum for sharing club-related information, for which purpose statements are an appropriate topic introduction technique. The same is true of the Auxiliary meetings, in which two introductions provide information that elicits discussion but presents no problem and requires no action.

The introductions made by the women in the joint board meetings differ somewhat. Of the six introductions including statements, three report on matters that have been discussed in the Auxiliary and call for action by the joint board or the men's club. For example, in the November Auxiliary meeting the women agree to change the date of their next meeting pending the availability of the clubhouse on the date required. In the joint board meeting that follows, two of the women jointly construct an introduction that presents this decision to the men, as the following excerpt shows.

Excerpt 11

AY: The Auxiliary has changed our meeting date till December fifth, uh,

AB: For that

AY: For December [only]

AB: [December]

AY: which'll move it up a week. Cause there's nothing going on here we'd like to have on New Year's Eve.

AB: ( ) Our meeting's usually the second, and because, our party's the eleventh and we need to wrap everything, our par- meeting would be after the party? So we've moved it to December fifth.

AY: Is there anythi- any schedule conflict with that?

IM: *I- I- I got to go out and recheck the [schedule.]*

The introduction concludes with a question that specifies the action required, making sure that the clubhouse is available.

The women's other three introductions, which involve matters relating to the joint board or the whole club rather than the Auxiliary specifically, also end with questions. I. e. the statements give background information for questions. In one case a speaker inquires as to what went wrong with a recent event; this introduction can therefore be taken as presenting a problem to be dealt with. The second inquires as to the status of a project discussed in a previous joint board meeting. The third may be an indirect suggestion in the form of a question; although a discussion follows, the pragmatic force of the introduction is not made clear to me, although of course it may be to the participants.

Thus, across genders and meeting types it can be said that the statements in introductions often present problems to be dealt with and/or serve as background to questions, requests, or suggestions. The structure of the relationship between the Auxiliary and the men's club is reflected in the specific nature of these introductions. In the joint board meetings, both women and men produce declaratives in connection with problems or projects of the joint board or the club as a whole. However, the women also inform the men of matters discussed in the Auxiliary in order to gain necessary cooperation; the men, on the other hand, inform the women on projects undertaken by the men's club in order simply to share information. In this way, the introductions reflect the fact that the Auxiliary members' plans are subject to the approval of and require the cooperation of the men's club, while the converse is not true.

A difference also appears between the Auxiliary and the joint board meetings, in that five introductions in the Auxiliary meetings include declaratives that share information on the speaker's personal life and open a topic not strictly related (although it may be conceptually linked) to club business. An example is shown in this excerpt from the February Auxiliary meeting:

Excerpt 12

>CD: Well, just a word in passing, she was telling she couldn't cash checks. I have a home equity loan at the Old Kent bank, and I cannot cash a check in there.
>
>AB: I'll be damned.
>
>F: At where ( )
>
>CD: At the Old Kent.
>
>F: That's terrible.

While personal topics do occur in the joint board meetings, albeit in lower proportions than in the Auxiliary meetings, all but one was excluded from the analysis in this chapter because they were gradual, stepwise changes, without clearly identifiable introductions.

The final difference concerns the number of introductions in which the declarative portion is followed by a question. This occurs in only three of the nineteen introductions in the Auxiliary meetings and one of the twelve men's introductions in the joint board meeting, but in five of the six introductions by women joint board participants. This finding accords with a higher frequency of questions in introductions produced by the women in the joint board meetings compared to the Auxiliary participants and the men, discussed in the following section. This may indicate that while the women in the mixed-gender setting do not use a remarkably lower proportion of declaratives in introductions than the women in the single-gender setting or the men, they are more inclined to give information when it is seen as background to a question.

Questions

Hypothesis 3 is that a higher proportion of the women's utterances first referencing the topic NP will include questions than will the men's. The numbers of introductions including questions for women in each meeting type and for men are shown in
Table 6.

Table 6. Introductions that include questions

Auxiliary	joint board women	joint board men	total
17/39 (43.59%)	10/16 (62.50%)	7/25 (28.00%)	24/80 (30.00%)

As the table shows, a higher proportion of the women's utterances in both settings contain questions than do the men's in the joint board meetings. The p-value is significant at the 0.1 level ($\chi 2 = 4.789$, $p = 0.091$), which suggests a difference among groups. To see if this result reflects a difference among all three groups, a Fisher's exact test was performed comparing the women in the single-gender context with the women in the mixed-gender context. Based on the descriptive finding that in the mixed-gender environment the women ask more questions, the one-sided alternative hypothesis version was applied. The resultant one-tailed p-value was 0.107, which is suggestive but not significant. It seems, then, that the significant difference is between the men and the women. Therefore, these data support previous findings that women are particularly likely to use questions in conversation and to introduce topics by means of questions, and they extend these findings to a context more formal than casual conversation.

Jones et al.'s (1999) finding that women open topics with questions in order to involve their partners in establishing the new topics is also upheld by the questions that appear in the introductions. This is particularly apparent when statements are followed by questions, as discussed in the previous section. This point is illustrated by the following example from the November Auxiliary meeting.

Excerpt 13

AY: Okay, let's get on with the meeting here.

AB: Okay, uh, tickets.

NA: The raffle's going very well. They're all s- tickets are almost sold out. I think you have a few books left?

F: Yeah. [Every]

NA: [Uh]

F: body else is out now.

This example shows a cooperative introduction in which the chair produces a focused NP that passes the introduction to another speaker, NA. NA opens with two statements but then asks a question eliciting another speaker's participation in the topic. Similarly, in the case represented in
Excerpt 14, AY opens a topic introduction with a statement pointing out a problem followed by a directive calling for the problem to be solved, then follows with a question.

Excerpt 14

AB: Is there any unfinished old business?

AY: Well, it's always on the ( ), as always, nothing ever happens, can't we, find somebody to do this communication ( )? Is that going to be, everlasting, the same way as it always is?

F: Probably

It is the question that succeeds in eliciting the participation of other speakers, as shown by the response in the last line of the excerpt.

However, questions also appear without other forms, as in this example from the May Auxiliary meeting.

Excerpt 15

AB: Um, up- we'll bring up the joint board meeting [at about]

AY: [have it in September]

AB: September for the next joint board instead of August.

F: mm.

NA: Are you going to go to the men's board meeting?

AB: I didn't go the last night, because, with the end of the month, when is it?

AY: [It was]

AB: [It's already]

AY: last Thursday

Following AB's and AY's joint closing of the topic *rescheduling the joint board meeting*, NA opens the topic *ensuring a women's representative will attend the men's board meeting* with a question to AB. Introductions consisting of only a question, sometimes preceded by a pre-signal, are in fact more common than introductions in which a question follows other forms.

A finding not predicted is that the women's introductions in the joint board meetings are considerably more likely to include questions than are introductions in the Auxiliary meetings. In fact, the majority of the women's introductions in the joint board meetings, 62.5%, include a question, compared to 28% of the men's and 43.59% of those in the Auxiliary. The reasons for this difference are not clear. The questions in the Auxiliary meeting introductions involve present activities, such as an inquiry on nomination procedure, possible projects, ongoing projects, people connected with the club in some way, matters incidental to club business, and other questions linked to institutional action. The range of women's questions in the joint board meetings is narrower. In three cases, speakers ask for information that will help the Auxiliary function better: whether the clubhouse is available for a meeting on a certain day, whether the men have made any progress in interesting more of their wives in joining the Auxiliary, and who on the men's club can be responsible for ensuring that the Auxiliary is kept informed about events. Other questions concern ongoing joint board projects, e.g. how to proceed or what the project status is. Finally women joint board participants also ask about projects directed by the men's club, e.g. when a party will be held and why a recent activity was unsuccessful, and in one case a speaker asks about the feasibility of a project that would be undertaken by the men's club or by the joint board (which of these is not clear to me, although it seems very clear to the participants). The men's questions in the joint board meeting address similar topics. Given this similarity, and the greater range of topics addressed by questions in the Auxiliary, there is no evidence that the different proportions are related to the quality of topics introduced.

A more likely explanation, then, based on previous research, is that women's observed tendency to produce more questions than men is more pronounced in mixed-gender settings than in all-women settings. To support this finding, comparisons need to be undertaken of speakers in casual conversation, particularly in naturalistic settings, and in other relatively formal situations.

Directives

The fourth hypothesis is that a lower proportion of the women's first-mention utterances will include directives than will the men's, and a higher proportion of the directives used by the women will propose joint action as opposed to action to be undertaken by the addressee(s). The numbers of introductions that include directives are shown in the first row of
Table 7; the proportions and percentages refer to the total number of introductions produced by the group in question; e.g. 15.38% of introductions produced by Auxiliary participants include a directive. The results of classifying the directives as joint action or addressee action appear in the second and third rows. Here the proportions and percentages refer to the total shown in the first row; e.g., of the six introductions with directives produced by Auxiliary members, 83.33% attempt to elicit joint action.

Table 7. Introductions that include directives

	auxiliary	joint board women	joint board men
total	6/39 (15.38%)	5/16 (31.25%)	8/25 (32.00%)
joint action	5/6 (83.33%)	2/5 (40.00%)	3/8 (37.50%)
addressee action	1/6 (16.67%)	3/5 (60.00%)	5/8 (62.50%)

Concerning the proportion of introductions that include directives, the women in the joint board behave very similarly to the men (31.25% compared to 32%), while the introductions of the women in the single-gender context include directives only 15.38% of the time. However, the difference among the three groups is not statistically significant ($\chi 2 = 2.944$, $p = 0.230$). On the premise that the lack of significance might be a result of the small number of introductions with directives, a Fisher's exact test was also applied, comparing the women in the single-gender context to the women in the mixed-gender context. The result of the one-tailed comparison is a p-value of .119, which is suggestive but not conclusive. Thus, the first part of the hypothesis, that the women will more often include directives in their topic introductions, is not clearly supported.

Concerning the proportion of directives referencing joint action, the descriptive pattern is very similar to the one seen with all directives: the proportions for the women and men in the joint board, 40% and 37.5% respectively, are close to each other, while the proportion for the women in the single-gender context, 83.33% is quite different, in the predicted direction. Again, however, the difference among the three groups is not significant ($\chi2$ =2.944, p = .190). Not surprisingly, the reliability of the analysis is compromised by the very small numbers analyzed. The Fisher's exact test of the difference between the women in the single-gender and mixed-gender contexts gives a one-tailed p-value of .181, which is not conclusive, and comparing the women in the single-gender context with the men yields only the slightly more suggestive value of .111.

The overall picture, then, is one in which the descriptive statistics strongly suggest a trend in support of the hypothesis, but the smallness of the sample precludes definite conclusions. The findings may be further mitigated by the fact that the six justifications in the introductions of women joint board participants occur in only three interactions; there are two in each. Similarly, in the Auxiliary the four justifications occur in three introductions. It is not clear how multiple justification clauses in the same introduction might affect the analysis. Therefore, these results are inconclusive and call for further investigation with more data.

Justifications

The final hypothesis is that the women's topic introductions in both meeting types will include more justifications than will the men's. Table 8 shows the proportional occurrences of justifications in the meetings. Since more than one justification may be counted in one utterance, ratios of justifications to utterances, rather than percents of introductions containing justifications, are given to normalize proportions. For example, the ratio for Auxiliary meetings indicates that there are 10.26 justifications for every 100 topic introductions; however, since more than one justification occurs in one utterance, it is not true that 10.26 of introductions include justifications.

Table 8. Justifications in introduction

Auxiliary	joint board women	joint board men
4/39 (10.26:100)	6/16 (37.5:100)	3/25 (12.00:100)

The hypothesis is partially supported; while the Auxiliary introductions include a slightly lower ratio of justifications than the men's in the joint board meetings, women's introductions in the joint board meetings include a considerably higher ratio of justifications than men's introductions. This difference may constitute evidence that in the mixed-gender setting the women are less sure that their topics will be accepted or be understood in the sense in which they are intended. However, the findings may be further mitigated by the fact that the six justifications in the introductions of women joint board participants occur in only three interactions; there are two in each. Similarly, in the Auxiliary the four justifications occur in three introductions. It is not clear how multiple justification clauses in the same introduction might affect the analysis. Therefore, these results are inconclusive and call for further investigation with more data.

Conclusions

The general question investigated in this article is whether the women use more introduction forms that draw attention to the topic introduction and evoke the participation of the other participants in establishing the topic. The results are quite complex and in some cases differ according to the gender composition of the group. Figure 2 shows a summary of the patterns found.

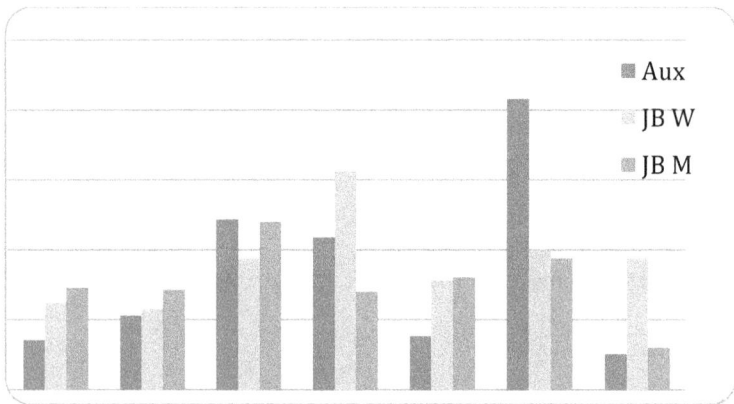

Figure 2. Summary of introduction elements comparison

As the figure shows, different patterns are established among the speaker-context groups. The proportional frequency of pre-signals is approximately equal across speaker gender and group gender when the post-elicitor contexts are excluded. In contrast, questions show an effect for both speaker gender and group composition; the women produce a higher proportion than the men, and a higher proportion in the joint board meetings than in the Auxiliary meetings. Declarative proportions are also affected by both factors, but differently than are questions. The joint board meeting data show men to use a higher proportion of declaratives and a lower proportion of justifications than the women do; however, the speech of the women in the Auxiliary meetings resembles that of the men in the joint board meetings rather than the women. Similarly, the women use more justifications than the men do only in the mixed-gender context. Therefore, these data cannot be described by saying that features of feminine speech style are more frequent in all-female speech or that the women accommodate to the mens' style. The functions of the features are important in the interpretation, as is the co-occurrence of certain features.

The similarity of pre-signals suggests that the speakers do not perceive any imbalance in the joint board meetings such that the women's topics are less likely to be addressed than the men's are. On the other hand, the women's increased use of justifications in the joint board meetings compared to the Auxiliary meetings suggests tentatively that they may be less sure that their topics will be seen as valid, or be understood in the way that the speaker intends.

The somewhat weak tendency (48% compared to 37.5%) for women to use fewer declaratives in their introductions in the joint board meetings than the men do is also in line with earlier studies that men tend to make more statements than women do in mixed-gender conversation. While in the Auxiliary meetings the frequency is higher, similar to that of the men in the joint board meetings, this appears to reflect the higher incidence of personal topics in these meetings. If the five declarative introductions that share personal information are removed from the Auxiliary data, the proportion of introductions with statements goes down to 41.18%, much closer to that in the joint board setting.

In addition, in the joint board meetings four of the six women's introductions that include statements end with questions; this tendency is not seen in the men's introductions, or in introductions in the Auxiliary meetings. This difference reflects the Auxiliary and joint board meetings' common function as a forum for sharing information related to club activities and pointing out problems or making suggestions, and also the institutional relationship between the Auxiliary and the men's club. Because one function of the joint board meetings is to provide a forum in which the women can obtain approval for and/or cooperation with projects initiated by the Auxiliary, the women often use statements to inform the men about these projects and follow the declaratives with requests or questions; half of the declarative introductions they produce are of this type. Moreover, the other half conclude with questions, thus eliciting input from the other participants. In the men's introductions, on the other hand, declaratives preceding directives typically support suggestions the men make for actions of the joint board; while the men do sometimes request the help of the Auxiliary with projects, they do not require the women's approval and these requests are less likely to be framed as the topic of conversation. Correspondingly, men's declarative introductions do not typically conclude with questions, since the joint board meeting is more a forum for the men to share information about their plans and activities than to elicit the women's input on them. Thus, the difference in frequency between the women's statements in the Auxiliary and joint board meetings reflects a number of situational constraints regarding appropriateness of different kinds of topics and institutional structure. Similarly, the women's use of relatively few directives in the single-gender context, often suggesting group action, contrasted to the similarity of their speech with the men's in the mixed-gender meetings, reflects the function of the directives in the joint board meetings. The women use directives to bring requests and suggestions from the Auxiliary meeting to the men's club members and attempt to ensure their cooperation with projects.

Finally, the women's use of questions supports earlier findings that women tend to open topics with questions to elicit the participation of the interlocutors. The higher frequency among the women in the joint board meetings, compared to the men, would seem to corroborate Fishman's (1987) finding that women use questions to require at least minimal participation from a male interlocutor in developing the topics the woman introduces. However, the still higher frequency among the women in the Auxiliary does not support this interpretation, nor does the similarity between the men and women on the use of pre-signals, discussed above. The difference between my findings and those of Fishman may simply reflect the difference between dyadic conversation and larger groups. Alternatively question frequency may be a feature noticeably affected by speakers' tendency to accommodate to each others' speech styles. That is, the Auxiliary participants may accommodate to each others' use of questions to elicit joint development of topics, resulting in the feature being intensified in the all-women setting. On the other hand, in the joint board meetings the women may accommodate to the men's tendency to use fewer questions in this way, resulting in greater similarity between the speech of the two groups (Smythe and Meyer 1994). This interpretation could be further supported if it were found that the men in their single-gender meetings use still fewer questions, and in the mixed-gender setting also accommodate to the women's style.

Thus, the data suggest that introduction features link to speaker gender, group gender, and local context and purposes in varying ways. While previous research predicts that women will use more questions and justifications and fewer declaratives than men, these results appear only or more strongly in the mixed-gender setting. For directives and pre-signals, the predicted higher frequency for men and women, respectively, is not confirmed. The preponderance of directives suggesting joint action does appear in the women's speech, but only in the single-gender context, which, along with the small number of directives in the samples, leaves the interpretation of this finding in doubt. More research is needed in similar situations

References

Berthoud, Anne-Claude and Lorenza Mondada. 1991. "Stratégies et marques d'introduction et de réintroduction d'un objet dans la conversation." *Bulletin CILA 54*: 159-79.

Button, Graham and Neil Casey. 1984. "Generating topic: The use of topic-initial elicitors." In *Structures of social action*, edited by J. Maxwell Atkinson and John Heritage, 167-90. Cambridge: Cambridge University Press.

Ervin-Tripp, Susan. 1976. "Is Sybil there? The structure of some American English directives." *Language in Society 5*: 25-66.

Fishman, Pamela. 1978. "Interaction: The work women do." *Social Problems 25*: 397-406.

Geluykens, Ronald. 1991. "Topic management in conversational discourse: The collaborative dimension." *Papers from the CLS Regional Meeting 27*: 182-95.

Geluykens, Ronald. 1993. "Topic introduction in English conversation." *Transactions of the Philological Society 91*: 181-214.

Geluykens, Ronald. 1999. "It takes two to cohere: The collaborative dimension of topical coherence in conversation," In *Coherence in Spoken and Written Discourse: How to create it and how to describe it: Selected papers from the International Workshop on Coherence, Augsburg, 24-27 April 1997*, edited by Wolfram Bublitz, Uta Lenk and Eija Ventola, 35-53. Amsterdam: John Benjamins.

Goodwin, Marjorie Harness. 1990. *He-said-she-said: Talk as social organization among black children*. Bloomington: Indiana University Press.

Haas, A. 1979. "The acquisition of genderlect, Language, sex, and gender: Does la difference make a difference?" edited by Judith Orsanu, Mariam Slater, and Leononer Loeb Adler, 101-13. New York: New York Academy of Sciences.

Hirschman, Lynette. 1994. "Female-male differences in conversational interaction." *Language in Society 23*: 427-442.

Jones, Elizabeth, Cynthia Gallois, Victor Callan, and Michelle Barker. 1999. "Strategies of accommodation: Development of a coding system for conversational interaction." *Journal of Language and Social Psychology 18*: 123-52.

Kalčik, Susan. 1975. "…like Ann's gynecologist or the time I was almost raped: Personal narratives in women's rap groups." *Journal of American Folklore 88:* 3-11.

Maltz, Daniel and Ruth Borker. 1982. "A cultural approach to male-female miscommunication." In *Language and social identity*, edited by John Gumperz, 196-216. Cambridge: Cambridge University Press.

McGarry, Theresa. 2004. "Speaking of topic introductions in the ladies auxiliary: A single-gender and mixed-gender comparative analysis." PhD Diss., University of South Carolina, Columbia.

Mulac, Anthony and Torborg Louisa Lundell. 1986. "Linguistic contributors to the gender-linked language effect." *Journal of language and social psychology 5*: 81-101.

Mulac, Anthony, John Wiemann, Sally Widenmann, and Toni Gibson. 1988. "Male/female language differences and effects in same-sex and mixed sex dyads: The gender-linked language effect." *Communication Monographs 44*: 185-90.

Smythe, Mary-Jeanette and Jasna Meyer. 1994. "On the origins of gender-linked language differences: Individual and contextual explanations." In *Differences that make a difference*, edited by Lynn Turner and Helen Sterk, 251-60. Westport, CT: Bergin and Garvey.

Stodtbeck, Fred and Richard Mann. 1956. "Sex role differentiation in jury deliberations." *Sociometry 19*: 3-11.

Tannen, Deborah. 1991. *You just don't understand: Women and men in conversation*. New York: Ballantine Books.

West, Candace. 1998. "Not just 'doctors' orders': Directive-response sequences in patients' visits to women and men physicians." In *The sociolinguistics reader vol. 2: Gender and discourse*, edited by Jenny Cheshire and Peter Trudgill, 99-126. London: Arnold.

Chapter 8: Metaphors in Distress: Gender Differences in Sudanese Arabic

Yousif Elhindi, East Tennessee State University

Abstract: This study investigates gendered linguistic differences in Sudanese Arabic, a variety spoken in Central and Northern Sudan. These linguistic differences are gender exclusive and they are associated with specific social gender roles that include story-telling, divorce initiation, and burial mourning. Crossing the linguistic gender boundary constitutes a violation of the sociolinguistic rules and it is regarded as signaling affiliation with the other gender.

Although these gendered linguistic differences in Sudanese Arabic are small in number, they are metaphoric in nature and are associated with the Sudanese women's social roles, e.g. 'cooking' and 'lamenting' deceased loved ones. And since these metaphors are used in 'distress' or 'agitation' situations, it is hypothesized that women employ them as a protest against the social roles which they have been forced to undertake.

The study concludes that these linguistic differences, which are gender exclusive, arose as a result of gender segregation and strictly defined social roles. However, these differences are being leveled as a result of education, modernization, and changing social roles in Sudanese society.

Introduction

Interest in gendered linguistic differences reached its heyday in the 1970s as a result of the women's movement, especially after the publication of Robin Lakoff's book *Language and Women's Place* in 1975. However, most of the studies in this field have focused on gender differences in the use of English and other European languages. And since these European languages only exhibited gender-preferential differences, earlier research has not looked into gender exclusive differences. Hence, it is important to investigate gender-linked linguistic differences in under-studied non-European languages in order to determine the factors that influence this phenomenon across diverse language communities.

Wolfram and Schilling-Estes (2006) categorize the approaches applied to the study of gender differences into three categories. The first approach, known as the deficit approach, was introduced in the early 1920s by the Danish linguist Otto Jespersen, whose sexist views relegate women's language to an inferior status. According to him, the language of women is syntactically simple, lexically impoverished, and spoken "with little prior thought." (248). Despite its obvious shortcomings, this viewpoint was dominant until the publication of Lakoff's article alluded to above. Lakoff catalogues a number of linguistic features that characterize women's speech. These include more frequent use of tag questions, statements with rising intonation, and 'weak' directives. Although Wolfram and Schilling-Estes subsume Lakoff's approach under the 'deficit approach', they argue that, unlike Jespersen's, it attributes these differences to the fact that men hold the societal power positions and their language is considered to be the norm.

The second approach applied to the explanation of gendered linguistic differences in English is the cultural differences approach. This approach attributes linguistic differences to the fact that in the American society, boys and girls are brought up as members of different groups. This sex-determined acculturation starts at a very early age and is manifested in a number of ways that include the way children are dressed, games they play, and general manners of interpersonal interaction. Proponents of this approach, such as Deborah Tannen, attribute cross-gender communication misunderstandings to the way that the sexes view conversation. While women regard it as a collaborative endeavor whose goal is to forge and maintain interpersonal relationships, men consider it a competitive task in which they have to 'do better' than the other participants because they have been brought up as members of a hierarchical subgroup (253-4).

The third approach, known as the dominance approach, explains differences in the way men and women talk in terms of dominance. Those who adhere to this theory believe that men introduce more topics, interrupt more frequently, and generally dominate conversation, not because they are members of a different subgroup, but they do that intentionally in order to serve their own purposes (255-256). Wolfram and Schilling-Estes conclude that these three approaches are not mutually exclusive. Furthermore, they point out their shortcomings, which include ignoring men's language, not taking socio psychological factors into account when studying gendered linguistic differences, and regarding gender as a static biological construct rather than a social dynamic that is constantly used to project the self.

This brief summary of the chapter "Gender and Language Variation", in Wolfram and Schilling-Estes's book, is representative of the variation approach inherent in the sociolinguistics tradition, an approach that is largely based on the concept of 'divergence'. This approach investigates different usages within this framework and attributes linguistic variation to social, spatial, and temporal distance between speakers. Associating linguistic variables with the gender of the speaker has often been criticized. McElhinny (2003), for instance, cites four controversial theoretical assumptions that are imbedded in this paradigm. These include equating gender with sex and considering it as an attribute (22).

Many of the current studies on gendered linguistics, especially in the field of anthropological linguistics, are based on the assumption that 'gender' is a dynamic, social construct, which is different from 'sex', which is a constant, biological construct. Foley (1998) emphasizes the notion of our 'engendered habitus', arguing that gender influences social behavior and daily cultural interactions and it is, at the same time, influenced by these interactions and social behaviors. Citing several studies that investigate the significance of gendered linguistic practices, Foley asserts that the thesis of "*universal* asymmetry in cultural evaluation of the sexes", despite being called into question, seems to be true over a wide range of cultures, even egalitarian ones (287). Reviewing a study by Keenan (1974), Foley states that *kabary* is a public style of speech used by men in Malagasy. In this indirect public style of speech, men criticize the speech of their opponents after commending its eloquence and other rhetorical skills, and then deliver their own speeches. *Kabary* is considered to be a valued style in Malagasy because its 'indirectness' is valued in that culture. The linguistic practices of women in Malagasy, on the other hand, are devalued as a result of their 'directness'. Women's linguistic practices in Malagasy include arguing, expressing anger, and haggling in the market. Another egalitarian society whose gendered linguistic practices reflect the bias against women's language is Javanese. Javanese language is characterized by terminology that reflects politeness and linguistic forms that denote the relative status of speakers and addressees. Although both men and women use politeness and status terms – men use these in the public realm whereas women use them in the domestic realm- men's language is valued more than women's. Foley concludes that the evidence suggests "male dominance is expressed and constructed through language" (293).

Linguistic Gender Differences in the Arab World

Before reviewing the studies addressing the question of gender and language in any specific Arab countries, it's important to briefly point out a few issues that have influenced language use and language policies all over the Arab world. The first of these is diglossia (Ferguson 1995), or the use of two different varieties in different social situations, a 'Low' (L) variety, usually used in casual situations such as conversing with family and friends, and a 'High' (H) variety, employed in formal settings like education and the media. According to Ferguson, Standard Arabic is the 'High' variety and Colloquial Arabic is the 'Low' one. Many sociolinguists (cited in Hachimi 2001) have challenged Ferguson's view arguing that there are more than two Arabic varieties, suggesting the term "multiglossia" as a substitute for "diglossia". Whether the linguistic situation in the Arab world is diglossic or multiglossic, it is true that the Standard varieties of Arabic are used in education, the media, and religious settings. Colloquial Arabic, on the other hand, is used in informal situations, such as conversing with family and friends or haggling at a market. Studies dealing with gendered linguistic differences in the Arab World, as the few reviewed below will show, conclude that the language of male speakers is characterized by more standard linguistic features than the language of women. This underscores that the Arab world is a patriarchal society in which men function in the public domain of religion, education, and the media, which are associated with using the 'H' variety, whereas women are confined to the domestic domain, in which using the 'L' variety is the norm.

The second factor that is often cited when social roles of women in the Arab World are discussed is Islam. Since the majority of Arabs are also Muslims, it is believed that Islam is the factor behind the traditional role of women as house wives confined to the domestic domain. Hachimi (2001) argues that, in Morocco, Quranic verses are cited to solidify the higher status of men in the society and to subjugate women and relegate them to an inferior position. She quotes the following two verses from the Quran[1]:

wa   li-r-riža:l-i   ʕalay- hinna   daraž-a   ni
and   for-det-men-gen   over-them-fem   degree-fem.sing   to
"The men are superior to them (women) by a degree." (Sura 2:228)

ʔar-riža:l-u   qawwa:m-u:na   ʕala n-nisa:ʔ-I   [bi-ma:
det-men-nom   powerful-pl.acc   over-det-women-gen   for-what

faḍḍal-a   l-La:h-u   baʕd-a-hum   ʕala: baʕd-i-n
prefer-acc   det-God-nom   some-acc-pl.masc   over some-gen-indef

wa   bi-ma: ʔanfaq-u: min   ʔamwa:l-i-h-im].
and   for-what   spent-they.masc   from   money-pl-gen-3pl.masc
"Men have more power than women [Allah has made the one of them to excel over the other and because they (the men) spend of their money]" (Sura 4:34).

Hachimi adds that despite the decontextualized interpretation of these verses, they are not challenged by anyone because they constitute a divine assertion. The inferior status of Moroccan women results in some gendered linguistic practices. These include the different ways men and women validate the credibility of their statements. While a male can say only *wa rah hdərt mʕak* "I am telling you!", a woman has to swear by almighty God and say *wa həq ilah lʕaliy lʕaḍim ila bṣṣħ* "By the truth of God the glorious and the great, it is true." This implies that Moroccan women lack credibility and trustworthiness; hence, unlike their men counterparts, they have to make an appeal to God in order to validate what they say.

De Ruiter (2007) uses data from his 2006 study in order to validate Sadiqi's claim that Standard Arabic in Morocco is a male language. Characterizing the languages used in Morocco in terms of gender, Sadiqi (2003) (cited in De Ruiter 2007) argues that Standard Arabic is a male language, whereas Amazigh is a female language. She adds that Moroccan Arabic and French are both male and female languages. However, the former is more a male language in rural areas and the latter a more female language in urban centers. Sadiqi's characterization of Standard Arabic as a male language is predicated upon its association with the religious domain, which is completely dominated by men. Using questionnaires, De Ruiter asked 569 Moroccan males and females questions about their Standard

---

[1] The abbreviations used in the glosses are as follows. acc: accusative; det: determiner; fem: feminine; gen: genitive; indef: indefinite; masc: masculine; nom: nominative; pl: plural; sing: singular; 3: third person

Arabic (SA) use, SA proficiency, and SA attitudes. Although the results indicated more positive attitudes by women towards SA, the differences between the male and female groups were not statistically significant. Hence, it could be concluded that in spite of the fact that Moroccan women are as proficient as men in SA, the language is considered to be male because men dominate the religious sphere with which it is associated. They are the ones who preach in mosques and discuss religious issues in the media.

Dahir (1997) investigates phonological variation in the speech of men and women in Damascus, Syria. He investigates the use of the standard variant, the voiceless uvular stop [q], and the colloquial variant, the glottal stop [ʔ], in the speech of Damascene men and women to realize the variable /q/. Analyzing the use of these two variables in the interviews of 23 men and 23 women, Dahir concludes that educated men favored the use of the standard variant more than educated women. He explains this finding by asserting the standard variant has been reintroduced into the colloquial through education, and men have had more access to education than women. He also concludes that the colloquial variant is favored by younger Damascenes because it is associated with more urbanization and modernization. Finally, Dahir cites an interesting study by Sawaie (1987), who investigated the use of these two variants in Aleppo. Sawaie observed that boys used the colloquial variant during the time that they were taken care of by their mothers in the 'women quarter'. However, as soon as they left that quarter and started to mingle more and more with men, they switched to the standard variant.

Similar results were reached by Abdul-Jawad (1981) who investigated lexical and phonological variation in Amman, Jordan. Analyzing a hundred tapes of interviews, family talk, and public speeches, Abdul-Jawad concludes that using the standard voiceless uvular stop [q] or one of its nonstandard realizations (glottal stop [ʔ], voiced velar stop [g], and voiceless velar stop [k]) is determined by a number of sociolinguistic factors that include age, gender, education, and style. However, he asserts that men used the standard form [q] more than women. Using VARBRUL analysis, Abdul-Jawad finds out that the probability of men's using of the standard [q] was (.66), while that of women was only (.34). He concludes that men favor using the standard because it is associated with education, to which they have more access than women, and also because it is the language variety used in the public domain which they control, whereas women favor using the nonstandard forms because they have more limited access to education than men and as a result of their social functions, which are largely confined to the domestic context. These results, he concludes, contradict the findings of studies investigating gendered linguistic variation in western non diglossic settings which concluded that women used more standard forms than men.

These findings were reiterated by Haeri (1996), who investigated the effect of gender, class, and education on two phonological variables in the speech of Cairenes: 1) the use of *qaf*, the voiceless uvular stop [q], and 2) the palatalization of alveolar stops [t] and [d]. He concludes that educated men used more *qaf* in their speech than women, while women used more tokens of the Cairene Colloquial glottal stop [ʔ]. Although this result mirrors that of Dahir (1997) and Abdul-Jawad (1981), Haeri's explanation of the gender differences is different.

He argues that diglossia and the male dominance of the public sphere are not an adequate explanation of the differences because both Classical Arabic and Egyptian Arabic are languages of the public domain. Haeri concludes that the use of *qaf* is determined by the profession one has rather than the gender. And since more men hold jobs that require the use of standard variety, like teaching and journalism, they use more of this variable than women.

Linguistic Gender Differences in Sudanese Arabic

Introduction and Literature Review

Arabic is not an indigenous Sudanese language. It was introduced by the Arabs who started settling in the country in the seventh Century. It's now spoken by the majority of the population. The varieties of Arabic spoken in Sudan differ along the geographic and social dimensions in addition to their contact with the various native Sudanese languages. The variety investigated in this chapter is spoken in and around the Khartoum province.

Despite the linguistic diversity of the country, few linguistic studies have been carried out in the Sudan. According to my knowledge, only one paper addressing the issue of gendered linguistic differences in Sudanese Arabic has been published. It was written by Hurreiz in 1978. In it, he asserts that social stratification is not clearly defined in the Sudan. Hence, he adds, it cannot be considered a driver of linguistic variation. However, he points out that sex, gender, and education are all factors of linguistic variation. Since his article focuses on gendered linguistic differences in Khartoum and its vicinities, Hurreiz argues that there are two varieties of Sudanese Colloquial Arabic, one spoken by males and the other by females. This, he believes, is the result of the segregation of men and women because the community is predominantly Muslim, and Islam is a religion that "restricts and sanctions the mixing of the two sexes" (p. 42).

Hurreiz states the linguistic indoctrination of Sudanese children starts at a very early age. Boys are brought up to adhere to the language variety used by males, and any deviation from this norm would result in disapproval and punishment. A boy using a feminine linguistic expression would be considered a 'homosexual', a 'sissy', or lacking in masculinity and its attributes. Girls, on the other hand, are also brought up in a manner that ensures their usage of feminine expressions. If a girl uses a masculine expression, she would be reprimanded and accused of masculinity. Crossing the linguistic boundary becomes a more serious violation as children reach adolescence and adulthood. After explaining how social control results in the acquisition of the 'proper' variety, Hurreiz discusses a few linguistic expressions that are exclusively used by women and a couple of others that are exclusively used by men.

Hurreiz lists the following as expressions that are exclusively used by Sudanese women (43)[2]:

bari	'never'
sajam	'woe to [you/ me/ him, etc.]'
iTriʃni/itrishni	'may God make me deaf'
iʕamiini/ya'ameeni	'may God make me blind'
Ixaribni/yakharibni	'may God destroy me'

Then he cites another group of expressions that are also exclusively used by women, pointing out that although the individual lexical items are not gender specific, their collocation with specific words mark the expression as feminine. Examples of this are the words samaʕ (a participial noun which means 'hearing') and aDaan (a noun which means 'ear'). Although either noun can occur in the masculine variety of Sudanese Arabic, the combination samaʕ aDaani (I heard it with my own ears) is an exclusively feminine expression. Other examples of this cited by Hurreiz are the following (44):

ħaal assuuruur	'What a pleasing state!'
ħaal alʕadu/ħaal al'adu	'What a dreadful state!'
ʃofʕeini /shof'eini	'I have seen it with my own eyes.'

The last group of expressions that mark the feminine variety of Sudanese Arabic is what Hurreiz calls one-word sentences. These are exclamations that consist of single words uttered with a rising intonation. Examples include (44):

ħaalan!/halan!	'What a (x) state!'
ʃiitan!/sheetan!	'What a (x) thing!'

Hurreiz argues that the meaning of such exclamations is determined by the context of situation in which they are used. If a woman, for instance, sees something that pleases her, she might exclaim "ħaalan!" meaning "what a pleasing state!" And if she sees something she doesn't like, the same expression would be employed to express her disapproval. Men, on the other hand, react to the above situations by using full sentences like "da ħaal jiʕajib", meaning "this is a pleasing state", or "da ħaal jidʒannin", meaning "this is a maddening state".

Finally, Hurreiz attempts to explain switching between the two varieties in mixed gender interactions. He indicates that regardless of the degree of formality or age, men use the masculine variety when they address women. Hence, Sudanese men always employ the masculine variety in all situations because using a feminine expression is undesirable. Women, according to Hurreiz, switch from the feminine variety to the masculine variety when they are addressing strangers or elderly males. However, when they interact with male relative of the same age, they retain their feminine variety unless a stranger is present. Hurreiz argues that switching varieties can be explained using the framework of encounter and gathering proposed by the sociologist Erving Goffman (1963). More recent

---

[2] Both IPA and conventional transcriptions symbols are used to write the examples.

theories such as Speech Accommodation Theory (Giles, 1973) and Language Style as Audience (Bell, 1984) offer more adequate tools if applied to the explanation of switching. However, since the absence of feminine expressions is associated with the formal variety, it can be contended that a diglossic situation is in play. Hurreiz's assertion that women refrain from using feminine expressions in institutions of education and government offices supports this argument. Since these domains constitute situations in which a more formal variety of the language is functionally appropriate, it is highly unlikely for women to use the feminine expressions discussed above because they are markers of the colloquial associated with the "low variety". However, it should be pointed out that even in institutions of education and government offices the language of interaction is not a highly codified variety that can be labeled 'Standard Arabic'. It is a hybrid that has markers of both. This phenomenon is common all over the Arab world where speakers use multiple varieties in different social situations, which led many sociolinguists to suggest the term 'multiglossia' to explain it.

Subjects and Data

The subjects for this study are 12 native Sudanese, 6 males and 6 females between 30 and 80 years of age. I explained the research objectives to them and asked them to list all the expressions that are exclusively used by one gender in a blue examination notebook that was given out to each one of them. Two weeks later, I collected the notebooks and tabulated the expressions.

Ideally, data for sociolinguistic research should be collected from a larger sample of subjects using the language in authentic situations. However, this was not possible for this research because of the small Sudanese community residing in the town where the author of this chapter lives. Moreover, corpora and data banks for spoken Sudanese Arabic are nonexistent. And finally, it would be extremely difficult to use recorded data for the purpose of investigating exclusive gender differences. Not only are people suspicious of being recorded, but the expressions discussed in this chapter are also used in specific situations that may never arise during the course of an interview.

Feminine Expressions in Sudanese Colloquial Arabic

Before introducing feminine expressions in Sudanese Colloquial Arabic, it is important to reiterate that linguistic gender differences can be categorized into two broad classes. These are gender-exclusive differences, which include forms and expressions that are used by one gender. The other category is gender-preferential differences, which refers to forms and expressions that are preferred by one gender. Although these are used by both genders, they are statistically more frequently used in the dialect of the gender that prefers them. All the differences discussed here are of the former type.

Terms of Endearment.

As the title indicates, these are forms that express affection. These expressions have similar syntactic structures. First, they can all be preceded by the vocative "ya" if the speaker is addressing someone who is present. Second, no vocative is attached if the speaker is talking about someone who is not present in the situational context. And third, each of these expressions constitutes a noun phrase that starts with the word "wad", meaning "boy/son", or "bit", meaning "girl/daughter". However, the antecedent implied by the expression does not have to be of a certain age.

ya bit ummi	'O, my mother's daughter'
ya wad abui	'O, my father's son'
ya bit batni	'O, daughter of my abdomen/belly'
wad alhana	'son of bliss/happiness'
bit almuna	'daughter of good luck/tidings'
wad alsiroor	'son of delight/joy'
wad ridha	'son of contentment/satisfaction'
wad hashay	'son of my bowels/guts'
bit hashay	'daughter of my bowels/guts'

Although these expressions are grouped in one category, there are subtle differences in their usage. The first expression, which is "ya bit ummi" (O, my mother's daughter) is probably the most frequently used one. It's usually used to imply that the addressee is a dearly loved person, just like a 'sister', as the literal meaning of the expression indicates. Expressions that denote an indirect reference to the 'womb or uterus', i.e. "bit/wad batni" (son/daughter of my belly/abdomen) and "wad/bit hashay" (son/daughter of my bowels/guts) are mostly employed by mothers addressing their offspring, regardless of age. The remainder of the expressions, i.e. "wad/bit" (son/daughter) compounded with "alhan, almuna, alsiroor, and alridha" (bliss, good luck, delight, and contentment) are used to express approval or admiration.

As alluded to earlier, the explanation suggested by Hurreiz to explain linguistic gender differences in Sudanese Arabic is social stratification. He believes that because of Islam, which segregates the two sexes, and lack of women's education, the two sexes are brought up as two separate social groups; hence, they speak different varieties of the language. This view is supported by the studies reviewed above that attribute the frequency of certain linguistic forms in the language of women to their segregation and lack of education, which deprive them of the opportunity to acquire the more formal variety of the language used in education, government offices, and other jobs that require a formal education. Although the same may be true of Sudan, an explanation needs to be given as to why these linguistic differences are gender-exclusive in Sudan while they are gender-preferential elsewhere in the Arab World. Considering the expressions discussed in this section, it could be argued that the ones that have a second compounded element associated with the bowels, abdomen, or belly are used by women because they denote their child-bearing role. The remainder of the terms of endearment underscore that women are more verbal and eloquent in expressing their feelings and emotions. These terms are parallel to the ones discussed by Lakoff under 'empty adjectives', e.g. *gorgeous* and *adorable*. It is unfortunate that "empty", with all its negative connotations has been chosen to modify these meaningful adjectives.

Exclamations and Interjections

These are single-word utterances that express strong emotions. They include those cited by Hurreiz (1978).

halan (ḥaalan)	'what a (x) state'
sheetan (ſiitan)	'what a (x) thing'
ajjj	'gosh/gee'
barry	'absolutely not'
kur	'no misfortune'
wai	'ouch

The first two expressions have been discussed in detail in the literature review section above. *Aji* (gosh or gee) is a very common exclamation that expresses surprise or disbelief. Like the other expressions in this category, *aji* is uttered with rising intonation. The degree of disbelief or surprise is also indicated by other paralinguistic features, including tone, volume, and facial expressions like raised eyebrows and dropped jaw. To express surprise or disbelief, men use the expressions "ma/mush ma'agool" or "ma/mush mumkin", which mean "this cannot be true." The next exclamation, *barry*, indicates emphatic denial. If a remark or a deed is attributed to a woman who has not said or done it, she might emphatically deny it by remarking *barry*. A Sudanese male in the same situation would say "ma hasal" (this did not happen). The next to last expression, *kur*, is used to dispel evil or ward off bad happenings. It is employed when a misfortune befalls someone. *Kur* is exclaimed in a variety of situations ranging from a simple fall to a serious disease. This could be used to express the speaker's sympathy and her wish for a positive outcome, to dispel any evil that might inflict her with the same misfortune, or both. Since there is no other term in Sudanese Colloquial Arabic that has the pragmatic versatility of *kur*, what Sudanese males in situations of misfortune depends on the circumstance. A man would likely say "ya satir" ("O Protector God"!) if someone falls down. In more serious situations the likely response would be a supplication or prayer to alleviate the misfortune. Finally, the interjection *wai* is used for the expression of pain. Its male counterpart is *akh*.

As discussed above, *Halan* and S*heetan*, "what an 'x' state" and "what an 'x' thing", are used by women to express their extreme satisfaction or dissatisfaction with certain states or things. Again, it can be argued that women are not afraid of expressing their feelings and they can do that by employing a single word, with a rising intonation and the facial expressions that suit the situation. Since men never use these single-word expressions, they have to resort to longer utterances to achieve the same communicative goal. And since these same utterances used by men are not gender-exclusive, which makes their use by women possible, it could be argued that Sudanese women have a richer repertoire to choose from.

On the other hand, the interjections *kur*, *barry*, and *wai* do not seem to have any semantic significance, although they are pragmatically viable in the situations shown above. *Kur*, used to ward off misfortune and evil, is probably an incantation like the mystical word 'abracadabra'. Superstitions, the belief in magic, and the fear of the unknown are all widespread in Sudan, especially in uneducated communities. And since women have not had equal access to education, they have traditionally been the ones who sought fetishes and amulets, practiced fortune-telling and divination, and burned incense in their home, particularly at sunset when evil spirits are believed to be more active. Therefore, the interjection *kur* could be a remnant of an evil-dispelling ritual that Sudanese women used to perform.

Metaphors in Distress

Since the first five of the expressions discussed in this section include the words *ramad* 'ashes' or *sajam* 'soot', it is important to explain the source domain from which they are derived. One of the basic responsibilities of a Sudanese woman as homemaker or house wife is to cook for her family. Before the introduction of cooking gas and modern utensils, wood was used as fuel. And when the wood was burnt inside these traditional kitchens in an already hot climate, the conditions become unbearable. In addition to this, women have to tolerate the flying sparks, ashes, and smoke. This source domain gave rise to the following metaphoric expressions that are used in distress situations.

sajami	'my soot/soot on me'
sajam khashmi	'soot of my mouth/soot in my mouth'
sajami wa ramadi	'my soot and my ashes/soot and ashes on me'
museebat alsajam	'calamity of soot'
museebat alsawad wa alramad	'blackness and ashes calamity'
wob alay	'woe !'
hai wob	'lamentation interjection'

These metaphors, except the last one, are used in a variety of distress situations ranging from minor unfortunate accidents to the passing away of loved ones. The last one is only used to mourn dead people. *Sajami* is probably the most frequently used one. If a woman hears about a relative or a friend encountering a mishap such as falling ill or losing a job, she remarks '*sajami*'! This term may be repeated for emphasis to denote a higher degree of distress. Moreover, it can also be compounded with *khasmi*, 'my mouth', or *ramadi*, 'ashes', to achieve the same result, i.e. expressing a more profound degree of desolation. *Museebat alsajam*, 'calamity of soot', and *museebat alsawad wa alramad*, 'blackness and ashes calamity' mean that this mishap is as distressful as the passing away of a dear person. Black color, soot, and ashes are all metonyms of lamentation and mourning. In Sudan, like all Islamic countries, women are not permitted to go to the cemetery. However, when the body is prepared for burial they follow it for a distance, wailing and scattering ashes over themselves. Although this latter practice is no longer common, the expression alluding to it still exists.

It is evident that the source domain of most of the expressions is associated with the traditional Sudanese kitchen and women's social role of cooking. Metonyms derived from this domain are used by Sudanese women to express grief and distress. Needless to say, men also experience the same emotions; however, in Sudanese culture it is completely undesirable for men to cry or express their emotions. The culture stipulates certain characteristics for males. These include being stern and the ability to keep emotions suppressed.

Masculine Expressions in Sudanese Colloquial Arabic

The feminine expressions discussed above are diverse and vivid. They express a variety of situations that reflect women's social roles, e.g. child bearing and rearing, cooking, lamenting and mourning. However, the masculine expressions discussed below are limited in scope and they only reflect a single social role of men, which is divorce initiation.

Divorce Expressions

alay altalaq	'divorce is upon me'
alay alharam	'my wife/wives is/are prohibited for me'
tallaq	'divorce is upon me'
harram	'my wife/wives is/are prohibited for me'

All these terms denote an oath in which a male swears that he will divorce his wife if she doesn't carry out a certain act. For example, a man may swear that he will divorce his wife if she ever talks to someone again. The expressions are also used in situations where the person who swears beseeches someone else to do something. For instance, a man may say "divorce is upon me that you have dinner with us". Muslim scholars regard these oaths as baseless, unlawful, and unbinding for several reasons. First, they argue that when a Muslim swears, he or she should do so by "Allah", the creator because he is the only entity worthy of being sworn by. Second, although divorce is permitted in Islam, it is advised that it should only be sought in extreme cases where all options for reconciliation have been explored. And third, since the person who swears has no control over what other people do, it is unwise and futile to swear that somebody else does something or refrains from doing it. Nevertheless, married Sudanese males continue to employ these oaths. Most of them, however, do not follow through and divorce their wives if the oath is not fulfilled. Women never use these expressions because divorce is always initiated by men.

Interaction and Code-Switching

Hurreiz discusses the situations in which women use or refrain from using what he calls 'the feminine variety'. The account he presents is by and large true. However, it is inaccurate to refer to the variety used by women in formal situation or in the presence of strangers as 'the masculine variety'. By the same token, 'the feminine variety' is not a precise reference to the language employed by women in informal settings where they intimately interact with family and friends. Both men and women speak the colloquial variety in informal settings and they may employ gender-exclusive expressions in the situations alluded to above. Since these gender-exclusive expressions are few in number, that does not warrant designating the varieties as male or female.

Hurreiz also claims that as women break the segregation barrier, get admitted into institutions of higher education, and become employed, their exposure to the 'male variety' increases. Moreover, he adds, they are also expected to use that variety at government offices, businesses, and universities. Although it is true that the variety used in such formal situations is more formal, calling it a masculine variety is not an accurate nomenclature. Because of the diglossic, or multiglossic, situation in the Sudan, different varieties of the language are used in different social situations. As a consequence of the male dominance of these situations in which the "H" variety is employed, i.e. education, the media, government offices, and businesses, it is unjustifiably called 'the masculine variety'. If it were, then it would be spoken by all males, which is not true because uneducated ones do not acquire it.

Conclusion

This chapter investigated gender-exclusive differences, an uncommon linguistic phenomenon, in Sudanese colloquial Arabic. It is hypothesized that factors such as patriarchy and biased interpretations of Islamic texts resulted in the segregation of women, limiting their education and prescribing to them specific social roles confined to the domestic domain. Consequently, women developed a number of expressions associated with these roles. These expressions have been classified into three classes, which are "terms of endearment", "exclamations and interjections", and "metaphors of distress.

Terms of endearment are expressions that display the speaker's affection to a loved one. Some of these include words that denote the uterus, or womb. It is argued that such terms originated as a result of the child-bearing and child-rearing experiences. Since mothers are the ones who get pregnant, give birth, nurse and nurture the children, they use terms and expressions that reflect their affection by evoking these experiences. The second category, which includes exclamations and interjections, has miscellaneous expressions that include *kur*, which may be a remnant of an evil-expelling ritual. Warding off evil from the domestic domain is one of the social roles of Sudanese women. Incense burning during certain times of the day is still practiced by women in the Sudan and it is widely believed that it guards against evil and misfortune. The third and last class of exclusive feminine expressions is metaphors of distress. These are expressions that include words associated with the traditional Sudanese kitchen such as *sajam* and *ramad* "soot and ashes" which are employed to express misery, suffering, and grief. Although men use these two terms, they never use them in the same situations discussed in section 3.3.3. A Sudanese male may refer to someone or address him/her as *sajam*, meaning 'worthless'. Women, however, use the kitchen experience as a source domain from which they create several vivid metaphors that they use in stressful conditions.

Men, on the other hand, use a few gender-exclusive terms, all of which are oaths. They employ such expressions to swear that they will divorce their wife/wives if they don't do or if somebody else does not do something that is specified at the time the oath is undertaken. Since divorce in the Sudanese society is initiated by males, such oaths are never sworn by women.

If a member of one gender uses an expression that is exclusively used by the other, this will be considered a violation of the sociolinguistic rules. Since the exclusively male expressions are few in number, and because women never employ them, the possibility of a male using a female expression is more likely. When that happens, the individual will be reprimanded. For instance, if a male expresses pain by saying *wai*, the female exclamation, instead of *akh*, the male one, he will be called *khayib* or *batil*, which are very stigmatized terms that means the person is not straight or gay. Therefore, from a very early age, as Hurreiz pointed out, boys are instructed to make the right linguistic choice by avoiding feminine expressions. If they fail to do so, they are not only reprimanded, but they may also be physically punished, Hurreiz also states that the same is not true for girls. As alluded to above, male–exclusive expressions are few in number and limited to swearing. Therefore, the only possibility for a female to use them is mimicking or playing the role of a male.

Since these gender-exclusive expressions are associated with the traditional gender roles in the Sudan, and because more and more women are entering the public domain, it seems that the younger generations are using these expressions less frequently. This, however, needs to be verified by further research that investigates the frequency of occurrence of these linguistic forms by different age groups.

References

Abdul-Jawad, Hassan R. "Lexical and Phonological Variation in Spoken Arabic in Amman." Ph.D. diss., University of Pennsylvania, 1981.

Bell, Allan. "Language Style as Audience Design." *Language in Society,* vol. 16, no 2 (1984): 145-204.

Dahir, Jamil. "Gender in Linguistic Variation: The Variable (q) in Damascus Arabic." *Perspectives on Arabic Linguistics XI; Papers from the Eleventh Annual Symposium on Arabic Linguistics,* no. 1 (1998): 183-206.

de Ruiter, Jan Jaap. "The Gender of Standard Arabic." In *O ye Gentlemen: Arabic studies on Science and Literary Culture,* edited by Arnoud Vrolijk and Jan P. Hogendijk, 407-19. Leiden, the Netherlands: Brill, 2002.

Ferguson, Charles. "Diglossia." *Word,* no. 15 (1959): 325-40.

Foley, William. *Anthropological Linguistics: An Introduction.* Malden, MA: Blackwell Publishing, 1997.

Giles, Howard. "Accent Mobility: A Model and Some Data." *Anthropological Linguistics,* vol. 15 (1973): 87-105.

Goffman, Erving. *Stigma.* London: Penguin. 1963.

Hachimi, Atiqa. "Shifting Sands: Language and Gender in Moroccan Arabic." In *Gender Across Languages: The Linguistic Representation of Women and Men,* edited by Marlis Hellinger and Hadmund Bubmann, 27-51. Amsterdam: John Benjamins, 2001.

Haeri, Niloofar. *Sociolinguistic Variation in Cairene Arabic: Palatalization and the qaf in the Speech Men and Women.* Ph.D. diss., University of Pennsylvania, 1991.

Hurreiz, Sayyed Hamid. "Social Stratification and Linguistic Variation in Khartoum and Its Vicinity." In *Aspects of Language in the Sudan,* edited by Robin Thelwall, 41-9. Ulster, Northern Ireland: The New University of Ulster, 1978.

Lakoff, Robin. *Language and Women's Place.* New York: Harper and Row, 1975.

McElhinny, Bonnie. "Theorizing Gender in Sociolinguistics and Linguistics Anthropology. In *Handbook of Language and gender,* edited by Janet Holmes and Miriam Meyerhof, 21-42. Oxford: Basil Blackwell, 2003.

Sadiqi, Fatima. *Women, Gender, and Language in Morocco.* Leident and Boston: Brill, 2003.

Wolfram, Walt, and Schilling-Estes, Natalie. *American English*, 2nd edition, Oxford: Blackwell, 2006.

Chapter 9: Naming Places, Establishing Divides: Gender and Linguistic Territorialization among Sri Lankan Students

Cala Zubair, State University of New York—Buffalo

Abstract: A Sri Lankan student group known as The Sinhalese Raggers has developed terms to describe designated "Ragger" areas of campus (place names). These place names infuse sites with significance in relation to the Raggers community, additionally creating ethnic boundaries that carve out monolingual, mono-ethnic spaces amidst a diverse student population. While males provide positive descriptions of Ragger place names and the ethnic boundaries they create, females question their exclusivity. This paper explores how students' distinctive interpretations of place names represent varying attitudes towards circulating public ideologies as well as differing tolerances towards non-Sinhalese ethnicities. By associating geographic space with linguistic terms connected to ethnopolitical divides, place names infuse sites with ideologies available for group members to variably orient towards.

The Sinhalese Raggers and Linguistic Territorialization

As one of the primary media through which we express our connection to our surroundings, language attaches us to a place. The phenomenon I'll explore in this presentation focuses on how university youth interpret their surroundings through the naming of places and what I call *linguistic territorialization* - that is, the discursive processes involved in claiming a space as one's own, or using language to *territorialize* a place. Speakers achieve this first by expressing interlocutors' unique relationship and understanding of a place, and second, by addressing and altering the relationship of outside or othered individuals to that place.

The term linguistic territorialization comes easily enough. The community I studied for this project – a group of Sinhalese university students in central Sri Lanka who call themselves Raggers – have many community practices (in addition to language use) that pivot around demarcating campus space as Ragger territory. The Raggers group name comes from their practices of ritual hazing, which range from the mildly comical (forcing groups members to cross dress or recite sappy love poems to strangers) to the overtly cruel (stonings, beatings, and other forms of punitive physical action). Raggers hazing practices crucially center on specific campus places Raggers demarcate as their own. The community's goals of forming a cohesive group include familiarizing Raggers with Ragger campus space and terms for Ragger campus space. Thus, one of the linguistic ways Ragger territory is set apart from other areas of campus is through place names. This process of naming campus space so as to claim it for their own is part of Raggers' linguistic territorialization. But this process is not only a process of naming.

Territorialization is also overwritten with community discourses that encapsulate Ragger ideologies within the name of a territory and are readily available for group members to engage with through discursive acts such as stance-taking, aligning or disaligning with overarching Ragger discourses, or language use indexing facets of a speaker's identity, such as gender, ethnicity, and religion. As we'll see through interview conversations with the four speakers I examine here (two males and two females), linguistic territorialization involves using similar place names, but with different interpretations and different assessments of the other. This results in variation of the imagined boundaries of campus space and variation in orientation to group specific ideologies.

Place Names as Self-Conscious Language Use

Work on language and personal identity has considered place insofar as language varies based on locale, functioning to reflect a person's dialect. In other words, regional features may read New Englander or Upper Midwesterner (Wolfram and Schilling-Estes 2006, Chapter 5), where people speak in ways that give the perception they are from a particular place (Preston 1989; Niedzielski and Preston 2003; Johnstone, Andrus, and Danielson 2006).

Places, however, are not monolithic spaces inhabited by individuals who all share the same identities or linguistic habits. This is particularly true in multilingual societies like Sri Lanka, where competing ethnicities (Sinhalese, Tamil, and Muslim) inhabit the same spaces and are often identified based on language use. In Sri Lanka, the Sinhalese ethnic majority usually identifies Sinhala as a native or primary language, while Muslim and Tamil minorities often identify with the Tamil language. When it comes to place names in areas with mixed Sinhalese, Muslim, and Tamil communities, places often have two closely related but variable names, one in Tamil and one in Sinhalese. The name a speaker uses in discourse aligns them with a recognizable ethnic population. Thus, when space is under dispute or co-habited by diverse groups, speakers may self-consciously use language to lay claim to a place. Studies such as Schilling-Estes (1998, 2002), Johnstone (1999), and Coupland (2001) analyze how self-conscious speech is a way for speakers to express ties to a place during acts of identity construction. As Johnstone (2011) indicates, "place identity [can be] evoked through self-conscious use of linguistic features," in turn playing a role in individual or group identity building. Using language to territorialize a space (linguistic territorialization), Sinhalese Raggers provide an example of how speakers overtly express their ties to a place through language.

Modan (2007) describes processes similar to territorialization in her discussion of "turf wars" in a multi-ethnic, multi-class neighborhood of Washington, DC. In Mt. Pleasant, old and new residents create discourses that mimic their battles for neighborhood territory, using language to legitimize themselves as community members while discrediting others. Raggers' linguistic choices in relation to place names are a similar means to stake claim to university campus spaces, both through their choice of names for a particular place, as well and through the links they make between a place name and facets of group identity. These claims relate most directly to ethnicity, but also reveal gender dynamics within the community. In the following section, I examine the way four speakers discuss the territories they imagine Ragger place names to create, exploring the links between language, ethnicity, place, and the way males versus females ideologically divide campus territory.

Variable Interpretations of Place Names

The following list represents a sample of the most commonly used place names Ragger subjects identified: *Ala Gadans, Banti Wimana, Gemba Kantima, Jeppa Wila, Maessa Kantima, Polonnaruwa,* and *Thatta place*. For the purpose of this study, I focus only on the last two terms: *Thatta place* and *Polonnaruwa*. While other place names were used frequently in conversation, *Thatta place* and *Polonnaruwa* generated the most controversy between speakers as male and female subjects created different ethnic territories through their discourses about them.

	Term	*Meaning*
1	අල ගඩාන්ස් (*Ala Gadans*)	The garden of students not involved with the Raggers
2	බන්ටි විමන (*Banti Wimana*)	Area used by Raggers to engage in sexual activities
3	ගෙම්බා කැන්ටිම (*Gemba Kantima*)	Canteen or lunch area for the Raggers
4	ජෙප්ප විල (*Jeppa Wila*)	Raggers' lake
5	මැස්සා කැන්ටිම (*Mæssa Kantima*)	Canteen or lunch area for non-Raggers
6	පොලොන්නරුව (*Polonnaruwa*)	Open space for Ragger gatherings
7	තට්ට ප්ලේස් (*Thatta place*)	Creek used by Raggers for hazing

Thatta place

Thatta place literally means "bold place" and is a term which names an area of the creek that flows across the university used by seniors Raggers to haze junior Raggers. Junior students are often asked to wash in the often cold water of the creek, or may be brought here to wash seniors' clothes. Raggers also use this place to store alcohol – which is prohibited on campus - and often involved in hazing. In many ways, this location is a Ragger headquarters of sorts and a training ground for enculturating incoming students. As such, the use of the term presents speakers with an opportunity to align with hazing, which is central to group's behavior and identity. This is how two male speakers (whom I call 'Buddhika' and 'Harendra') discuss *Thatta place*.

Thatta place – males (Buddhika = B; Harendra = H)

1   Cala: When do incoming freshers learn to use the name *Thatta place*?

2   B: All know *Thatta place* by the first few weeks – even most freshers come to know by the end of the first week-

3   H: …or first few days, *mee* [discourse marker]…

4   B: And Anti-Raggers will know as well…*mee* because they are **not welcome** at the *Thatta place*.

5   Cala: Why do you think Raggers started using this term to describe the area by the creek?

6   H: The name shows how **ragging is important** – we need a place for it – away from watching eyes who don't understand the importance. Ragging is *thatta* ["<u>bold</u>"] because to be a Ragger a fresher needs to learn this. That's what the **Sinhalese** are.

7   B: If you are not a Ragger, you are **not welcome** in the *Thatta place* because you cannot **endure** being a part of the group.

(Note on code choice: Speakers often chose to use English when speaking with me. I was perceived by the community as an outsider, and my ties to English were apparent. Some younger subjects indicated that senior Raggers instructed them not to speak in Sinhala, warning that I might be an invasive presence. This is an example of how the community was often very secretive and protective of its practices.)

Exclusivity: In line 4, male 1 (Buddhika) identifies Thatta place as an exclusive space, a space for Raggers where Anti-Raggers (those not in the Raggers group) are unwelcome. He reiterates this in line 7: "**if you are not a Ragger, you are unwelcome**". Using the term to territorialize the space by interpreting it as a place where only certain students may frequent, Buddhika expresses the Raggers' relationship to the place by creating an othered group who Raggers do not allow to have a physical connection with the place.

Ragging as important & bold: But more specifically, what sets Raggers apart from Anti-Raggers? As Harendra indicates in line 6, ragging sets them apart, an "important" activity (line 6) that is central to how the group members adopt and shape younger students. Harendra tells us that *thatta* means "**bold**", something freshmen are taught through ritual hazing at the *Thatta place*. Thus, the word *thatta* in *thatta place* functions to evaluate ragging as a practice for which this space is demarcated.

Sinhalese endurance: Harendra further connects being a "bold" Ragger to being a member of the Sinhalese ethnicity. The othered category is not just students who chose not to join the Raggers group, but non-Sinhalese ethnicities – Tamil and Muslim students. Buddhika supports Harendra's statement in line 7, suggesting non-Raggers, and by extension non-Sinhalese, cannot "**endure**" ragging processes that group members undergo.

For Buddhika and Harendra the name *Thatta place* invokes an exclusive space where bold Sinhalese endure ragging. Rather than seeing *thatta place* as a name that upholds the dignity of the Raggers group and the Sinhalese ethnicity, in the example below, female speakers Buddhi and Eranga view the name as a contradiction.

Thatta place – females *(Buddhi = B; Eranga = E)*

1 B: *Thatta place* is a **silly name**. **Biagulu ["coward"]** would be more like it because senior Raggers get drunk on their power and abuse poor, little freshers-

2 E: We were lucky that our seniors last year showed us things about Raggers, but we didn't do too much ragging-

3 B: not like the guys!

4 Cala: What sort of ragging did you und- have?

5 E: Mostly with dress – a few times we had to pro-protest an instructor-

6 B: English instructor – and I had to sing a love song to some *modaiya* ["stupid person"].

7 Cala: Is the term *Thatta place* important for Raggers?

8 E: It's important to know – but it just shows how **silly** ragging can be sometimes.

Silly: Rather than demarcating this space as a place of boldness, both Buddhi and Eranga indicate that it is a place of sillyness (line 1 & 8). In line 1, Buddhi calls the word *thatta* a "silly" name. She explains that activities that occur in that place relate to fear the freshermen Raggers have and bullying by the seniors. The new term she offers up is "coward" (*biagulu*). This term encompasses both seniors who "get drunk on their power and abuse poor, little freshers" (line 1) and freshmen who may feel fear during hazing. In line 8, Eranga extends the descriptor "silly" to ragging itself. By rejecting a central practice of the Raggers community, Eranga distances herself from the Sinhalese Ragger identity we saw expressed by Harendra and Buddhika. Neither female views ragging as "bold," nor *Thatta place* as a place of boldness that glorifies the Sinhalese Raggers. In choosing a new name, Buddhi questions the territorialization the male conversation constructed.

Polonnaruwa

Polonnaruwa is the name of a vacationing and tourist spot in Northern, central Sri Lanka known for housing the ruins of an 11th century Sinhalese-Buddhist city. Raggers use this term to name the open space next to the Faculty of Arts building said to resemble the ancient city of *Polonnaruwa* because of the building ruins located here. Males see the use of the term as opportunity to align with a nationalist, pro-Sinhalese-Buddhist ideology that promotes pro-Sinhalese Buddhist ethnicity/religion at the expense of Tamil and Muslim minority ethnicities, including English language speaking groups.

Polonnaruwa – males *(Buddhika = B; Harendra = H)*

1 Cala: Where does the term *Polonnaruwa* come from?

2 B: *Polonnaruwa* is famous ruin –ruins- the North -

3 H: In the North, central province. What we have on campus doesn't compare….but saying our hang out spot is *Polonnaruwa…ithing, ithing* ["this, this"] respects our history as **Sinhalese** – as *mee* [discourse marker] **disciples of Buddha**…*mee*

4 Cala: What other history could your group be associated with if this term wasn't used?

5 B: The Tamil tiger terrorists.

6 H: Or their supporters – The English.

7 B: We are all Sinhalese – we don't mix with non-Sinhalese or Buddhist or Anti-Raggers who have chosen English over their roots.

8 Cala: Does anyone outside your group know the term *Polonnaruwa*, do you think?

9 B: The **Sinhalese** [language] is on the rock- on the lawn there [*pointing across the courtyard*]. They know **who it belongs to and what we stand for**.

Sinhalese: In line 3, Harendra tells us that he perceives the name *Polonnaruwa* as having a direct link with Sinhalese-Buddhist history: "**saying our hang out spot is *Polonnaruwa…ithing, ithing* ["this, this"] respects our history as Sinhalese – as *mee* disciples of Buddha**". For him *Polonnaruwa* indexes a Sinhalese identity. This Sinhalese identity is transferred to the Ragger's campus spot through use of the name. In case an outsider or Ragger forgets what this territory is, or who it belongs to, Buddhika indicates that it is literally written in stone: "The **Sinhalese** [language] is on the rock- on the lawn there [*pointing across the* *courtyard*]. They know **who it belongs to and what we stand for**". On a rock that stands out from the pile of ruins, the name *Polonnaruwa* is spray-painted in white Sinhala script. For these males, the place name territorializes the space as Sinhalese.

The place name also territorializes this space as Ragger. Buddhika notes in line 7 that "**we are all Sinhalese**" – meaning all Raggers – and non-Raggers are unwelcome: "**we don't mix with non-Sinhalese or Buddhist or Anti-Raggers**". Two lines earlier, Buddhika has specified that "non-Sinhalese" include Tamils (whom he refers to as "**terrorists**"). In line 7, he also excludes those "**who have chosen English over their roots**". In using *Polonnaruwa* to territorialize this space, Buddhika defines an othered group prohibited from accessing the place. Taken together, lines 3, 7, and 9 show a clustering of the descriptors "Sinhalese". Line 3 links Sinhalese to the place name, line 7 to Raggers, and line 9 ties Ragger space to *Polonnaruwa* as in the diagram below.

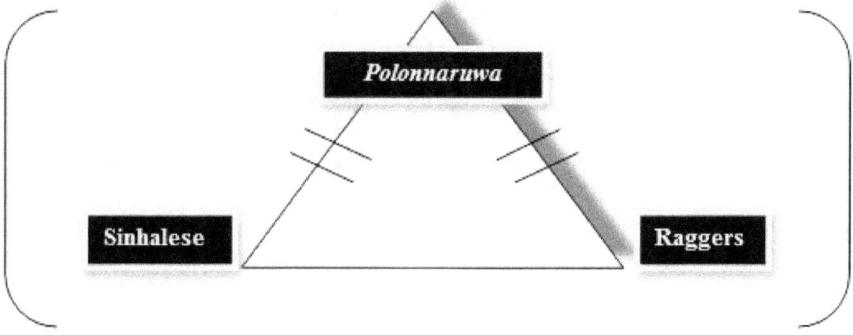

Figure 1: Buddhika and Harendra discursively link the Raggers with *Polunnaruwa* and *Polunnaruwa* with the Sinhalese ethnicity

For males, the name *Polonnaruwa* overwrites the space with pro-Sinhalese-Buddhist sentiment, anti- everyone else. Again, the females are not so rigid in drawing the boundaries of Ragger territory. Instead, they question the legitimacy of applying the place name *Polonnaruwa* to a spot on campus that is exclusively accessible to Raggers.

***Polonnaruwa – females** (Buddhi = B; Eranga = E)*

1   Cala: Can you comment on how Raggers use the word *Polu- Polonnaruwa*?

2   B: It's sad that the **Sinhalese word there is spelled wrong** [referring to the rock where the term *Polonnaruwa* is spelled *Polunaruwa*].

3   E: [*laughs*] We really **have to use the name-** but **the misspelling shows it's backwards**. If seniors think this means we are more Buddhist, they forget that Buddhism is tolerance.

4   B: And those few rocks **can't compare** to the actual *Polonnaruwa* – up North.

5   E: And you have **Tamils, Muslims, Burghers, tourists, all sorts of races and individuals** – not just Sinhalese!

6   Cala: Would you pick a different name for the spot?

7   E: *Polonnaruwa* is fine – only **campus is open to all and some Raggers can't see that *Polonnaruwa* means this**.

Legitimacy: In line 2, Buddhi immediately draws into question the legitimacy of using the term *Polonnaruwa* by pointing out that the spray painted script is incorrect if meant to resemble the ancient city (*Polonnaruwa* is incorrectly spelled *Polunaruwa*). Eranga backs Buddhi's assessment up by saying, "**the misspelling shows it's backwards**" (line 3). Rather than embracing the use of the place name, Eranga indicates they "**have to use the name**" (line 3), "have" being an auxiliary that indicates a necessity we can assume comes from pressure within the community to know and use Ragger place names. Buddhi additionally questions the legitimacy of the place name by saying that the ruins on campus "**can't compare to the actual *Polonnaruwa***" (line 4).

Eranga then re-territorializes the Ragger *Polonnaruwa* by re-interpreting the term. The ancient ruins are open to all, "**Tamils, Muslims, Burghers, tourists, all sorts of races and individuals**" (line 5). She breaks the link in the chain that Buddhika and Harendra created where *Polonnaruwa* was equated with the Sinhalese ethnicity.

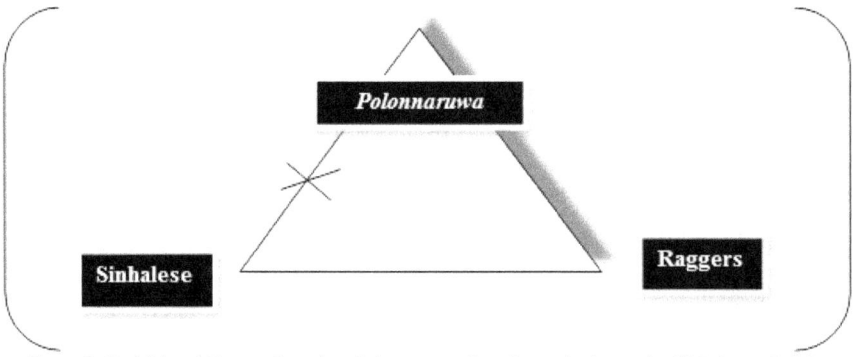

Figure 2: Buddhi and Eranga deny that *Polunnaruwa* is a site exclusive to the Sinhalese ethnicity

Since Raggers are all Sinhalese and have created exclusive physical territories, this makes the use of the place name inappropriate. The link between the name *Polonnaruwa* and the Raggers group is now broken. There is no othered group assumed by the name *Polonnaruwa* because the Northern ruins is not an exclusive territory.

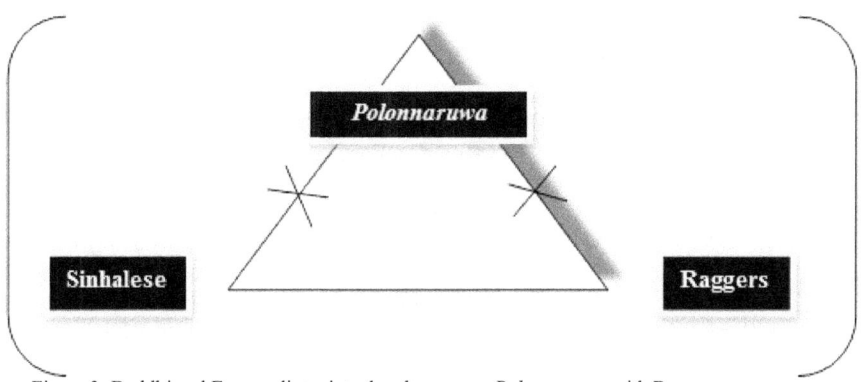

Figure 3: Buddhi and Eranga dissociate the place name *Polunnaruwa* with Ragger campus space

Conclusion

As an integral way for Raggers to claim certain spots of campus space as their own, place names are a discursive site where speakers may participate or protest assumed physical boundaries and their ideological links. While males use place names like *Thatta place* and *Polonnaruwa* to support their Sinhalese ragging community, females either question the names (*Thatta place*) or re-interpret their meaning (*Polonnaruwa*). For the latter term, speakers' distinctive interpretations represent varying attitudes towards circulating public ideologies of Sinhalese-Buddhist nationalism. Male interpretations of *Polonnaruwa* reflect an ethnopolitical territorialization that mirrors recent rises in nationalism. Females, on the other hand, show tolerance towards non-Sinhalese ethnicities, similar to how they show tolerance towards non-Ragger students in their discussion of *Thatta place*. These variable perspectives occur as part of a larger pattern in the community where males and females exhibit opposing opinions towards Ragger culture, thus varying in how they link language and physical space. By associating places on their campus with linguistic terms connected to ethnopolitical and student divisions, Raggers use place names to infuse sites with ideologies available for group members to variably territorialize and orient towards

References

Coupland, Nikolas. 2001. Dialect Stylization in Radio Talk. Language in Society 30: 3, pp 345-375.

Johnstone, Barbara. 1999. Uses of Southern-sounding Speech by Contemporary Texas Women. Journal of Sociolinguistics 3, pp 505-522.

Johnstone, Barbara, Jennifer Andrus and Andrew Danielson. 2006. Mobility, Indexicality, and the Enregisterment of "Pittsburghese" Journal of English Linguistics 34: 2, pp 77-104.

Johnstone, Barbara. 2011. Language and Place. Cambridge Handbook of Sociolinguistics. Ed. Rajend Mesthrie. Cambridge: Cambridge University Press.

Modan, Gabriella. 2007. Turf Wars: Discourse, Diversity, and the Politics of

Place. Oxford: Blackwell.
Niedzielski, Nancy and Dennis Preston. 2003. Folk Linguistics. Berlin: de Gruyter.
Preston, Dennis. 1989. Perceptual Dialectology: Nonlinguists' Views of Areal Linguistics. Berlin: de Gruyter.
Schilling-Estes, N. 1998. Investigating 'self-conscious' speech: The performance register in Ocracoke English. Language in Society 27: 53-83.
Schilling-Estes, N. 2002. Investigating stylistic variation. In Chambers, J.K., P. Trudgill, and N. Schilling-Estes (eds.), Handbook of Language Variation and Change. Malden, MA: Blackwell.
Wolfram, Walt and Natalie Schilling-Estes. 2006. American English: Dialects and Variation 2nd edition. Oxford: Blackwell.

Chapter 10: Linguistic Differentiation in the Ekegusii Language

Martha Michieka[1] and Hellen Ondari[2]

Abstract: Language use is clearly related to social meaning, and it is also true that language powerfully conveys cultural values. A significant amount of earlier research tended to focus on sexism in language and the argument that language use favors men over women. Such research sought to expose the male dominance in language regulation and other forms of sexist practices. These studies, such as work by Lakoff (1975), which were mainly done in literate western cultures, suggest that "Men signaled their authority in language through their roles in the dictionary making process, in the writing of normative grammars, in the establishment of language academies and other normative language institutions, ..." (Pauwels, 2011 p. 148). Some of the studies that have followed from other contexts such as gender studies from African contexts have used the same western ideologies to study gender variation (e.g. Choti 1995, Githinji 2008, Mukama 2002, Wango, 1998). This paper explores the gender differences in the Ekegusii language, an African Bantu language spoken by the Gusii people of South Western Kenya. The Ekegusii language, though rapidly changing due to globalization to incorporate a number of western values, is still firmly grounded in traditional values that are fundamentally different from the value systems that have shaped most of the theories governing gender studies. In our paper we argue that the gender differences in linguistic practices constructed through social practices within the Gusii community do not necessarily imply inequality. While there are specific linguistic forms that Gusii men tend to use more frequently in their speech, just like there are forms that women tend to use more frequently, we resist the orientation that gender studies imply study of female subordination versus male domination. We argue instead that the Ekegusii language presents evidence for gender difference rather than gender inequality. This study will focus on the lexicon used to refer to Gusii women, and how this lexicon when

---

[1] East Tennessee State University
[2] University of East Africa Baraton

carefully analyzed for meaning reflects difference instead of women's subordination.

Introduction

Language and Gender emerged as a serious discipline in its own right with the rise of feminist studies, especially those pioneered by Robin Lakoff in her 1975 book *Language and Woman's Place*. The discipline deals with two aspects of language. On the one hand, the discipline looks at how genders speak and write. On the other hand, it looks at how genders are spoken or written about. A significant amount of research conducted between the early 60s through the 90s on language and gender tended to focus on sexism in language and the argument that language use favors men over women. Such research was influenced by the Women's Liberation Movement which characterized that period, turning those years into a period of intense feminist activity in the United States of America and the Western World at large. As Lakoff (2004) states, "The women's movement first exploded taboos, speaking the unspeakable, thinking the unthinkable, occasionally even doing the undoable" (p.17). The movement was a social struggle which, through public demonstrations and other strategies for intervention, sought to sensitize people in the western world to the disadvantaged position of women in society, professionally, politically, culturally and socially. It was an intellectual commitment and political movement that sought justice for women and the end of sexism in all forms.

Studies have in the past also focused on the question "Do men and women speak differently?" Traditionally two explanations have been dominant in addressing this question about gender linguistic differences: the dominance approach and the difference approach. The dominance approach, spearheaded by Lakoff (1975), sees women as an oppressed group and interprets linguistic differences between women and men's speech as a reflection of men's dominance and women's subordination. Identifying some of the features of what she calls "women's language", Lakoff argues that women use these features, such as hedging, super polite forms and hypercorrect grammar in their language because they are denied means of strong expression within a male dominated society. Adherents to this dominant theory, however, have generalized Lakoff's impressionistic conclusions, which were not based on any empirical study, but rather on her own intuitions about language use and on limited data collected from the speech of heterosexual White Middle Class American women, to include women from other cultures in the world. As a result these claims have generated considerable debate and have been intensively investigated by various researchers. Her claims have been associated with "a deficit model of women's language use – she seems to be suggesting that the way women speak is inadequate in several aspects" (Swann p. 227). Lakoff's claims have also been criticized on the basis that they do not necessarily reflect the reality of the female speech community. Moreover, her lexical gender markers have been viewed as lacking accuracy and being mere stereotypes. The deficit model also fails to take into account the fact that society is dynamic, and there have been changes overtime on the outlook on women due to various influences such as education, religion and interaction with other cultures. Weatherall (2002) for example, cites

O'Barr and Atkins' 1980 study, which suggests that the features identified by Lakoff as characteristic of women's language were not necessarily "a function of gender but a function of power" (p. 65). These features were identified with people of lower status, and since not all women have lower status, the features were not restricted to women only. Men of lower status displayed the features when interacting with their bosses, just like women of lower status.

Eckert and McConnell-Ginet (2004) observe that although the proposals resulting from Lakoff's work have been supported by observations from everyday interactions, the proposals remain weak due to their lack of a coherent theoretical framework within which to define and further explore them. Eckert and McConnell-Ginet further observe that "gender and language suffer the problem of too much abstraction from the social practices of the communities that produce those particular speech forms" (484). Despite these weaknesses and criticisms of the dominance approach, the approach has continued to hold power in explaining gender linguistic difference and in influencing daily practices and interactions both positively and negatively. Weatherall (2002), for instance, cites an example of the negative influences of the dominance approach in work places where women are trained to speak like men as a way of trying to "empower" them.

The tendency for men and women to talk differently has been explained by the difference approach as being a result of diverse acculturation or due to cultural differences between the two genders. The difference approach emphasizes the idea that men and women belong to different subcultures. This view is based on the argument that whenever people from different cultures communicate, there are bound to be misunderstandings because each participant in the conversation brings his or her own rules to the conversation. This approach was proposed by Daniel Maltz and Ruth Borker in their 1982 paper "A cultural approach to male-female miscommunication". These researchers argued that women and men are socialized differently and that they belong to different gender subcultures. They argued that miscommunication between genders can be examined within the larger framework of miscommunication across cultures. Deborah Tannen (1990) has further developed this approach in her book *You Just Don't Understand: Women and Men in Conversation*. She contends that differences between women's and men's speech reflect the different subcultures within which men and women are brought up during their socialization process, by which they end up with varied communication patterns that complicate communication across gender. Tannen observes that whereas the female subculture uses language to build hierarchical relationships, men seek to dominate and assert their power. By such an argument Tannen seems to be apologetic about the men's dominance, and she has been heavily criticized for downplaying male domination in language use. Troemel-Ploetz (1991), for example, argues that by trying to avoid any negative assessment of men's speaking styles, Tannen is effectively cementing patriarchy. Troemel-Ploetz, like other critics of Tannen, argues that she has overstretched Maltz and Borker's difference approach. The approach has also been seen as a documented excuse to continue viewing female talk as inferior. Tannen, for example, states that women are socialized to be cooperative in their speech while men are socialized to be competitive. In a society where people consider assertiveness and competition to be positive qualities, arguing that women are socialized to be unassertive directly implies that women are socialized to be deficient while men are socialized to dominate in language and in other areas. Any suppressing acts from men can therefore be excused: "It is not their fault; that is how they have been raised".

Both of these approaches we have discussed, though different, try to explain the existence of linguistic differences between genders, and both approaches end up disadvantaging women in some way. The approaches seem to emphasize the role of socialization in creating the gender differences and both point out feminine talk as being deficient. Also, most of the research reviewed above argues from the feminist viewpoint with a major focus on gender inequality and not necessarily on gender difference. Many feminist critiques of language have concerned themselves with what languages reveal about gender inequality and especially about the subordination, discrimination and objectification of women as reflected in language. In this paper we argue that languages represent a wide range of cultural backgrounds, and each culture has unique values, beliefs and experiences. We propose that the values the Ekegusii language represent do not necessarily match those presented by most western world views, since this language of the Gusii people represents a unique cultural group with unique experiences and beliefs.

Gendered Linguistic Differences in Ekegusii Language

A Brief Introduction to the Ekegusii Language

Ekegusii is the language spoken by the Abagusii people of the Gusii community in the Kisii and Nyamira counties of Kenya. The traditional Gusii community is a patriarchal system in which men are perceived as heads of households, owners of family resources, and breadwinners. Women on the other hand are perceived as wives, mothers and nurturers expected to use the family resources provided by the men as husbands and fathers to nurture their families. Traditionally, cultural norms and values were inculcated in the children, and all family members were expected to know their place in society and what was expected of them. This order was valued as it was crucial for family harmony.

There is a general tendency to assume that patriarchal structures benefit males more than females and thus males "have often been viewed as winners and women as losers in those systems" Silberschmidt (1991). However, as Wamae (1999) observes, the patriarchal system in the African context does not necessarily subjugate women. Those who understand the system live in harmony within it. Language has always played an important role in the socialization process and in the instilling of order and harmony in the society. Clearly, if language is a major component of any human culture, and it definitely is, it encodes the values and preoccupations of that human culture. It is one of the main means by which these values are transmitted to the children and other incomers to the community (Cameron 1998 p.10). It will be wrong therefore to assume that what is represented by one language is going to stand true in all other cultures.

Most of the existing language and gender studies from Africa have tried to show how language has been used within the patriarchal society to marginalize women (Choti 1998, Githinji 2008, Mukama 1995, Wango, 1998). These studies have used the same western ideologies and feminist views to study gender variation in Africa. Relying on such ideologies, however, causes misrepresentation of African languages and language users. Gender linguistic differentiation analysis from this perspective assumes that the contexts are similar to those of the western world, and that the views that most of the feminist researchers had are shared by language users around the world. On the contrary, the middle class American women who provide data for most of the feminist studies do not represent a majority of African women, especially Gusii women, nor are the views the feminists held concerning men universally representative. Not everyone views men as power misogynists and culture as oppressive. Silberschmidt (1991), for example, reports that research findings in the Kisii district, unlike what most gender studies suggest " indicate that few men are 'winners' and that "women in Kisii have strength that men seem to lack" (p.6) .

Review of Gendered Linguistic Differences in Ekegusii

Not much research has been done among the Gusii people concerning the topic of gendered linguistic differentiation. Most of the research on the Gusii people is mainly in anthropology and does not necessarily focus on language issues (Silberschmidt (1991, 1999). The available work specifically focusing on gendered linguistic differences in Ekegusii that we found is Choti 1998's unpublished Master's thesis "Language and hierarchy: the linguistic portrayal of the Gusii woman". Choti argues that Ekegusii has inbuilt sexual biases manifested in the language the genders use in speech and the language used to speak about the genders. This fact creates asymmetry between men and women in the Gusii society. He analyzes the grammatical categories and narrative stylistic forms in which sexism has been encoded. These include grammatical devices, such as nouns, pronouns and verbs, and stylistic forms such as similes and metaphors. He also analyses the meanings implied in men's and women's names, observing that there are four categories of names: (i) names exclusively for men, (ii) names exclusively for women, (iii) names that label people because of the circumstances surrounding their birth and (iv) nicknames which echo certain qualities in an individual. Choti, however, focuses on names used exclusively for women. He then establishes that while names given to males magnify such qualities as hardness, toughness, wealth and strength, women's names, on the other hand, emphasize goodness, softness, tenderness, swiftness in completing tasks, politeness, sweetness and obedience, love for aesthetic value and beauty. Choti concludes that the use of such names with contrasting values reflects the gender hierarchy in the society. As Choti admits, the evaluation of his research was entirely based on the "theory of feminism which attributes any differences in men's and women's social ranks to social forces rather than biological ones" (p.vii). Unfortunately the feminist theory that influences his evaluation and research as mentioned earlier follows ideologies that do not fully represent the African view. How and why for example is toughness a better trait than swiftness? What is especially interesting is the fact that Choti's work is set in a context where in the existing folklore the hare, not the lion or the elephant, is always the hero. Most people grow up with the knowledge that swiftness and intelligence, qualities attributed to the hare, are more important than toughness or physical strength as embodied in the lion or elephant. Therefore, naming a boy Nchogu (Elephant) or Simba (Lion) is not necessarily placing men higher in a hierarchy.

Going beyond the Gusii community, we stretch this review to include gendered linguistic differentiation works from two other contexts in East Africa, which are relatively similar to that of the Gusii community. Wango (1998) in his unpublished thesis "Language and gender: a case study in social semiotics of the lexicon of the Gikuyu language" explored the extent to which the Gikuyu language is sexist. The Gikuyu language, like Ekegusii, is a Bantu language spoken in Central Kenya. Wango concludes that several terms used in the Gikuyu language continue to produce negative perceptions about women and their image while promoting the male image. Wango, like Choti, uses western feminist theory to analyze his data, and male and female images and self perceptions take a western perspective.

Mukama (1995) in her paper entitled "Gender Stereotyping in African Languages" analyzes language about women, as found in proverbs, idioms, conventional similes and sayings, innuendos, and direct moralizations. She cites Cameron (1990) who contends that these linguistic features (proverbs, idioms, conventional similes and sayings, innuendos, and direct moralizations) are "authorities" by themselves and they are therefore nearly always stated in discourses as unquestionable matter-of-fact presuppositions. Mukama looks at the imposing features in African languages which show males as invincible. For instance, men are compared to a fierce indomitable lion (or to those animals whose maleness is visibly imposing, like that of the he-goat, cock, bull and lion). She observes that the equivalent comparison for women is lacking and interprets this gap to be due to the assumption that fierceness and excessive authoritativeness are not feminine attributes in those cultures. She also examines proverbs and sayings which according to her argument tend to endorse sexual inequality by creating an asymmetry of powerful men and powerless women. One of the examples of the difference in language use that she gives from the Runyankore/Rukiga is "A woman is a woman... she is never a man." She interprets this saying to mean that women are regarded as lesser beings in this culture (Mukama 1995 p. 378).

We argue, though, that while indeed there are features of language in these cultures that denigrate and marginalize women, the above example simply shows that men and women are different and this difference does not necessarily imply power or powerlessness. There is no reason why the above saying cannot have a converse "a man is a man, he is never a woman." This paper contends that men's and women's roles in the Gusii society are not competitive but complementary - a man cannot be a woman and a woman cannot be a man, but they can complement each other. We look at language as a tool that enables speakers to accomplish these roles in order to foster social harmony.

Linguistic Gender Differences as Illustrated in the Gusii Lexicon

We argue that the Ekegusii language presents evidence for gender difference rather than gender inequality. This study focuses on lexical items used to refer to Gusii women as contrasted or compared to those used for men and how this lexicon when carefully analyzed for meaning reflects difference instead of women's subordination. This next section analyzes common lexical items used to refer to women and whenever applicable compares the equivalent reference for men to provide evidence that the Ekegusii language reflects difference instead of inequality.

Pronouns

This discussion focuses more on nouns than it does on other forms of lexicon such as pronouns and adjectives. Ekegusiidoes not have grammatical gender and therefore pronouns will not inflect for gender. In place of the third person pronouns he/ she, the Ekegusii language normally has just one pronoun, which inflects for noun class.

(i) *Amache*   **aye**
    water   [possessive pronoun]
    His or her water
(ii) *Amaino* **aye**
    teeth   [possessive pronoun]
    His /her teeth
(iii) *Omosacha* **oye**
    man   [possessive pronoun]
    Her husband
(iv) *Omokungu* **oye**
    woman   [possessive pronoun]
    His wife
(v) *Ere*   no   *muya*
    [third person sing pronoun] is   nice
    He/ she is nice

The pronouns are inflected for noun classes but not for gender. Pronouns alone do not indicate gender, and it is up to the addressee to seek further clarification where necessary. In example (v) the third person singular pronoun is not gendered, and like the other pronouns above the addressee is assumed to know the referent.

Nouns Used to Refer to Women

One of the key controversies in the English language relating to gender has been the use of masculine generic where the male terms are used to refer specifically to males and generically to human beings (Martyna 1983 p.25). Among the accomplishments of the feminist movement is the push for nonsexist language such as *humankind* instead of *mankind*, *he/she*, and nonsexist job titles such as *police officer* instead of *policeman*. Ekegusii does not have such masculine generic terms. The generic term *mwanyabanto* which roughly translates as *humankind* is unmarked for gender.

Ekegusii, however, does have gender specific referents. Some of the common lexicon that is gender specific include *omokungu* 'woman', *omosacha* 'man', relationship names such as *tata* 'father', *baba* 'mother', *tatamoke* 'uncle', and *makomoke* 'aunt'. In the next section we analyze the semantics of the terms used to talk about women to show how these very terms reflect difference instead of male domination and women subordination.

(i) Omokungu (woman) vs omosacha (man)

These two terms if well understood denote balanced roles in the Gusii community, and do not suggest subordination on the part of the woman. The term *omokungu* 'woman' literally means the treasurer. Other terms derived from the same root word include *omokungi*, which means a treasurer of an organization, e.g company treasurer or church treasurer, and *ekungo* 'treasure'. The term *omosacha* (man) on the hand is literally translated as the gatherer/ hunter. A verb from the same source, *gosacha*, literally translates as to gather/ hunt.

The role of a woman as a wife and a mother in traditional Kisii was to properly manage what the husband provided in order to ensure that the family was well fed. In contemporary Kisii, even if a man has a good and well-paying job but does not have a wife, he will be perceived as a squanderer of resources. This is because the society perceives women as "treasurers", and men are complete and purposeful only if they work with a treasurer of what they gather. So while one gathers (*omosacha)*, the other carefully manages (*omokungu*). The word does not have any slight implication of women being wasteful or careless spenders as many could want to interpret the term. On the contrary, the term emphasizes the significance of the role of men and women to complement each other. Unlike the English terms that may give the impression that *woman* is derived by adding a prefix to *man*, the Ekegusii language treats the two as separate yet complementary.

Often parents of a hard-working unmarried man will suggest that he marry so that he can find someone to manage his wealth; otherwise it will be wasted. Along the same lines, close relatives of a well-to-do unmarried man get wary when a man marries because they understand that his "woman" will be the treasurer and they might not have free access to his wealth as they used to.

The term *omukungu*, however, simply means woman and not necessarily a married woman. Lakoff (1975) argues that "women are always defined in terms of the men to whom they are related" (p.35). *Omokungu* is not associated to a male. A woman is still *omokungu* whether she is single, married, divorced or even widowed.

(ii) Omorugi

Omorugi, a term used specifically for married women poorly literally translates into a cook. When Kisii men introduce their wives as "this is my *omorugi*" there is no derogative intention implied. It is almost as endearing as using terms like honey, darling or sweetheart. People will refer to someone's wife as X's *omorugi* (X's cook). However, in the western mindset, the word *omorugi* has been misconstrued to suggest an oppressed, servitude position. Most people who assess gender difference from a western point of view will likely question an article that evaluates the term *omorugi* as anything less than an embodiment of female subordination. The term *omorugi*, on the contrary, is one that portrays the powerful role a woman plays in the Gusii community. This power is recognized and even illustrated in the Kisii saying *"omosacha nenda"* which literary translates into "A man is his stomach."

The saying is similar to the English proverb "The way to a man's heart is through his stomach". The Kisii saying, however, emphasizes the fact that a man cannot survive if his stomach is not catered to; what makes him is his stomach. If he is full then he is contented, but if he is hungry he is grumpy and helpless. The role of the woman as a "cook" is not just a subservient role; she is not viewed as a man's servant, but one who plays a sustaining role for her family.

The traditional Kisii community had clearly defined gender roles, and cooking was not a man's domain. If a man cannot cook, and it is food that makes him, then he depends on the woman for survival. No Kisii man looks down upon the role of a woman as the cook and housekeeper. As Akama discusses in his extensive ethnographical essay of the Gusii people, traditionally children were introduced to gender specific roles and functions at a very early age. The gender roles were very clearly marked: "males were taught specific roles such as herding, hunting, and clearing fallow land to make it ready for cultivation, while girls were introduced to roles such as cleaning the homestead and housekeeping, fetching water and collecting firewood, and how to use a hoe for crop cultivation and weeding" (p. 110). Although men don't herd and hunt anymore, traditional Kisii families still consider cooking and housekeeping as a woman's chore and many men, unless living away from home in some urban setting, will not cook or engage in housekeeping. As Egejuru (1997) argues

> The mistake is often made when those who assert that the African woman in general is oppressed because she plays a minor role in her society and that she has no real saying in important decisions that affect her. It is doubtful that any objective Igbo man would say that his wife plays a minor role in his family. In Africa as a whole, roles are not categorized as major or as minor or as inferior and superior. There is a clear division of labor, but all roles are complementary and interdependent. Like many things in Africa, the designation of a woman's role as inferior came with colonization (p. 17).

House-keeping for example was never regarded as an inferior role. The idea of some chores being considered inferior has evolved partly due to paid employment. Traditionally men were not paid for hunting or working outside the home to provide for their families. Their roles as hunters and gatherers were not considered superior. Since men were not taught how to cook, and were in fact discouraged from spending time in the kitchen, they could not eat any of the game they caught until it was prepared by the woman. So *omosacha* (hunter, man) hunted for game, *omorugi* (cook, woman) prepared it, and together the family had a meal. Egejuru (1997) observes rightfully that, "Both the man and the woman know that a woman symbolizes the hearth where she cooks and distributes the food. Thus, she can starve her husband into submission by withholding food and sex" (p.16). It is from her kitchen that a woman wages power and being called a cook therefore is in no way a subordinate term.

Unlike the English language, where occupations are marked for gender, such as policeman vs. policewoman, among the Gusii people most occupations are gender neutral. In contemporary Kisii, men no longer hunt or gather and neither do all women stay home and do all the cooking and cleaning. The terms *omorugi* and *omosacha* are no longer literal in meaning. While *okoruga* "to cook" was a strictly gendered role in traditional Kisii most of the other jobs, as seen in the few examples below, have always remained gender neutral.

Omorwaria	(the one who heals) 'physician'
Omonyabiasara	(the one who does business) 'businessman/business woman'
Omorubi	(the one who fishes) 'fisherman/fisherwoman'
Omoremi	(the one who farms) 'farmer'
Omogesi	(the one who harvests) 'reaper'
Omorendi	(the one who watches) 'watchman/ watchwoman'

(iii) Omongn'ina

Omongn'ina is a difficult term to translate into the English language because it does not have a direct equivalent. The literal translation is 'an old/ elderly lady' but the connotations are completely different. *Omongn'ina* in the kisii language is an endearing term that connotes maturity, wisdom and mother of all. Until recently, the Gusii community was mainly an oral community and all forms of education were transmitted orally. *Omongn'ina* along with *omogaka* (an old/ elderly man) was the family historian and carrier of traditional wisdom. Younger women who show wisdom and maturity in handling matters can be praised as o*mongn'ina*. Fathers sometimes call their daughter's *omong'ina* as a way of praising the wisdom and maturity that the young person is already demonstrating. The use of the term o*mongn'ina* in the Ekegusii language challenges Lakoff's (1975) proposition that the language used to describe women "submerges a woman's personal identity… by treating her as an object – sexual or otherwise - but never as a serious person with individual views" (p.7).

(iv) Relational nouns : *baba*

Baba (mother): this word is not only used to refer to one's mother, it is also an honorific term used when addressing elderly women, older than the speaker. The word is endearing to refer to women of any age. *Baba* is not just honorific but almost sacred. Both men and women swear in Mother's name: *aki baba bori*, literally "It is the truth in Mother's name." Both men and women are cautious not to utter Mother's name in vain. Similarly, when someone is shocked the Gusii equivalent of "Oh my God" is *Baba ominto* 'Oh our mother!' It is possible to argue that using *baba* or Mother in swearing is a form of abuse of the female gender, but considering that in most cultures people swear in the name of God or gods, this usage could on the contrary suggest that the Ekegusii language ranks women/*baba* close to God; mother is supreme.

Conclusion

We do not intend to underestimate the dominance of men in the Gusii community, but, as we have shown, the Ekegusii language does not support this dominance. The lexicon used to refer to women reflects that women are different and play various roles in society, but they are not in any way inferior. While woman abuse and male dominance is not an uncommon occurrence in the Gusii community, the language itself does not support female subordination or male dominance. As shown in the examples above, most of the lexicon used to refer to women has complementing masculine terms.

We have shown that the western based feminist framework does not correctly explain the Kisii reality. While we agree that human beings everywhere are inherently the same, and that their basic needs are generally the same, issues of gender arise as a result of socialization and each culture socializes its people differently. What one culture might view as discrimination and male dominance may be an accepted gender differentiation in another culture. An African based theoretical framework is needed to analyze and discuss gendered linguistic differentiation in the Ekegusii language.

References

Akama, S. (2006). The indigenous education system: The making of a Gusii man or woman. In J. S. Akama & R. Maxon (Eds.), *Ethnography of the Gusii of western Kenya: A vanishing heritage* (pp. 105- 114). New York: Edwin Mellen Press.

Cameron, D. (1998). *The Feminist critique of language: A reader*. London: Routledge.

Choti, J. (1998). *Language and hierarchy: The linguistic portrayal of the Gusii woman*. (Unpublished master's thesis). Egerton University, Kenya.

Eckert, P. & McConnell-Ginet, S. (1988). Communities of practice: Where language, gender, and power all live. In J. Coates (Ed.), *Language and gender: A reader* (pp. 484-494). Oxford: Blackwell.

Egejuru, P. (1997). The paradox of womanhood and the female principle in Igbo cosmology. In P. Egejuru & K. Katrak (Eds.), *Nwanyibu: Womanbeing and African literature* (pp.11-19). Trenton, NJ: Africa World Press.

Githinji, P. (2008). Sexism and (mis)representation of women in Sheng. *Journal of African Cultural Studies*, 20 (1), 15-32.

Lakoff, R. (1975). *Language and woman's place*. New York: Harper & Row.

Lakoff. R (2004). Author's introduction: Language and woman's place revisited. In R. Lakoff, *Language and woman's place: Text and commentaries* (pp. 15-28). M. Bucholtz (Ed). New York: Oxford University Press.

Maltz, D. & R. Borker (1982). A cultural approach to male-female miscommunication. In J. Gumperz (Ed.), *Language and social identity* (pp. 196-216). Cambridge: Cambridge University Press.

Martyna, W. (1983). Beyond the he/ man approach: The case for nonsexist language. In B. Thorne, C. Kramarae, & N. Henley (Eds.), *Language, gender and society* (pp.25-37). Cambridge: Newbury House Publishers.

Mukama, R. (1995). Gender stereotyping in African languages. In A. Akinlabi (Ed.), *Theoretical approaches to African linguistics* (pp. 375-392). Trenton, NJ: Africa World Press.

Pauwels, A. (2011). Linguistic sexism and feminist linguistic activism. In A. Mooney, J.S. Peccei, S. LaBelle, B. E. Henriksen, E. Eppler, A. Irwin, ... & S. Soden (eds), *The language, society and power reader* (pp. 484-494). New York: Routledge.

Silberschmidt, M. (1991*). Rethinking men and gender relations: An investigation of men, their changing roles within the household, and the implications for gender relations in Kisii district, Kenya*. Centre for Development Research.

Silberschmidt, M. (1999). *Women forget that men are the masters: Gender antagonism and socio-economic change in Kisii district, Kenya*. Uppsala: Nordic Africa Institute.

Swann, J. (2009) Gender and language use. In R. Mesthrie, J. Swann. A. Deumert, and W. Leap, *Introducing sociolinguistics* (2nd ed.) (pp.213-241). Philadelphia: John Benjamins.

Tannen, D. (1990). *You just don't understand: Women and men in conversation*. New York: Ballantine.

Troemel-Ploetz, S. (1991). Selling the apolitical. *Discourse and society* 2. 489-502.

Wango, M. (1998). *Language and gender: A case study in social semiotics of the lexicon of the Gikuyu language*. (Unpublished master's thesis). Kenyatta University, Kenya.

Weatherall, A. (2002). *Gender, language and discourse*. New York: Routledge.

Index

A

Abdul-Jawad, 160
accommodation, 3, 129
adjective, 37, 47, 164, 187
adverb, 64
Africa, 186, 189
Agha, 29
Agreement Maxim, 3, 86, 88, 92, 93, 94, 95, 96, 97
Ainworth-Vaughn, 129
Aizawa, 52, 71, 77
Aleppo, 160
Al-Khatib, 87, 91
alveolar stops, 160
Amazigh, 159
Andersen, 105
Anderson, 6
Andrus, 172
anthropological linguistics, 157
Aotearoa. *See* New Zealand
Arabic, 41, 48, 89
    Classical Arabic, 161
    Egyptian Arabic, 161
    French Arabic, 159
    Jordanian Arabic, 91
    Moroccan Arabic, 159
    Sudanese Arabic, 4, 156–69
Arifin, 90, 96, 97
Arndt, 55
Asano, 58, 59, 63, 64, 65
Azman, 90

B

Baba, 90, 91
back formation, 42, 46
Barron, 104
Bauer, 7, 14, 18
Ben Yehuda, 40
Benton, 7, 18
Berthoud, 131–34
Besnier, 55
Bible, 38, *See* Hebrew, Biblical Hebrew
Biggs, 6
Blum-Kulka, 102, 103, 104, 107, 120, 121
Blust, 6
Borker, 52, 72, 183
Bourdieu, 6
Brown, 87
Bucholtz, 4, 105
Buddhism, 176
Bybee, 17
Byon, 104

C

Cajun, 28
Cameron, 104, 184, 186
Canary, 105
Carroll, 27
Chen, 88, 90, 91
Cheng, 51, 52, 55, 58, 60, 61, 67, 105
Cheshire, 5
Chinese, 3, 102–23
Chinese culture, 88
Chino, 54, 61, 68
Choti, 181, 184, 185, 186
Choueka, 40
Coates, 1, 2, 5, 71, 129
code-switching, 27
comics, 53
Community of Practice, 3
compliment, 3, 86–97
Confucianism, 74
conversation, 50–79
Conversational Principles, 86, 92
Coupland, 172

Crawford, 72
Cross-Cultural Speech Act Realization Project, 3, 102, 104, 107
cultural differences approach. *See* difference approach

D

Dahir, 160
Dahl, 106
Damascus, 160
Daneš, 55
Danielson, 172
daroo, 63, 64
David, 87, 90
De Ruiter, 159
declarative clause, 134
deficit approach, 157
dictionary, 2, 39, 41, 181
difference approach, 72, 182, 183, *See* cultural differences approach
diglossia, 158, 160, 161, 163, 168
directive, 3, 131, 136, 139, 140, 141, 150, 153, 154, 157
Discourse Completion Test, 3, 86
dislocation, 134
divorce, 4, 156, 167, 168
dominance approach, 52, 72, 157, 182, 183
Dubois, 26, 28
dyad, 140, 153
Dybala, 27

E

Eckert, 5, 22, 26, 52, 72, 183
Economidou-Kogetsidis, 104
Egejuru, 189
Ekegusii, 4, 181–91
Elbert, 6
elicitor, 141, 142, 143, 152
Endo, 72, 75, 76
English, 1, 3, 41, 42, 104, 133, 156, 157, 174, 176, 177, 187, 188, 189
   American English, 89
   New Zealand English, 2, 19, 73, 90
   South African English, 89
essentialism, 73
ethnicity, 172, 175, 176
Even-Shoshan, 40
evidentiality, 63
external modification, 107, 112, 118, 119, 120, 122, 123

F

face-threatening act, 103
Falconer, 52, 71, 73, 74, 77
Farghal, 87, 91
feminism, 4, 39, 184, 185, 186, 191
Ferguson, 158
Fishman, 129, 138, 153
Foley, 158
formulaic speech, 131
French, 42, 131, 133
Fukushima, 91

G

Gajaseni, 87, 90
García, 104
gay, 169, *See* LGBT, *See* LGBT
Geluykens, 129
genbunitchi, 50, 75, 76, 77, 78
gender-exclusive differences, 3, 163, 168
gender-preferential differences, 156, 163
German, 42
Githinji, 181, 184
Golato, 87
Gordon, 5, 7, 9, 12, 18
grammatical gender, 39, 42, 46, 187
grounder, 118, 119
Gumperz, 25
Gusii, 190, 181–91

H

Hachimi, 158, 159

Haeri, 160
Hall, 4
Han, 87
Hanks, 25
Harlow et al, 6
haru, 2, 22–33
Hasunuma, 54
Hattori, 52
Hause, 105
Hawaiian, 6
Hay, 12
Hayashi, 50, 52, 54
hazing, 172, 173, 174
head act, 106–23
Hebrew, 2, 36–48
    Biblical Hebrew, 45
hedge, 120
Herbert, 87, 90
Hokkaido, 53
Holmes, 2, 6, 19, 52, 72, 73, 87, 90, 103, 105, 112, 115, 120
Holtgraves, 105
Hong, 104
honorific, 2, 22–33, 40, 77, 190
Horii, 25
Horvath, 26, 28
House, 102, 103
Hurreiz, 161, 162, 164, 165, 167, 168, 169

I

Ide, 23, 24, 50, 51, 52, 55, 61, 68, 71, 74
ideology, 2, 4, 22, 23, 24, 25, 29, 30, 33, 73, 75, 172, 176, 181, 185
idiom, 40, 41, 186
illocution, 61, 108, 110, 119, 121
inanimacy, 36
incorporative attitude, 54–58
India, 89
in-group, 4, 32
Inoue, 72, 74, 76
interruption, 157
intonation, 52, 71, 157, 162, 165
involvement, 53, 55, 56, 57, 69, 70
Ishikawa, 76

Islam, 159, 161, 164, 167
Italian, 42
Iwasaki, 26
Izuhara, 54, 55

J

Jamaliah, 88
Janney, 55
Japan, 50–79
Japanese, 1, 2, 3, 50–79
    Osaka Japanese, 22–33
Japanese culture, 88
Javanese, 158
Johnson, 63, 64, 65, 67, 87, 97
Johnstone, 22, 33, 172
Jorden, 24
Jugaku, 52, 71
Junichiro, 24
justification, 109, 111, 120, 131, 136, 140, 141, 143, 151, 152, 154

K

kabary, 158
Kabashima, 53
Kansai, 53
Kashiwagi, 59, 71
Kasper, 102, 103, 106
Katagiri, 50, 52, 54
Kawasaki, 71
Keenan, 158
Kendall, 72
Kenya, 181–91
Khartoum, 161
Kiesling, 22, 33
Kim, 104
Kisii. *See* Ekegusii
Korean, 3, 102–23
Kose, 54
Koyama, 53
Krupa, 6
Kuki, 6
Kuwayama, 61, 68

L

Labov, 5
Ladino, 41
Lakoff, 52, 72, 121, 156, 157, 164, 181, 182, 183, 188, 190
Lee, 104
Leech, 3, 86, 88, 92, 93, 94, 96
lesbian, 38–39, *See* LGBT
Levinson, 87
Levon, 38
Lewis, 5
lexicon, 4, 160, 162, 186
LGBT, 1
linguistic territorialization, 171
Livnat, 41, 42, 43
Lorenzo-Dus, 87, 91

M

Maeda, 22, 25
Maegaki, 29
Malagasy, 158
Malayalees, 88
Maltz, 52, 72, 183
Manes, 87
manga. *See* comics
Mangaian, 6
manzai, 31
MAONZE, 7
Māori, 19
marae, 7
Masuoka, 55, 61, 63, 64, 65, 68, 71, 77
Matsumoto, 72
Maynard, 54, 55, 71
McConnell-Ginet, 52, 72, 183
McDonough, 106
McDougall, 71
McElhinny, 52, 72, 106, 157
McGloin, 50, 51, 52, 54, 55, 61, 69, 71, 74
McIlvenny, 72
media, 22, 27, 29, 44, 158, 160, 168
Meiji era, 3, 50, 74, 77, 78
merger, 17
metalinguistics, 131, 134

metaphor, 185
metapragmatics, 25, 29
metonym, 166
Meyer, 104, 154
Mills, 122
Miyaji, 23
Miyazaki, 51, 52, 55, 58, 59, 63, 64
Mizutani, 51, 55, 71
modal, 50, 58, 59, 62, 64, 65, 78
Modan, 173
Modesty Maxim, 3, 86, 88, 92, 93, 94, 95, 96, 97
modification, 118, 119
Mondada, 131–34
monopolistic attitude, 53–58, 62, 69, 70, 78
Morita, 65, 66
Moriyama, 63, 65
Morocco, 159
morphology, 38, 39, 46
mourning, 156, 166, 167
Mukama, 181, 184, 186
Mulac, 138
multiglossia, 158, 163, 168
Murphy, 129
Mursy, 87, 88
Muslim, 167, 172, 175, 176

N

Nakamura, 72, 74, 75, 76
Nakazaki, 52
name, 44, 171–79, 190
Narrog, 63, 67
Nelson, 87
Niedzielski, 172
Nitta, 63, 64
Niyekawa, 24
Noda, 24
numeral, 37

O

Ochs, 79
Oda, 61, 68, 71
Oishi, 54, 55
Okamoto, 22, 23, 25, 71, 77, 121

Okuda, 75
Olshtain, 104, 120, 121
onna-kotoba, 72, 74, 75
onna-rashisa, 3, 50, 52, 53, 72, 75, 74–78, 78, 79
Ooka, 76
Oota, 52, 55, 71
Osaka-no obachan, 29, 33
Owen, 104
Ozaki, 76

P

Pair, 104
Pākehā, 8, 9
paralinguistic features, 165
particle, 3, 32, 37, 50–79
Pauwels, 42
performative, 110
Phillips, 17
phonetics, 19
phonology, 5–19, 160
Pichler, 1, 2
politeness, 3, 23, 24, 29, 77, 86, 87, 88, 89, 90, 96, 105, 158, 185
Politeness Principle, 3, 86, 88, 92, 93, 94, 96
Polonnaruwa, 176, 177, 178
Polynesia, 6, 9
Pomerantz, 86, 87, 89
pōwhiri, 7
pragmatics, 3, 43, 79, 87, 89, 165
preposition, 37
pre-signal, 131, 134, 135, 140, 142, 149, 152, 153
prestige, 2, 36, 43
Preston, 172
pronoun, 4, 17, 37, 71, 133, 185, 187
proverb, 186, 189
Pukui, 6
Punjabis, 88

Q

qaf, 160
Quran, 159

R

Raggers, 175, 177
Ramazanoglu, 87, 90
register, 38
religion, 158, 161, 172, 176, 182
request, 3, 59, 102–23, 136
Reynolds, 51, 52, 55, 71, 77
Roen, 87, 97
role-play, 103, 106, 107, 114
role-enactment, 106
Rosenhouse, 48
Rosenthal, 40, 41
Ruātoki valley, 7
Rue and Zhang, 111
ryoosai-kenbo, 50, 74–79

S

Sa'ar, 45
Sadiqi, 159
Saito, 72
Sakuma, 54
Sakurai, 50, 52
salience, 2, 29, 36, 37, 43, 46, 103, 134
Sato, 23
Sawaie, 160
Schilling-Estes, 5, 157, 172
Schneider, 104
Schwarzwald, 39
Seiichi, 23
semantics, 43, 46, 48, 64, 165
sentence-final particle, 50–79, *See* particle
sexism, 182, 185
Shanmuganathan, 87, 90
Shibamoto, 24, 29, 71
Shibamoto Smith, 71
Shibata, 6
Shibatani, 24
Silberschmidt, 184, 185
Silverstein, 25
Sinhala, 4, 174, 171–79
Sinhalese, 175, 171–79
slang, 41

Smythe, 154
social class, 182
social construction approach, 52, 72, 73
socio-cultural aspect, 55
sociolinguistics, 157, 160, 163
solidarity, 31, 32, 89, 97
Southern Cook Islands, 6
Spanish, 42
Speech Accommodation Theory, 163
Spender, 37
Sri Lanka, 4, 88, 171–79
stance, 172
standardization, 27
stigmatization, 169
story-telling, 156
Straight, 87
Stubbe, 52, 72, 73
SturtzSreetharan, 22, 23, 25, 26, 29
Sudan, 4, 161, 165, 156–69
suffix, 2, 23, 22–33, 36, 37, 39, 45, 46
Sugimoto, 24
Sunderland, 103, 122
suppositional, 63
Suzuki, 55, 61, 68, 71, 77
Swann, 182
symbolic capital, 6
syntax, 5, 18, 19, 37, 163
Syria, 160

T

Takubo, 61, 63, 64, 68, 71, 77
Talbot, 103
Tamil, 86–97, 172, 175, 176
    Malaysian Tamil, 3, 86–97
Tanaka, 51, 52, 55, 61, 69, 74
Tannen, 52, 72, 129, 157, 183
Telegus, 88
Teramura, 63, 65, 67
terms of endearment, 164
Tobin, 45
topic introduction, 3, 128–54
Troemel-Ploetz, 183
Trosborg, 104, 106

Trudgill, 6, 52, 72
truth-value, 63, 64
Tsui, 105
Tuamotuan, 6
Turkish, 41

U

Umar, 104
Urano, 87
Usami, 53, 61, 68
Uyeno, 51, 52, 54, 55, 58, 59, 61, 69

V

Van Mulken, 104
variation approach, 157
verb, 37, 108, 185
vocabulary. *See* lexicon
vocative, 163

W

Wamae, 184
Wango, 181, 184, 186
Weatherall, 103, 182, 183
West, 52, 72, 105, 129, 140
Wilkins, 105
Wilson, 87, 88
Wolfram, 5, 157, 172
Wolfson, 87
Women's Liberation Movement, 182
Wong, 104
Woods, 5

Y

Yaeger-Dror, 6
Yamaji, 25
Yang, 105
Ye, 90
Yiddish, 41
Yonezawa, 54

Yuan, 87
Yukawa, 72

Z

Zhang, 104
Zimmerman, 52, 72, 105, 129

www.ingramcontent.com/pod-product-compliance
Lightning Source LLC
Chambersburg PA
CBHW070831300426
44111CB00014B/2515